MORE ADVANCE PRAISE FOR **STANDARD DEVIATIONS**

"Gary Smith's *Standard Deviations* is both a statement of principles for doing statistical inference correctly and a practical guide for interpreting the (supposedly) data-based inferences other people have drawn. Cleverly written and engaging to read, the book is full of concrete examples that make clear not just what Smith is saying but why it matters. Readers will discover that lots of what they thought they'd learned is wrong, and they'll understand why."

—BENJAMIN M. FRIEDMAN
William Joseph Maier Professor
of Political Economy, Harvard University

"*Standard Deviations* shows in compelling fashion why humans are so susceptible to the misuse of statistical evidence and why this matters. I know of no other book that explains important concepts such as selection bias in such an entertaining and memorable manner."

—RICHARD J. MURNANE
Thompson Professor of Education and Society,
Harvard Graduate School of Education

"We all learn in school that there are three kinds of lies: lies, damn lies, and statistics. Gary Smith's new book imparts true substance to this point by setting forth myriad examples of how and why statistics and data-crunching at large are susceptible to corruption. The great risk today is that the young will forget that deductive logic is vastly more powerful than inductive logic."

—HORACE "WOODY" BROCK
President, Strategic Economic Decisions, Inc.

"Statistical reasoning is the most used and abused form of rhetoric in the field of finance. *Standard Deviations* is an approachable and effective means to arm oneself against the onslaught statistical hyperbole in our modern age. Professor Smith has done us all a tremendous service."

—BRYAN WHITE
Managing Director, BlackRock, Inc.

STANDARD DEVIATIONS

STANDARD DEVIATIONS

FLAWED ASSUMPTIONS, TORTURED DATA, AND OTHER WAYS TO LIE WITH STATISTICS

GARY SMITH

OVERLOOK DUCKWORTH
NEW YORK · LONDON

This edition first published in hardcover in the United States and the United Kingdom in 2014 by
Overlook Duckworth, Peter Mayer Publishers, Inc.

New York
141 Wooster Street
New York, NY 10012
www.overlookpress.com
For bulk and special sales, please contact sales@overlookny.com,
or write us at the above address.

London
30 Calvin Street
London E1 6NW
info@duckworth-publishers.co.uk
www.ducknet.co.uk

Library of Congress Cataloging-in-Publication Data

Smith, Gary, 1945- author.
Standard deviations : flawed assumptions, tortured data, and other ways
to lie with statistics / Gary Smith.
pages cm
Includes bibliographical references and index.
1. Standard deviations. I. Title.
QA279.S638 2014   519.5--dc23   2014017052

Book design and typeformatting by Bernard Schleifer
Manufactured in the United States of America
FIRST EDITION
ISBN 978-1-4683-0920-1
2 4 6 8 10 9 7 5 3 1

To my wife Margaret and my children Josh,
Jo, Chaska, Cory, Cameron, and Claire

CONTENTS

INTRODUCTION *3*

1. Patterns, Patterns, Patterns *7*
2. Garbage In, Gospel Out *25*
3. Apples and Prunes *43*
4. Oops! *55*
5. Graphical Gaffes *71*
6. Common Nonsense *91*
7. Confound It! *105*
8. When You're Hot, You're Not *123*
9. Regression *137*
10. Even Steven *159*
11. The Texas Sharpshooter *163*
12. The Ultimate Procrastination *175*
13. Serious Omissions *185*
14. Flimsy Theories and Rotten Data *201*
15. Don't Confuse Me With Facts *213*
16. Data Without Theory *233*
17. Betting the Bank *263*
18. Theory Without Data *281*
19. When to Be Persuaded and When
    to Be Skeptical *289*

SOURCES *299*

INDEX *321*

STANDARD DEVIATIONS

INTRODUCTION

WE LIVE IN THE AGE OF BIG DATA. THE POTENT COMBINATION of fast computers and worldwide connectivity is continually praised—even worshipped. Over and over, we are told that government, business, finance, medicine, law, and our daily lives are being revolutionized by a newfound ability to sift through reams of data and discover the truth. We can make wise decisions because powerful computers have looked at the data and seen the light.

Maybe. Or maybe not. Sometimes these omnipresent data and magnificent computers lead to some pretty outlandish discoveries. Case in point, serious people have seriously claimed that:

- Messy rooms make people racist.
- Unborn chicken embryos can influence computer random-event generators.
- When the ratio of government debt to GDP goes above 90 percent, nations nearly always slip into recession.
- As much as 50 percent of the drop in the crime rate in the United States over the past twenty years is because of legalized abortion.
- Drinking two cups of coffee a day substantially increases the risk of pancreatic cancer.
- The most successful companies tend to become less successful, while the least successful companies tend to become more successful, so that soon all will be mediocre.
- Athletes who appear on the cover of *Sports Illustrated* or

Madden NFL are jinxed in that they are likely to be less successful or injured.

- Living near power lines causes cancer in children.
- Humans have the power to postpone death until after important ceremonial occasions.
- Asian Americans are more susceptible to heart attacks on the fourth day of the month.
- People live three to five years longer if they have positive initials, like ACE.
- Baseball players whose first names began with the letter D die, on average, two years younger than players whose first names began with the letters E through Z.
- The terminally ill can be cured by positive mental energy sent from thousands of miles away.
- When an NFC team wins the Super Bowl, the stock market almost always goes up.
- You can beat the stock market by buying the Dow Jones stock with the highest dividend yield and the second lowest price per share.

These claims—and hundreds more like them—appear in newspapers and magazines every day even though they are surely false. In today's Information Age, our beliefs and actions are guided by torrents of meaningless data. It is not hard to see why we repeatedly draw false inferences and make bad decisions. Even if we are reasonably well informed, we are not always alert to the ways in which data are biased or irrelevant, or to the ways in which scientific research is flawed or misleading. We tend to assume that computers are infallible—that no matter what kind of garbage we put in, computers will spit out gospel. It happens not just to laymen in their daily lives, but in serious research by diligent professionals. We see it in the popular press, on television, on the Internet, in political campaigns, in academic journals, in business meetings, in courtrooms, and, of course, in government hearings.

Decades ago, when data were scarce and computers nonexistent, researchers worked hard to gather good data and thought carefully before spending hours, even days, on painstaking calculations. Now with data so plentiful, researchers often spend too little time distinguishing between good data and rubbish, between sound analysis and junk science. And, worst of all, we are too quick to assume that churning through mountains of data can't ever go wrong. We rush to make decisions based on the balderdash these machines dish out—to increase taxes in the midst of a recession, to trust our life savings to financial quants who impress us because we don't understand them, to base business decisions on the latest management fad, to endanger our health with medical quackery, and—worst of all—to give up coffee.

Ronald Coase cynically observed that, "If you torture the data long enough, it will confess." *Standard Deviations* is an exploration of dozens of examples of tortuous assertions that, with even a moment's reflection, don't pass the smell test. Sometimes, the unscrupulous deliberately try to mislead us. Other times, the well-intentioned are blissfully unaware of the mischief they are committing. My intention in writing this book is to help protect us from errors—both external and self-inflicted. You will learn simple guidelines for recognizing bull when you see it—or say it. Not only do others use data to fool us, we often fool ourselves.

1

PATTERNS, PATTERNS, PATTERNS

OUTH SOCCER IS A VERY BIG DEAL WHERE I LIVE IN SOUTHERN California. It's a fun, inexpensive sport that can be played by boys and girls of all sizes and shapes. I initially didn't know anything about soccer. All I knew was that, every weekend, the city parks and school grounds were filled with kids in brightly colored uniforms chasing soccer balls while their parents cheered. When my son was old enough, we were in.

By the time the 2010 World Cup came around, my son was playing on one of the top soccer teams in Southern California. I was the manager and a fanatic about soccer, so naturally he and I watched every World Cup match we could. The opponents in the 2010 championship game were Netherlands and Spain, two extraordinarily talented teams from underachieving nations that often disappointed their supporters. Which country would finally win the World Cup? I loved the Dutch, who had won all six of their World Cup games, scoring twelve goals while allowing only five, and had knocked out the mighty Brazil and Uruguay. But then I heard about Paul the octopus, who had correctly predicted the winners of seven World Cup games by choosing food from plastic boxes with the nations' flags on them. Paul the Oracle had picked Spain, and the world now seemed certain of a Spanish victory.

What the heck was going on? How could a slimy, pea-brained invertebrate know more about soccer than I did? I laughed and waited for Paul the Omniscient to get his comeuppance. Except he didn't. The Dutch did not play with their usual creativity and flair. In a brutal, cynical match, with fourteen yellow cards—nine given to the dirty Dutchmen — Spain scored the winning goal with four minutes left in the game.

How could an octopus living in a tank have predicted any of this? Had Paul ever seen a soccer game? Did Paul even have a brain?

It turns out that octopuses are among the most intelligent invertebrates, but that isn't saying much—sort of like being the world's tallest midget. Still, Paul made eight World Cup predictions and got every single one right. Not only that, Paul made six predictions during the 2008 European Football Championships and got four right. Overall, that's twelve out of fourteen correct, which in the eyes of many would be considered statistical proof of Paul's psychic abilities. But were there really enough data?

If a fair coin is flipped fourteen times, the chances of twelve or more heads are less than one percent. In the same way, if Paul were just a hapless guesser with a 50 percent chance of making a correct prediction, the probability that he would make so many correct predictions is less than 1 percent, a probability so low that it is considered "statistically significant." The chances of Paul being correct so many times are so small that, logically, we can rule out luck as an explanation. With his consistency, Paul had demonstrated that he was not merely a lucky guesser. He was truly Paul the Psychic Octopus!

And yet, something didn't seem quite right. Is it really possible for an octopus to predict the future? Paul's performance raises several issues that are endemic in statistical studies. Paul was not a psychic (surprise, surprise), but he is a warning of things to watch out for the next time you hear some fanciful claim.

■ CONFOUNDING EFFECTS

First, let's look at how Paul made his predictions. At feeding time, he was shown two clear plastic boxes with the national flags of the opposing teams glued to the front of the boxes. The boxes contained identical yummy treats, such as a mussel or an oyster. Whichever box Paul opened first was the predicted winner.

Octopuses don't know much about soccer, but they do have excellent eyesight and good memories. One time, an octopus at the New

England Aquarium decided he didn't like a volunteer and shot salt water at her whenever he saw her. She left the aquarium to go to college, but when she returned months later, the octopus remembered her and immediately drenched her with salt water again. In an experiment at a Seattle aquarium, one volunteer fed the octopuses while another wearing identical clothes irritated the octopuses with a stick. After a week of this, most of the octopuses could tell who was who. When they saw the good person, they moved closer; when they saw the bad person, they moved away (and sometimes shot water at him for good measure).

Paul the Psychic Octopus happened to be living in an aquarium in Germany and, except for the Spain-Netherlands World Cup final, Paul only predicted games involving Germany. In eleven of the thirteen games involving Germany, Paul picked Germany—and Germany won nine of these eleven games. Was Paul picking Germany because he had analyzed their opponents carefully or because he had an affinity for the German flag? Paul was almost certainly color blind, but experiments have shown that octopuses recognize brightness and are attracted to horizontal shapes. Germany's flag has three vivid horizontal stripes, as do the flags of Serbia and Spain, the only other countries Paul selected. Indeed, the Spanish and German flags are pretty similar, which may explain why Paul picked Spain over Germany in one of the two matches they played and picked Spain over the Netherlands in the World Cup final. The only game in which Paul did not choose the German or Spanish flag was a match between Serbia and Germany.

The flag was apparently a confounding factor in that Paul wasn't picking the best soccer team. He was choosing his favorite flag. Paul the Omniscient was just a pea-brained octopus after all.

Figure 1.1: Paul's Favorite Flags

Germany (eleven times)   Spain (twice)   Serbia (once)

■ SELECTIVE REPORTING AND MISREPORTING

Another explanation for Paul's success is that too many people with too much time on their hands try stupid pet tricks, using animals to predict sports, lottery, and stock market winners.

Some will inevitably succeed, just like among thousands of people flipping coins, some people will inevitably flip heads ten times in a row. Who do you think gets reported, the octopus who picked winners or the ostrich who didn't?

Several years ago, a sports columnist for *The Dallas Morning News* had a particularly bad week picking the winners of National Football League (NFL) football games—he got one right and twelve wrong, with one tie. He wrote that, "Theoretically, a baboon at the Dallas Zoo can look at a schedule of 14 NFL games, point to one team for each game and come out with at least seven winners." The next week, Kanda the Great, a gorilla at the Dallas Zoo, made his predictions by selecting pieces of paper from his trainer. Kanda got nine right and four wrong, better than all six *Morning News* sportswriters. The media descended on the story like hungry wolves, but would Kanda's performance have been reported if he had gotten, say, six right and seven wrong?

Not to be outdone, officials at the Minnesota Zoo in Apple Valley, Minnesota, reported that a dolphin named Mindy successfully predicted the outcomes of NFL games by choosing among pieces of Plexiglas, each bearing a different team's name. The opponents' Plexiglas sheets were dropped into Mindy's pool and the one she brought back to her handler was considered to be her "prediction." The handlers reported that Mindy had gotten thirty-two of fifty-three games correct. If so, that's 60 percent, enough to make a profit betting on football games.

How many other birds, bees, and beasts tried and failed to predict NFL games and went unreported because they failed? We don't know, and that's precisely the point. If hundreds of pets are forced to make pointless predictions, we will be misled by the successful ones that get reported because we don't take into account the hundreds of unsuccessful pets that were not reported.

This doesn't just happen in football games. A Minneapolis stock broker once boasted that he selected stocks by spreading *The Wall Street Journal* on the floor and buying the stock touched by the first nail on the right paw of his golden retriever. The fact that he thought this would attract investors says something about him—and perhaps his customers.

Another factor is that people seeking fifteen minutes of fame are tempted to fudge the data to attract attention. Was there an impartial observer monitoring the Minneapolis stockbroker and his dog each morning? Back when bridge was the most popular card game in America, a mathematically inclined bridge player estimated that far too many people were reporting to their local paper that they had been dealt a hand with thirteen cards of the same suit. Given the chances of being dealt such a hand, there were not nearly enough games being played to yield so many wacky hands. Tellingly, the suit reported was usually spades. People were evidently embellishing their experiences in order to get their names in the paper.

After Paul the octopus received worldwide attention, a previously obscure Singapore fortune teller reported that his assistant, Mani the parakeet, had correctly predicted all four winners of the World Cup quarterfinal matches. Mani was given worldwide publicity, and then predicted that Uruguay would beat Netherlands and that Spain would beat Germany in the semifinals, with Spain defeating Uruguay in the championship game. After Netherlands defeated Uruguay, Mani changed his finals prediction, choosing Netherlands, which turned out to be incorrect. Nonetheless, the number of customers visiting this fortune teller's shop increased from ten a day to ten an hour—which makes you wonder whether the owner's motives were purely sporting and whether his initial reports of Mani's quarterfinal predictions were accurate.

Why did Paul and Mani become celebrities who were taken seriously by soccer fans celebrating and cursing their predictions? Why didn't they stay unnoticed in the obscurity they deserved? It's not them, it's us.

■ HARDWIRED TO BE DECEIVED

More than a century ago, Sherlock Holmes pleaded to his long-suffering friend Watson, "Data! Data! Data! I can't make bricks without clay." Today, Holmes's wish has been granted in spades. Powerful computers sift through data, data, and more data. The problem is not that we don't have enough data, but that we are misled by what we have in front of us. It is not entirely our fault. You can blame it on our ancestors.

The evolution of certain traits is relatively simple. Living things with inheritable traits that help them survive and reproduce are more likely to pass these traits on to future generations than are otherwise similar beings that do not have these traits. Continued generation after generation, these valuable inherited traits become dominant.

The well-known history of the peppered moth is a simple, straightforward example. These moths are generally light-colored and spend most of their days on trees where they are camouflaged from the birds that prey on them. The first dark-colored peppered moths were reported in England in 1848, and by 1895, 98 percent of the peppered moths in Manchester were dark-colored. In the 1950s, the pendulum started swinging back. Dark-colored moths are now so rare that they may soon be extinct.

The evolutionary explanation is that the rise of dark-colored moths coincided with the pollution caused by the Industrial Revolution. The blackening of trees from soot and smog gave dark-colored moths the advantage of being better camouflaged and less likely to be noticed by predators. Because dark-colored moths were more likely to survive long enough to reproduce, they came to dominate the gene pool. England's clean-air laws reversed the situation, as light-colored moths are camouflaged better on pollution-free trees. Their survival advantage now allows them to flourish.

Other examples of natural selection are more subtle. For example, studies have consistently found that men and women are more attracted to people with symmetrical faces and bodies. This isn't just cultural—it is true across different societies, true of babies, and even found in other animals. In one experiment, researchers clipped the tail feathers of some male barn swallows to make them asymmetrical. Other males kept their symmetrical tail feathers. When female swallows were let loose in this mating pool, they favored the males with symmetrical feathers. This preference for symmetry is not just a superficial behavior. Symmetry evidently indicates an absence of genetic defects that might hamper a potential mate's strength, health, and fertility. Those who prefer symmetry eventually dominate the gene pool because those who don't are less likely to have offspring that are strong, healthy, and fertile.

Believe it or not, evolution is also the reason why many people took Paul and Mani seriously. Our ingrained preference for symmetry is an example of how recognizing patterns helped our human ancestors survive and reproduce in an unforgiving world. Dark clouds often bring rain. A sound in the brush may be a predator. Hair quality is a sign of fertility. Those distant ancestors who recognized patterns that helped them find food and water, warned them of danger, and attracted them to fertile mates passed this aptitude on to future generations. Those who were less adept at recognizing patterns that would help them survive and reproduce had less chance of passing on their genes. Through countless generations of natural selection, we have become hardwired to look for patterns and to think of explanations for the patterns we find. Storm clouds bring rain. Predators make noise. Fertile adults have nice hair.

Unfortunately, the pattern-recognition skills that were valuable for our long-ago ancestors are ill-suited for our modern lives, where the data we encounter are complex and not easily interpreted. Our inherited desire to explain what we see fuels two kinds of cognitive errors. First, we are too easily seduced by patterns and by the theories that explain them. Second, we latch onto data that support our theories and discount contradicting evidence. We believe stories simply because they are consistent with the patterns we observe and, once we have a story, we are reluctant to let it go.

When you keep rolling sevens at the craps table, you believe you are on a hot streak because you want to keep winning. When you keep throwing snake eyes, you believe you are due for a win because you want to *start* winning. We don't think hard enough about the fact that dice do not remember the past and do not care about the future. They are inanimate; the only meaning they carry is what we hopeful humans ascribe to them. If the hot streak continues or the cold streak ends, we are even more convinced that our fanciful theory is correct. If it doesn't, we invent excuses so that we can cling to our nonsensical story.

We see the same behavior when athletes wear unwashed lucky socks, when investors buy hot stocks, or when people throw good money after bad, confident that things must take a turn for the better. We yearn to make an uncertain world more certain, to gain control over things that we do not control, to predict the unpredictable. If we did well wearing these socks, then it must be that these socks help us do well. If other people made money buying this stock, then we can make money buying this stock. If we have had bad luck, our luck has to change, right? Order is more comforting than chaos.

These cognitive errors make us susceptible to all sorts of statistical deceptions. We are too quick to assume that meaningless patterns are meaningful when they are presented as evidence of the consequences of a government policy, the power of a marketing plan, the success of an investment strategy, or the benefits of a food supplement. Our vulnerability comes from a deep desire to make sense of the world, and it's notoriously hard to shake off.

■ PUBLISH OR PERISH

Even highly educated and presumably dispassionate scientists are susceptible to being seduced by patterns. In the cutthroat world of academic research, brilliant and competitive scientists perpetually seek fame and funding to sustain their careers. This necessary support, in turn, depends on the publication of interesting results in peer-reviewed journals. "Publish or perish" is a brutal fact of university life.

Sometimes, the pressure is so intense that researchers will even lie and cheat to advance their careers. Needing publishable results to survive, frustrated that their results are not turning out the way they want, and fearful that others will publish similar results first, researchers sometimes take the shortcut of manufacturing data. After all, if you are certain that your theory is true, what harm is there in making up data to prove it?

One serious example of this kind of deception is the vaccine scare created by the British doctor Andrew Wakefield. His 1998 coauthored paper in the prestigious British medical journal *The Lancet* claimed that twelve normal children had become autistic after being given the measles, mumps, and rubella (MMR) vaccine. Even before the paper was published, Wakefield held a press conference announcing his findings and calling for the suspension of the MMR vaccine.

Many parents saw the news reports and thought twice about what was previously a de rigeur procedure. The possibility of making their children autistic seemed more worrisome than the minute chances of contracting diseases that had been virtually eradicated from Britain. More than a million parents refused to allow their children to be given the MMR vaccine.

I live in the United States, but my wife and I read the news stories and we worried, too. We had sons born in 1998, 2000, and 2003, and a daughter born in 2006, so we had to make a decision about their vaccinations. We did our homework and talked to doctors, all of whom were skeptical of Wakefield's study. They pointed out that there is no evidence that autism has become more commonplace, only that the definition of autism has broadened in recent years and that doctors and parents have become more aware of its symptoms. On the other hand, measles, mumps, and rubella are highly contagious diseases that had been effectively eliminated in many countries precisely because of routine immunization programs. Leaving our children unvaccinated would not only put them but other children at risk as well. In addition, the fact that this study was so small (only twelve children) and the author seemed so eager for publicity were big red flags. In the end, we decided to give our children the MMR vaccine.

The doctors we talked to weren't the only skeptics. Several attempts to replicate Wakefield's findings found no relationship at all between autism and the MMR vaccine. Even worse, a 2004 investigation by a London *Sunday Times* reporter named Brian Deer uncovered some suspicious irregularities in the study. It seemed that Wakefield's research had been funded by a group of lawyers envisioning lucrative personal-injury lawsuits against doctors and pharmaceutical companies. Even more alarmingly, Wakefield himself was evidently planning to market an alternative vaccine that he could claim as safe. Were Wakefield's conclusions tainted by these conflicts of interest?

Wakefield claimed no wrongdoing, but Deer kept digging. What he found was even more damning: the data in Wakefield's paper did not match the official National Health Service medical records. Of the nine children who Wakefield reported to have regressive autism, only one had actually been diagnosed as such, and three had no autism at all. Wakefield reported that the twelve children were "previously normal" before the MMR vaccine, but five of them had documented developmental problems.

Most of Wakefield's coauthors quickly disassociated themselves from the paper. *The Lancet* retracted the article in 2010, with an editorial comment: "It was utterly clear, without any ambiguity at all, that the statements in the paper were utterly false." The *British Medical Journal* called the Wakefield study "an elaborate fraud," and the UK General Medical Council barred Wakefield from practicing medicine in the UK. Unfortunately, the damage was done. Hundreds of unvaccinated children have died from measles, mumps, and rubella to date, and thousands more are at risk. In 2011, Deer received a British Press Award, commending his investigation of Wakefield as a "tremendous righting of a wrong." We can only hope that the debunking of Wakefield will receive as much press coverage as his false alarms, and that parents will once again allow their children to be vaccinated.

Vaccines—by definition, the injection of pathogens into the body —are a logical fear, particularly when they relate to our children's safety. But what about the illogical? Can manufactured data persuade us believe the patently absurd?

Diederik Stapel, an extraordinarily productive and successful Dutch social psychologist, was known for being very thorough and conscientious in designing surveys, often with graduate students or colleagues. Oddly enough for a senior researcher, he administered the surveys himself, presumably to schools that he alone had access to. Another oddity was that Stapel would often learn of a colleague's research interest and claim that he had already collected the data the colleague needed; Stapel supplied the data in return for being listed as a coauthor.

Stapel was the author or coauthor on hundreds of papers and received a Career Trajectory Award from the Society of Experimental Social Psychology in 2009. He became dean of the Tilburg School of Social and Behavioral Sciences in 2010. Many of Stapel's papers were provocative but plausible. Others pushed the boundaries of plausibility. In one paper, he claimed that messy rooms make people racist. In another, he reported that eating meat—indeed, simply thinking about eating meat—makes people selfish. (No, I am not making this up!)

Some of Stapel's graduate students were skeptical of how strongly the data supported his half-baked theories and frustrated by Stepel's refusal to show them the actual survey data. They reported their suspicions to the chair of the psychology department, and Stapel soon confessed that many of his survey results were either manipulated or completely fabricated. He explained that, "I wanted too much too fast."

Stapel was suspended and then fired by Tilburg University in 2011. In 2013, Stapel gave up his PhD and retracted more than 50 papers in which he had falsified data. He also agreed to do 120 hours of community service and forfeit benefits worth 18 months' salary. In return, Dutch prosecutors agreed not to pursue criminal charges against him for the misuse of public research funds, reasoning that the government grants had been used mainly to pay the salaries of graduate students who did nothing wrong. Meanwhile, the rest of us can feel a little less guilty about eating meat and having messy rooms.

Another example of falsified data involved tests for extrasensory perception (ESP). Early ESP experiments used a pack of cards designed by Duke psychologist Karl Zener. The twenty-five card pack features five symbols: circle, cross, wavy lines, square, or star. After the cards are shuffled, the "sender" looks at the cards one by one and the "receiver" guesses the symbols.

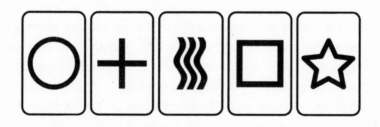

Figure 1.2: The five Zener cards

Some skeptics suggested that receivers could obtain high scores by peeking at the cards or by detecting subtle clues from the sender's behavior, such as a quick glance, a smile, or a raised eyebrow. Walter

J. Levy, the director of the Institute for Parapsychology established by ESP pioneer J. B. Rhine, tried to defuse such criticism by conducting experiments involving computers and nonhuman subjects. In one experiment, eggs containing chicken embryos were placed in an incubator that was heated by a light turned on and off by a computer random-event generator. The random-event generator had a 50 percent chance of turning the light on, but Levy reported that the embryos were able to influence the computer in that the light was turned on more than half the time.

Some of Levy's colleagues were skeptical of these telepathic chicks (I would hope so!) and puzzled by Levy's fussing with the equipment during the experiments. They modified the computer to generate a secret record of the results and observed the experiment from a secret hiding place. Their fears were confirmed. The secret record showed the light going on 50 percent of the time, and they witnessed Levy tampering with the equipment to push the reported light frequency above 50 percent. When confronted, Levy confessed and resigned, later explaining that he was under tremendous pressure to publish.

■ CHASING STATISTICAL SIGNIFICANCE

The examples we're most interested in, though, do not involve fraudulent data. They involve practices more subtle and widespread. Many concern statistical significance, an odd religion that researchers worship almost blindly. Suppose we want to test whether daily doses of aspirin reduce the risk of a heart attack. Ideally, we compare two random samples of healthy individuals. One sample takes aspirin daily, the second sample takes a placebo—an inert substance that looks, feels, and tastes like aspirin. The test should be double-blind so that the subjects and the doctors do not know who is in each group. Otherwise, the patients might be more likely to report (and the doctors more likely to hear) the "right results."

When the study is finished, the statisticians move in. The statistical issue is the probability that, by chance alone, the difference between the two groups would be as large as that actually observed. Most researchers consider a probability less than 0.05 to be "statistically significant." Patterns in the data are considered statistically persuasive if they have less than a 1-in-20 chance of occurring by luck alone. Paul the Octopus's record was statistically significant because he had less than a 1 percent chance of being that lucky.

In the first 5 years of an aspirin study of involving 22,000 males doctors, there were 18 fatal heart attacks in the placebo group, compared to 5 in the aspirin group. The probability of this large a disparity by chance alone is less than 1 percent. What about nonfatal heart attacks? Here, there were 171 in the placebo group and 99 in the aspirin group. The chances of this large a disparity by luck alone is about 1 in 100,000. These results were statistically significant and the American Heart Association now recommends daily aspirin for those with a high risk of suffering a heart attack.

On the other hand, not finding a statistically significant result is sometimes more interesting than finding one. In 1887 Albert Michelson and Edward Morley measured the speed of light both parallel and perpendicular to the earth's motion, expecting to find a difference that would confirm a theory that was popular at the time. But instead they found no statistically significant difference at all. Their research laid the groundwork for the development and the acceptance of Einstein's special theory of relativity. Their "failed" study helped revolutionize physics.

Closer to home, later in this book we will discuss arthroscopic surgery, a routine procedure performed hundreds of thousands of times each year for knee osteoarthritis. Recent studies have found no statistically significant benefits, a conclusion that could save millions of dollars each year in unnecessary surgery, not to mention the inconvenience and risk of complications from the surgical procedure. Not finding statistical significance for this widespread procedure was undoubtedly more valuable than many studies that have found statistical significance for the treatment of uncommon ailments.

Nonetheless, a study of psychology journals found that 97 percent of all published test results were statistically significant. Surely, 97 percent of all the tests that were conducted did not yield statistically significant results, but editors generally believe that tests are not worth reporting unless the results are statistically significant.

The same is true outside academia. A business or government researcher trying to demonstrate the value of a certain strategy, plan, or policy feels compelled to present statistically significant empirical evidence. Everywhere, researchers chase statistical significance, and it is by no means an elusive prey. With fast computers and plentiful data, finding statistical significance is trivial. If you look hard enough, it can even be found in tables of random numbers.

One way to find it is to test many theories but only report the results that are statistically significant. Even if only worthless theories are considered, one out of every twenty tests of worthless theories will be statistically significant. With mountains of data, powerful computers, and incredible pressure to produce publishable results, untold numbers of worthless theories get tested. Hundreds of researchers test thousands of theories, write up the statistically significant results, and discard the rest. The problem for society is that we only see the tip of this statistical iceberg. We see the statistically significant result, but not the tests that didn't work out. If we knew that behind the reported test were hundreds of unreported tests and remember that, on average, one out of every twenty tests of worthless theories will be statistically significant, we would surely view what does get reported with more skepticism.

Pharmaceutical companies, for example, test thousands of experimental drugs and, even in well-designed, unbiased studies, we can expect hundreds of worthless drugs to show statistically significant benefits—which can in turn generate immense profits. Drugmakers have a powerful incentive to test, test, and test some more. There is a much smaller incentive to retest an approved treatment to see whether the initial results were just a fluke—one of those one out of every twenty worthless treatments that turn out to be statistically significant.

When approved treatments do get retested, it is not at all surprising that the results are often disappointing. John Ioannidis holds positions at the University of Ioannina in Greece, the Tufts University School of Medicine in Massachusetts, and the Stanford University School of Medicine in California. (Imagine the frequent flier miles! Imagine the lack of sleep!) Ioannidis has devoted his career to warning doctors and the public about naively accepting medical test results that have not been convincingly replicated. In one study, he looked at 45 of the most widely respected medical studies during the years 1990 through 2003 that claimed to have demonstrated effective treatments for various ailments. In only 34 cases were attempts made to replicate the original test results with larger samples. The initial results were confirmed in 20 of these 34 cases (59 percent). For seven treatments, the benefits were much smaller than initially estimated; for the other seven treatments, there were no benefits at all. Overall, only 20 of the 45 studies have been replicated, and these were for the most highly respected studies! In the same year that Ioannidis published these unsettling findings, he wrote another paper with the damning title, "Why Most Published Research Findings Are False."

Another way to secure statistical significance is to use the data to discover a theory. Statistical tests assume that the researcher starts with a theory, collects data to test the theory, and reports the results—whether statistically significant or not. Many people work in the other direction, scrutinizing the data until they find a pattern and then making up a theory that fits the pattern. Ransacking data for patterns is fun and exciting—like playing Sudoku or solving a murder mystery. Examine the data from every angle. Separate the data into categories based on gender, age, and race. Discard data that muddle patterns. Look for something—anything—that is interesting. After a pattern is discovered, start thinking about reasons.

As researchers sift through the data, looking for patterns, they are explicitly or implicitly doing hundreds of tests. Imagine yourself in their shoes. First, you look at the data as a whole. Then you look at males and females separately. Then you differentiate between children and adults; then between children, teenagers, and adults; then between children, teenagers, adults, and seniors. Then you try different age cutoffs. You let the senior category be 65+, and when that doesn't work, you try 55+, or 60+, or 70+, or 75+. Eventually, something clicks. Even if researchers don't do formal statistical tests with every permutation of the data, they are still doing casual tests by looking for arrangements of the data that appear to be statistically significant. If we knew that the researcher obtained the published results by looking at the data in a hundred different ways, we would surely view the results with suspicion.

These practices—selective reporting and data pillaging—are known as *data grubbing*. The discovery of statistical significance by data grubbing shows little other than the researcher's endurance. We cannot tell whether a data grubbing marathon demonstrates the validity of a useful theory or the perseverance of a determined researcher until independent tests confirm or refute the finding. But more often than not, the tests stop there. After all, you won't become a star by confirming other people's research, so why not spend your time discovering new theories? The data-grubbed theory consequently sits out there, untested and unchallenged.

Many important scientific theories started out as efforts to explain unearthed patterns. For example, during the 1800s, most biologists believed that parental characteristics were averaged together to determine the characteristics of their offspring. For example, a child's height is an average of the parents' heights, modified perhaps by environmental influences.

Gregor Mendel, an Augustinian monk, conducted meticulous studies of tens of thousands of pea plants over an eight-year period. He looked at several different traits and concluded that the blending theory didn't work. When he cross-pollinated green-seeded plants with yellow-seeded plants, the offspring's seeds were either green or yellow, not yellowish-green. When he cross-pollinated smooth-seeded plants with wrinkly-seeded plants, the offspring's seeds were either smooth or wrinkled, not something in between. To explain the results of his experiments, he proposed what are now known as Mendel's Laws of Inheritance, an elegant probabilistic model of how traits pass from one generation to the next and sometimes skip generations. He conceived a theory to fit his data and thereby laid the foundation for modern genetics.

However, data grubbing has also been the source of thousands of quack theories. How can we tell the difference between a good theory and quackery? There are two effective antidotes: common sense and fresh data. If it is a ridiculous theory, we shouldn't be persuaded by anything less than overwhelming evidence, and even then be skeptical. Extraordinary claims require extraordinary evidence. Unfortunately, common sense is an uncommon commodity these days, and many silly theories have been seriously promoted by honest researchers. Have you heard the one about a baseball player's life expectancy falling by five years once he is elected to the Hall of Fame? Or the Chinese people who die of heart disease because they were born in a "fire year"? You will later in this book.

The second antidote is fresh data. It is not sensible to test a theory with the very data that were ransacked to concoct the theory. If a theory was made up to fit the data, then of course the data support the theory! Theories should be tested with new data that have not been contaminated by data grubbing.

When data-grubbed theories are tested with fresh data, the results are usually disappointing, which is not at all surprising. It is surely misleading to use the data that inspired a theory to test the theory, and it is surely unsurprising that the theory does not fit new data nearly as well as it fit the original data.

Case in point, I just flicked a quarter off my desk with the baby finger on my left hand, and the quarter landed tails. After seeing the quarter land tails, my theory is that if I flick a quarter off my desk with the baby finger on my left hand, it will always land tails. After all, my data support it. This theory is obviously stupid and useless, but no more so than some theories we will examine in detail in later chapters that are harder to see through even though they are derived in essentially the same way as my quarter-flicking theory. If children who died of cancer lived near power lines, then electromagnetic fields (EMFs) from power lines must cause cancer, right? If a theory sort of makes sense and you don't know that the theory came after looking at the data—after the quarter landed on the floor—it is tempting to believe that a theory that fits the data must be correct. After all, the data confirm the theory! This is one of those temptations that should be resisted.

Fortunately, we can resist. We can overcome the predilections we inherited from our distant ancestors as they struggled to survive and reproduce. We don't have to be duped by data.

■ **Don't be Fooled:** We are genetically predisposed to look for patterns and to believe that the patterns we observe are meaningful. If a baseball player plays a good game after wearing new socks, he shouldn't change socks. If the stock market does well after NFC teams win the Super Bowl, watch the game before investing. If a basketball player makes four shots in a row, he is hot and is very likely to make the next shot. If a heart-attack victim recovers after being sent healing thoughts from a thousand miles away, distant healing works. If a customer satisfaction survey finds that people living in homes with three bathrooms are more enthusiastic than are people living in homes with two bathrooms, that is the target market. If a country has a recession when federal debt was high, then government debt causes recessions. Throughout this book, we will debunk dozens of such examples.

Don't be fooled into thinking that a pattern is proof. We need a logical, persuasive explanation and we need to test the explanation with fresh data.

2

GARBAGE IN, GOSPEL OUT

CHARLES BABBAGE WAS BORN IN LONDON ON DECEMBER 26, 1791, a time of great change in technology and social mobility. He was keenly interested in mathematics, but frustrated by mistakes he found in mathematical and astronomical tables that were based on human calculations. The mistakes were not only intellectually frustrating, they had serious consequences, including causing captains to sail their ships into rocks and other hazards.

It was considered unpatriotic for an honorable Englishman to pay attention to French mathematicians. Nonetheless, Babbage did. He discovered that the French government had produced several mathematical tables using an automated human system. Senior mathematicians determined the formulas needed to fill in a table, and junior mathematicians respecified these formulas so that the calculations could be done by simple addition and subtraction. For example, to calculate 4 times 8, we can add 8 + 8 + 8 + 8 = 32. The menial work of adding and subtracting was done by specialists who were called "computers."

Babbage realized that, in theory, machines could be designed that would add and subtract with 100 percent accuracy, thereby eliminating human error. Babbage also knew about the calculating machines designed by two Germans (Wilhelm Schickard and Gottfried Wilhelm Leibniz) and the great French mathematician Blaise Pascal. As a teenager, Pascal had invented a mechanical calculator called the *Aritmatique* (or *Pascaline*) to help his father, a French tax collector. The *Aritmatique* was a box with visible dials connected to wheels hidden inside the box. Each dial had ten digits labeled 0 through 9. When the dial for the 1s column moved from 9 to 0, the dial for the 10s column moved up one notch; when the dial for the 10s column moved from 9 to 0, the dial for the 100s column moved up one notch; and so on. The *Aritmatique* could do addition and subtraction, but the dials had to be turned by hand.

Babbage put together these two ideas (converting complex formulas into simple calculations and automating the simple calculations) and designed a mechanical computer that could do the calculations perfectly every time. Called the Difference Engine, Babbage's first design was a steam-powered behemoth made of brass and iron that stood eight feet tall, weighed fifteen tons, and contained twenty-five thousand distinct parts. The Difference Engine could make calculations up to twenty decimals long and could print formatted tables of the results. After a decade tinkering with the design, Babbage began working on plans for a more powerful calculator he called the Analytical Engine. This design had more than fifty thousand components, used perforated cards to input instructions and data, and could store up to one thousand fifty-digit numbers. The Analytical Engine had a cylindrical "mill" fifteen feet tall and six feet in diameter that executed instructions sent from a twenty-five-foot-long "store." The store was like a modern computer's memory, with the mill the CPU.

Babbage's core principles were sound and similar to how modern computers work. However, given the technology of his time, his proposed machines were mechanical beasts and he was continually frustrated by limited financial resources and an inability to secure the precision components he needed. Nonetheless, his vision was so grand and his attention to detail so astonishing that his brain—the brain that invented the computer—is preserved to this day and displayed at the English Royal College of Surgeons.

On the 200th anniversary of his birth, in 1991, the London Science Museum made several of Babbage's computers from his original plans, including the Second Difference Engine, which worked as accurately as he intended and made calculations to 31 digits. In 2011, a private nonprofit project called Plan 28 was launched to build Babbage's Analytical Engine so that we can be inspired by Babbage's vision, which was literally a hundred years ahead of its time. The goal is to have it built by 2021, the 150th anniversary of Babbage's death.

Being a century ahead of his time, it is not surprising that many people were mystified by Babbage's vision. In his autobiography, he recounted that,

> On two occasions I have been asked [by members of parliament], "Pray, Mr. Babbage, if you put into the machine wrong figures, will the right answers come out?" . . . I am not able rightly to apprehend the kind of confusion of ideas that could provoke such a question.

Even today, when computers are commonplace, many well-meaning people still cling to the misperception that because computers do not make arithmetic mistakes, they are infallible. A 2014 article in Harvard's alumni magazine claimed that, "Whenever sufficient information can be quantified, modern statistical methods will outperform an individual or small group of people every time." That statement is either so hopelessly circular as to be meaningless or it is flat-out wrong.

The reality is that if we ask a computer to do something stupid, it will faithfully do it. Garbage in, garbage out is a snappy reminder of the fact that, no matter how powerful the computer, the value of the output depends on the quality of the input. A variation on this saying is garbage in, gospel out, referring to the tendency of people to put excessive faith in computer-generated output without thinking carefully about the input. If a computer's calculations are based on bad data, the output is not gospel, but garbage.

There are, unfortunately, far too many examples of people worshipping calculations based on misleading data. Here are a few.

■ GO TO THE BEST SCHOOL

David Leonhardt, Washington Bureau chief of *The New York Times*, has won several awards, including the Pulitzer Prize, for his writing on economic topics. In 2009 he wrote a *Times* column about *Crossing the Finish Line*, a book by William Bowen and Michael McPherson (two former college presidents) and a doctoral candidate who presumably did the heavy lifting by analyzing data for two hundred thousand students at sixty-eight colleges. The book's core argument is that the United States does a great job persuading students to go to college, but a lousy job getting students to graduate from college. Half of those who go to college don't graduate.

The first culprit they identify is under-matching: students who could go to colleges with high graduation rates choose instead to go to colleges with low graduation rates. Professor Bowen told Leonhardt, "I was really astonished by the degree to which presumptively well-qualified students from poor families under-matched." Overall, about half the low-income college-bound students with GPAs above 3.5 and SAT scores above 1200 could have gone to better colleges, but chose not to.

For example, 90 percent of the students at the University of Michigan graduate within six years, compared to only 40 percent at Eastern Michigan, yet many students with good enough grades to go to Michigan choose Eastern Michigan. An economic solution to under-matching would be to make Eastern Michigan more expensive or Michigan less expensive so that students would have an incentive to choose the school with the higher graduation rate.

If only it were that easy. These data are garbage and the conclusion is not gospel. Getting these so-called under-matched students to go to Michigan might actually lower their chances of graduating. The researchers assumed that the students were randomly assigned to Michigan or Eastern Michigan, much like the doctors who were randomly given aspirin or a placebo. College decisions are not a science experiment.

Self-selection bias occurs when people choose to be in the data—for example, when people choose to go to college, marry, or have children. When this happens, comparisons to people who make different choices are treacherous. For example, we are often told that college graduates earn more than high school graduates, suggesting that the observed difference in incomes measures the financial return from going to college. However, part of the reason college graduates earn more may be that they are brighter and more ambitious than those who choose not to go to college. People who make different choices may in fact be different.

Similarly, the under-matching argument is undermined by self-selection bias. Students not only choose to go to college, they choose which college to go to. Many students who choose Eastern Michigan over Michigan may do so because they believe they would have trouble graduating from Michigan. This may be the right choice. After all, they know themselves better than we do. Even though Eastern Michigan has a low overall graduation rate, perhaps every student who could have gone to Michigan, but chooses Eastern Michigan instead, does actually graduate. We cannot tell this from the data.

Self-selection bias is pervasive in "observational data," where we collect data by observing what people do. Because these people chose to do *what* they are doing, their choices may reflect who they are. This self-selection bias could be avoided with a controlled experiment in which people are randomly assigned to groups and told what to do. Fortunately for all of us, researchers seldom have the power to make us do things we don't want to do simply because they need experimental data.

For a valid under-matching study, students who are admitted to both Michigan and Eastern Michigan could be randomly assigned to each university. Then the graduation rates of the two groups could be compared. As unlikely as it seems, something similar was actually done in the 1960s in Ypsilanti, Michigan, where black children from low socioeconomic households were selected or rejected for an experimental preschool program based on the outcome of a coin flip. This study found that those who attended the preschool program were more likely to complete high school, less likely to be arrested, and more likely to have jobs. It may seem heartless to those who lost the coin flip, but this experiment demonstrated the value of the preschool program.

Oddly enough, Eastern Michigan University is located in Ypsilanti. An even odder coincidence is that in 2012, Eastern Michigan erroneously sent e-mails to 7,700 students (one third of the student body) telling them that they had flunked out. The school president apologized for this "inexcusable mistake," which would have pushed the school's graduation rate even lower.

A reader of Leonhardt's *New York Times* column posted a comment arguing that the quality of the education is more important than the graduation rate. (Otherwise, we could increase the graduation rate to 100 percent simply by passing out diplomas to every student—with no annoying requirements like papers, exams, or class attendance.) Leonhardt's response: "Well, college graduates earn 54 percent more on average than college dropouts, so the degree certainly seems to have economic meaning." Self-selection bias again! Surely, students who choose to go to college and choose to work hard enough to graduate from college are systematically different from college dropouts.

■ THE MORE VOTERS, THE BETTER?

Only about half of all eligible Americans vote in presidential elections. An interesting proposal to boost this percentage is to shame people who don't vote by posting their names in local newspapers or on the Internet. A more radical solution is suggested by this argument that appeared in the *New York Times* in 2014:

> Punishment and surveillance by itself causes people to withdraw from political participation—acts of engagement like voting or political activism. . . . In a large survey of mostly marginal men in American cities, the probability of voting declined by 8 percent for those who had been stopped and questioned by the police; by 16 percent for those who had experienced arrest; by 18 percent for those with a conviction; by 22 percent for those serving time in jail or prison.

The apparent implication is that voting would increase greatly if there were fewer arrests and convictions.

Before firing the police, consider that these are observational data. Perhaps the people being questioned, arrested, and convicted are not randomly selected from the population. Perhaps they have committed crimes. Perhaps people who do not vote are also more likely to commit crimes, and not because either causes the other.

■ FILL 'ER UP

Drinking is a chronic problem at many colleges, and very often a contributing factor to the dropout rate. Even when alcohol is not permitted on campus, there can be unfortunate incidents involving drunken students arrested in the surrounding neighborhoods. Students are upset about being arrested. Professors are upset that students are not studying. Parents are upset that the college is not monitoring and protecting their sons and daughters.

The principle of *in loco parentis* ("in the place of a parent") means that a college has a legal authority and responsibility to protect students, even from their own poor decisions. The application of this principle has waxed and waned but many colleges have good reason for concern. Students and parents have sued schools for being, in essence, bad parents. Arrests and deaths also have a chilling effect on admissions applications, which are the lifeblood of a college.

In 1984, E. Scott Geller, a psychology professor at Virginia Tech presented a research paper at the annual convention of the American Psychological Association, reporting what he saw at three bars near the Virginia Tech campus. (More fun than a science lab!) He found that, on average, drinkers who ordered beer by the pitcher consumed more than twice as much beer than did drinkers who ordered beer by the glass or bottle. His conclusion, reported nationwide, was that, "If we banned pitchers of beer we would have a significant impact on drinking."

Geller has published more than 350 research articles and among his many awards are the University Alumni Award for Excellence in Research and the Alumni Outreach Award from Virginia Tech for his exemplary real-world applications of behavioral science. But this was not one of his better studies. Common sense tells us that there is self-selection bias here in that people who order pitchers of beer are surely planning to drink a lot and generally fulfill their objective. There may be some psychological pressure to finish what has been paid for, but surely big drinkers will still be big drinkers even if they are forced to do so by the glass or the bottle.

Geller has done many studies of college drinking during his long and productive career and at the 2011 American Psychological Association convention, twenty-seven years after his bar study, he admitted the obvious: Many college students "intend to get intoxicated . . . We have shown in several studies that their intentions influence their behavior. If they intend to get drunk, it's difficult to stop that."

■ PUT DOWN THE REMOTE

So many television channels, so little worth watching. Scripted reality shows; talent contests with untalented contestants; Dr. Somebody telling people (who may be actors) that they are okay; Judge Somebody telling people (who may be actors) that they are jerks; comedies with incessantly annoying laugh tracks. Is it less painful if you watch television with the sound turned off?

Edward R. Murrow, one of America's most respected radio and television journalists, once said, "Television in the main is being used to distract, delude, amuse and insulate us." And this was in 1958, during the so-called golden age of television. It hasn't gotten better.

Scientists have long known that watching television causes a viewer's brainwaves to switch from beta waves (alert, logical) to alpha waves (relaxed, unfocused). A great Gary Larson cartoon with the caption "In the days before television" shows a family sprawled on the floor and couch staring at a blank wall.

Whether you're looking at a blank wall or a flickering light box, mindless staring (often accompanied by mindless eating and drinking) cannot be good for you. In 2011, a group of researchers reported that Australians who watch six hours of television a day die, on average, five years younger than people who don't watch any television. Doing the math, every hour of television past the age of twenty-five reduces life expectancy by twenty-two minutes. Not only do you waste an hour staring blankly, you lose an additional twenty-two minutes of your life. Taking into account people's lifetime television habits, they concluded that outlawing television would increase life expectancy by about two years.

The now familiar problem is that these are observational data with self-selection bias. Perhaps the people who choose to watch TV all day are less active, more depressed, or in worse health than are people who have more interesting things to do and are healthy enough to do them. For a valid experiment, we could randomly select two groups of people, with one group prohibited from watching TV and the other group forced to watch TV six hours a day. I'd hate to lose that coin toss.

■ PARDON MY FRENCH

At breakfast before the disastrous Battle of Waterloo, Napoleon declared, "Wellington is a bad general, the English are bad soldiers; we will settle this matter by lunchtime." For many, this is just another example of the unjustified arrogance that makes the French so annoying. However, a study by American Express and the French tourist bureau found that most Americans who have visited France more than once for pleasure in the past two years do not think the French are unfriendly. How in the world did they come to this conclusion?

Here is one way. Suppose that a researcher is hired to demonstrate that France is a fun travel destination. The researcher might conduct a simple survey:

1. How many business trips have you taken to France in the past two years?
2. How many pleasure (nonbusiness) trips have you taken to France in the past two years?
3. Do you think the French are unfriendly?

Suppose that most people who only take business trips to France think the French are unfriendly. This is why they never go to France unless they have to. The researcher throws out these responses.

Suppose that most people who have never been to France think the French are unfriendly. This is why they never go there. The researcher throws out these responses.

Suppose that most people who have taken just one pleasure trip to France think the French are unfriendly. This is why they never went back. The researcher throws out these responses too.

Suppose that most people who have taken more than one pleasure trip to France do not think the French are unfriendly. Finally! The answers the researcher wanted. The French tourism bureau can use these responses as the basis for their ad campaign: Most Americans who have visited France more than once for pleasure in the past two years do not think the French are unfriendly.

This statement is literally true, yet deceptive. There is self-selection bias in that those who chose to go back to France almost certainly had a good time on their previous visits. The false implication is that most people who go to France once want to go back.

This bias is inherent in all customer satisfaction surveys. An airline once advertised that 84 percent of the frequent business travelers from New York to Chicago preferred this airline to another airline. The puzzling thing about this ad was that only 8 percent of the people flying from New York to Chicago flew on this airline. If 84 percent of travelers prefer this airline, why were only 8 percent flying on it?

The answer to this puzzle is that the 84 percent figure was based on a survey of passengers who were on one of this airline's flights from New York to Chicago. It is not surprising that travelers who choose this airline prefer it. It *is* surprising is that 16 percent of the passengers prefer another airline. But we can hardly expect the airline to advertise that, "Sixteen percent of the people flying on our planes wish they weren't."

■ ONLY THE WEAK SURVIVE

Self-selection bias isn't the only potential problem with observational data. In the 1970s, a class-action lawsuit alleged that the Georgia-Pacific sawmill in Goss, Mississippi, discriminated against blacks in their initial job assignments and promotions. Fifty percent of the mill's labor force was black, but most black employees were hired in the lowest job classification ("utility") and never promoted.

At trial, the plant manager admitted that chief electrician was the only job at the mill that required any prior skills. The skills needed for all other positions could be learned on the job. The company's management also testified that hiring and promotion decisions were subjective and not based on any written procedures or specific criteria. The plant manager's explanation for why there were relatively few blacks in upper-level jobs included this gem: "black people are . . . contented more so in a semi-skilled job than taking on the responsibility and extra hard work and long hours."

The Fifth Circuit of the US Court of Appeals was not persuaded by this insult. They cited the US Supreme Court, in *Hazelwood School District v. United States*, "Where gross statistical disparities can be shown, they alone may . . . constitute prima facie proof of a pattern or practice of discrimination," and added that, "Although proof of discriminatory motive is generally required in disparate treatment cases, the evidence of subjective, standard-less decision-making by company officials, which is a convenient mechanism for discrimination, satisfies this requirement."

While the court's conclusion was no doubt correct, one part of the statistical evidence had a subtle flaw that was overlooked by everyone. The court was shown the 1976 wages of eleven employees who had been hired six years earlier to entry-level utility positions paying the same wages. In 1976 the five white employees earned an average of $3.88 per hour while the six black employees earned an average of only $2.99. This appeared to be clear evidence of salary discrimination. However, it is not that simple.

These data are backward-looking in that the study took a group of employees and looked backward instead of forward. In a forward-looking study, the researcher selects a sample and monitors it as time passes. One thousand people could be given medical checkups every year to see if there is a relationship between diet and heart disease. Or one thousand companies could be observed every year to see if there is a relationship between dividend policy and stock performance. In a backward-looking study, in contrast, the researcher selects a sample and looks at its history—for example, the medical records of one thousand elderly women or the past performance of one thousand companies.

Backward-looking studies often have *survivor bias* in that, when we choose a sample today and look backward, we only see the survivors. Medical histories of the elderly exclude those who did not live long enough to become elderly. Corporate financial histories exclude companies that went bankrupt.

A comparison of the 1976 salaries of people hired in 1970 is backward looking because it only includes those employees still with the company in 1976, thereby excluding those who were hired in 1970 and left the company voluntarily or involuntarily. Suppose the company hired ten whites and ten blacks in 1970 at exactly the same salary, and that half of each group are productive and half unproductive. Suppose, further, that over this six-year period salaries increased by 30 percent for productive employees and 10 percent for unproductive employees, independent of race. If all twenty employees were still with the company in 1976, average white and black salaries would be equal. If, however, unproductive white employees were fired, the average salary of the remaining whites would be higher than the average black salary. The same would happen if productive black employees left the company for better jobs elsewhere. We don't know if either of these things happened. The point is that a backward-looking study does not give a complete picture of what happened to everyone who was hired in 1970.

Many observational studies are tainted by survivor bias. For example, an HMO survey found that more than 90 percent of its members were satisfied. There are two kinds of survivor bias here, both of which bias the reported satisfaction rate upward: people who left the plan because they were dissatisfied and people who died.

Red Lion Hotels once ran full-page advertisements claiming that, "For every 50 business travelers who try Red Lion, a certain number don't come back. But 49 of 50 do." The basis for this claim was a survey of people staying at Red Lion, 98 percent of whom said "they would usually stay in a Red Lion Hotel when they travel." Obviously, people who stayed at Red Lion and didn't come back were excluded from this survey.

Here's a tricky one. A study of 115 cats that had been brought to New York City veterinary hospitals after falling from high-rise apartment buildings found that 5 percent of the cats that fell 9 or more stories died, while 10 percent of the cats that fell from lower heights died. The doctors speculated that this was because cats falling from higher heights are able to spread out their bodies and create a parachute effect. What's an alternative explanation?

There is survivor bias here in that those cats that died from their falls were not brought to the hospital. In addition, many cat owners may have given up on cats that were still alive, but badly injured in high falls, while cat owners whose pets fell shorter distances tended to be more optimistic and more willing to pay for treatment at a hospital.

■ DAMAGED PLANES

In World War II, the British Royal Air Force (RAF) planned to attach heavy plating to its airplanes to protect them from German fighter planes and land-based antiaircraft guns. The protective plates weighed too much to cover an entire plane, so the RAF collected data on the location of bullet and shrapnel holes on planes that returned from bombing runs. Figure 2.1 is a stylized representation, showing most holes on the wings and rear of the plane, and very few on the cockpit, engines, or fuel tanks—suggesting that the protective plates should be put on the wings and rear. Do you agree?

Figure 2.1: Which Places Need Protection?

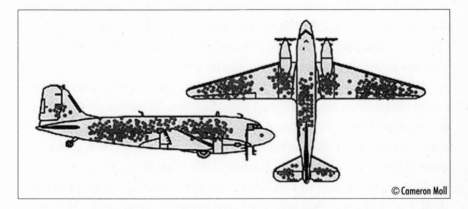

© Cameron Moll

Abraham Wald, a Hungarian Jew who had fled to the United States, had the insight to recognize that these data suffered from survivor bias. Returning planes seldom had holes in the cockpit and fuel tanks because those planes that were hit there did not survive and return to Britain. Returning planes were more likely to have holes in the wings because these holes did little damage. Wald's advice was exactly the opposite of the initial conclusion. Instead of reinforcing the locations with the most holes, they should reinforce the locations with no holes.

It worked. Far fewer planes were shot down and far more returned safely, ready to continue the war effort. Wald's clear thinking helped win the war.

■ SUCCESS SECRETS

In writing his bestselling book *Good to Great*, Jim Collins and his research team spent five years looking at the forty-year history of 1,435 companies and identified 11 stocks that clobbered the average stock:

Abbott Laboratories	Kimberly-Clark	Pitney Bowes
Circuit City	Kroger	Walgreens
Fannie Mae	Nucor	Wells Fargo
Gillette	Philip Morris	

After scrutinizing these eleven great companies, Collins identified several common characteristics and attached catchy names to each, like Level 5 Leadership—leaders who are personally humble, but professionally driven to make their company great.

Collins described his work as a "search for timeless, universal answers that can be applied by an organization." His search yielded the treasure he sought: "Almost any organization can substantially improve its stature and performance, perhaps even become great, if it conscientiously applies the framework of ideas we've uncovered." Readers who wanted to believe did believe. *Good to Great* sold more than four million copies and appeared on several lists of the best management books of all time.

The problem, of course, is that this is a backward-looking study undermined by survivor bias. Here is how the study should have been done. Start with a list of companies that existed at the beginning of this forty-year period. It could be all the companies in the S&P 500 index, all the companies traded on the New York Stock Exchange, or some other list. The important point is that the list starts forty years ago. Then, use plausible criteria to select eleven companies predicted to do better than the rest. These criteria must be applied in an objective way, without peeking at how the companies did over the next forty years. It is not fair or meaningful to predict which companies will do well *after* looking at which companies did well! Those are not predictions, just history.

After the chosen eleven are identified, their subsequent performance can be compared to other companies over a forty-year period. If Collins had done this, no doubt some of the eleven companies would have disappointed. Some might have gone bankrupt. So would some of the companies he did not select. That is the nature of the beast. But it would have been a fair comparison.

Collins did not do this. He insured that his eleven companies would not disappoint by choosing them at the *end* of the forty-year period based on their success. Collins wrote that he "developed all of the concepts . . . by making empirical deductions directly from the data." He thought he was boasting that his study was unbiased and professional. He didn't just make this stuff up. He went wherever the data took him.

In reality, Collins was admitting that he had no clue why some companies do better than others. And he was revealing that he was blissfully unaware of the perils of deriving theories from data. To buttress the statistical legitimacy of his theory, Collins talked to two professors at the University of Colorado. One said that, "the probabilities that the concepts in your framework appear by random chance are essentially zero." The other professor was more specific. He asked, "What is the probability of finding by chance a group of eleven companies, all of whose members display the primary traits you discovered while the direct comparisons do not possess those traits?" He calculated this probability to be less than 1 in 17 million. Collins concluded that, "There is virtually no chance that we simply found eleven random events that just happened to show the good-to-great pattern we were looking for. We can conclude with confidence that the traits we found are strongly associated with transformations from good to great."

I don't know how this probability of 1 in 17 million was calculated—I contacted the professor and he couldn't remember—but I do know that it is incorrect. The professor's calculations assume that the five traits were specified *before* looking at the data. They were not, and thus the calculations are irrelevant. The correct probability is not 1 in 17 million. It is 1. That's right: 100 percent.

Suppose that I am dealt five playing cards: the three of clubs, eight of clubs, eight of diamonds, queen of hearts, and ace of spades. Isn't that amazing? The chances of being dealt these particular cards is about one in three million and, yet, there it is! If I had correctly predicted these five cards *before* they were dealt, that would have been amazing. Not so in predicting the cards *after* they have been dealt. After I look at the cards, the probability of having these five cards is one, not one in three million.

When we look back in time at any group of companies, the best or the worst, we can *always* find some common characteristics. Look, every one of those eleven companies selected by Collins has either an *i* or an *r* in its name, and several have both an *i* and an *r*. Is the key for going from good to great to make sure that your company's name has an *i* or *r* in it? Of course not.

Finding common characteristics *after* the companies have been selected is not at all unexpected and not at all interesting. The interesting question is whether these common characteristics are of any use in predicting which companies will succeed in the future.

For these eleven companies, the answer is no. Fannie Mae stock went from above $80 a share in 2001 to less than $1 a share in 2008. Circuit City went bankrupt in 2009. The performance of the other nine stocks following the publication of *Good to Great* was distinctly mediocre. From the publication of the book through 2012, five stocks did better than the overall stock market, six did worse.

Twenty years earlier, another best-selling business book did something very similar and had exactly the same problems. The real lesson from this recurring cycle is that the authors who write these books and the millions of people who buy them do not realize that the books are fundamentally flawed.

McKinsey, one of the world's top consulting firms, asked two obscure consultants, Tom Peters and Robert Waterman, to take a look at several successful companies. Peters and Waterman talked to other McKinsey consultants and came up with a list of forty-three companies with good reputations and strong financials. They then talked to managers and read magazine stories, looking for common themes. This rather casual study was the basis for their wildly influential and successful book, *In Search of Excellence*, which identified eight common factors that Peters and Waterman found in these forty-three excellent companies—for example, a bias for action and being close to the consumer. This, too, was a backward-looking study. There is no way of knowing whether companies with a "bias for action," whatever that means, were more successful than other companies, or whether companies that had been excellent in the past would be excellent in the future.

Thirty-five of these forty-three companies have publicly traded stock. Since the book was published, fifteen have done better than the overall stock market, twenty worse. Collins, Peters, and Waterman do not provide any evidence that the characteristics they describe were responsible for these companies' past success. To do that, they would have had to provide a theoretical justification for these characteristics, select companies *beforehand* that did and did not have these characteristics, and monitor their success according to some metric established beforehand. They did none of this.

This problem plagues the entire genre of books on formulas/secrets/recipes for a successful business, a lasting marriage, living to be one hundred, and so on and so forth, that are based on backward-looking studies of successful businesses, marriages, and lives. There is inherent survivor bias. If we think we know any secrets for success, a valid way to test our theory would be to identify businesses or people with these traits and see how they do over the next ten or twenty or fifty years. Otherwise, we are just staring at the past instead of predicting the future.

■ **Don't be Fooled:** We observe people working, playing, and living, and we naturally draw conclusions from what we see. Our conclusions may be distorted by the fact that these people chose to do what they are doing. The traits we observe may not be due to the activity, but may instead reflect the people who chose to do the activity.

If we are told that kids who play competitive sports are confident, we shouldn't assume that playing competitive sports builds confidence. It may be that confident kids like to play competitive sports. If we are told that people who work on Wall Street are aggressive, we shouldn't assume that Wall Street nurtures aggression. It may be that Wall Street attracts aggressive people. If a Pulitzer Prize–winning journalist and the winner of a university award for excellence in research can be duped by self-selection bias, we all need to be wary.

We naturally draw conclusions from what we see—workers' wages, damaged aircraft, successful companies. We should also think about what we do not see—the employees who left, the planes that did not return, the companies that failed. The unseen data may be just as important, or even more important, than the seen data. To avoid survivor bias, start in the past and look forward. Look at people who were hired twenty years ago, planes that were sent on bombing missions, companies that were in business forty years ago—and see what happened next.

3

APPLES AND PRUNES

I HAVE A FRIEND NAMED STEVE WHO DROPPED OUT OF CAL TECH TO join the Army Rangers, an elite group of US soldiers sent on high-risk, close-combat missions. Part of the Ranger Creed is, "My country expects me to move further, faster and fight harder than any other soldier."

Steve's unit specialized in airborne assault missions and his knees took a beating from hundreds of parachute jumps. One time, his team was ambushed and pinned down in some rice paddies in Vietnam. They couldn't lift themselves up to fight or run, so they stayed as low as possible while they waited for helicopters to come in and disperse the enemy. Luckily, a sniper nicknamed Wild Bill had stayed on high ground for just this situation. Bill was three hundred yards from the rice paddies, but he routinely hit targets at three times that distance. Wild Bill picked off the enemy solders one by one as they peeked out of their hiding places. By the time the choppers arrived, all the enemy soldiers were either dead or had fled. Another time, Wild Bill shot an enemy general in his car from a hundred yards away. The bullet was so powerful that it pierced the car's supposedly bulletproof windshield, passed through the driver, and killed the general sitting in the backseat.

Steve retired from the Rangers with a pair of bad knees and a collection of amazing stories. Back in the States, he lived a peaceful but active life playing sports and teaching scuba diving until his osteoarthritic knees slowed him down. Osteoarthritis is a degenerative disease and Steve was frustrated by bleak predictions of a less-active future. One doctor told him, "You're too old to play sports," which is not what Steve wanted to hear.

Steve is hardly alone. Our knee joints are susceptible to tears, strains, and bits of loose cartilage after decades of supporting our overweight bodies while we stand, walk, run, jump, and dance. The most common treatment, used hundreds of thousands of times each year, is arthroscopic surgery. Two small incisions are made, one for a small fiberoptic camera and one for the miniature instruments used for the surgery. The surgeon removes the debris and then repairs, cleans, smooths, and trims what is left. Five thousand dollars later, the pain is gone. At least that's the theory.

Steve had arthroscopic surgery and raved about the results. He told me over and over that I should have an operation to repair my own tender knees. But I was skeptical. For decades, arthroscopic surgery had not been compared to anything. The doctors did the surgery, the patients said they felt better, and what more do we need to know? Well, for one thing, were their knees really improved? Perhaps the patients said they felt better because they thought they were supposed to feel better. Never underestimate the power of suggestion.

Wary of undergoing an unnecessary surgery, I looked into this further. The truly scientific way to tell if surgery makes a real difference is to do a controlled experiment in which randomly selected patients have arthroscopic surgery while others do not. A seemingly insurmountable difficulty is that the patients would know whether they had surgery, and this would influence their reports about how they felt.

To get around this problem, a controlled experiment conducted in the 1990s using 180 military veterans (not including Steve) set up an elaborate ruse. For those in the comparison group, two superficial incisions were made and the doctors acted out a charade that mimicked arthroscopic surgery. The patients did not know that they were part of an experiment. Nor did the doctors who independently assessed the veterans' conditions over the next two years. The study concluded that at no point did those patients who had real arthroscopic surgery feel less pain or function any better than the comparison group that had the phony surgery. Evidently, the reported pain relief was due entirely to the placebo effect that occurs when people who believe in the power of medicine and are hopeful of a medical cure respond positively to treatment, even if the treatment has no medical value.

After this study was published in 2002 in the *New England Journal of Medicine*, another study (published six years later in the same journal) confirmed that patients with knee osteoarthritis who received arthroscopic knee surgery, medication, and physical therapy fared no better on measures of pain, stiffness, and physical functions than did a comparison group that only received medication and physical therapy. Many doctors now advise patients to forego the surgery. This was the advice I received from my doctor—a sports medicine specialist—and I trusted him.

Something very similar happened with gastric freezing—a bizarre and now-discredited remedy for stomach ulcers. Stomach ulcers can be an excruciatingly painful ailment and were once commonly treated by surgically cutting off the supply of acid to the stomach. A doctor thinking outside the box thought that maybe the pain could be reduced by using ice to numb the stomach, in much the same way that ice is used to reduce the pain from a sprained ankle and other external injuries. However, swallowing dozens of ice cubes would not only be unpleasant but inefficient, since there was no way of ensuring that the ice cubes made sustained contact with the ulcer.

The proposed solution was to insert a balloon into the stomach of an ulcer sufferer and pump a supercooled fluid through this balloon. This would be certainly less expensive and less dangerous than surgery, though the effects would not be as long-lasting. Experiments done in the 1950s concluded that this wacky idea actually worked, in that patients reported reduced acid secretions and stomach pains. After the results were published in the prestigious *Journal of the American Medical Association*, gastric freezing was used for several years to ease the suffering of ulcer patients.

Like arthroscopic surgery for knee problems, there was no comparison group for gastric freezing and, thus, no way to know if it really worked. When asked about their stomach pains, the patients may have been inclined to give what they believed to be the right answer.

Again, what was needed was a controlled experiment in which randomly selected patients had supercooled fluid pumped into them while another group received a body-temperature fluid. Of course, none of the patients could be told which fluid they were receiving.

When this experiment was eventually done, the results were surprising. While 34 percent of those receiving the gastric-freezing treatment reported improvement, 38 percent of those receiving the body-temperature fluid did too. The placebo effect again! Subsequent studies confirmed that gastric freezing had no real benefits, and doctors have stopped stuffing icy balloons down people's throats.

As in these examples, well-designed empirical studies usually involve comparisons. However, comparisons are not always fair and valid, as illustrated by the next example. Sometimes it's like comparing apples to prunes.

■ THE MURDER CAPITAL OF MASSACHUSETTS

If the Dow Jones Industrial Average falls 100 points in a day, is that a lot or a little? We can put the change into perspective by calculating the percentage decline. If the Dow started the day at 1,000, a 100-point drop is a 10 percent decline (panic). If the Dow started the day at 10,000, a 100-point drop is a 1 percent decline (annoying). Percentage changes in stock prices are informative. However, some percentage changes are misleading, for example, when comparing the percentage change in something small to the percentage change in something big.

Wellfleet is a small Massachusetts town known for its oysters, artists, and tranquility. There was considerable surprise when a Boston newspaper reported that Wellfleet had the highest murder rate in Massachusetts, with forty murders per one hundred thousand residents that year—more than double the murder rate in Boston, which had only seventeen murders per one hundred thousand residents. A puzzled reporter looked into this statistical murder mystery and found that no Wellfleet police officer, including one who had lived in Wellfleet for fifty years, could remember a murder ever occurring in Wellfleet.

However, a man accused of murdering someone twenty miles away had turned himself in at the Wellfleet police station, and this Wellfleet arrest had been erroneously counted as a Wellfleet murder. Because Wellfleet had only 2,491 residents, this one misrecorded arrest translated into 40 murders per 100,000 residents. Boston, in contrast, had 98 murders, which is 17 murders per 100,000 residents.

This murder mystery shows how a statistical fluke can make a big difference if the base is small. A misrecorded murder in Boston has little effect on its murder rate. A misrecorded murder in Wellfleet puts a small village known for its oysters and artists on par with Detroit. One way to deal with a small base is to use data for several years to get a bigger base. Wellfleet's average murder rate over the past fifty years is one with the misrecorded arrest and zero without it—either way confirming that it is indeed a peaceful town. So relax, and pass the oysters.

■ PLEASE OPEN A QUARRY IN MY BACKYARD

Temecula is a Southern California community approximately equidistant from Los Angeles, San Diego, and Orange County. Although it is in an inland valley, Temecula is only twelve miles from the Pacific Ocean and daily ocean breezes carry cool air through a gap in the mountains, giving the Temecula Valley a moderate Mediterranean climate.

Blessed with wonderful weather, can-do enthusiasm, and a strongly pro-business attitude, Temecula's population grew from under 2,000 in 1980 to over 100,000 in 2010, with a median family income over $80,000. The small town also boasts a 128-acre sports facility with 10 baseball fields (5 with lights), 2 lighted football/soccer fields, a swimming pool, a gymnasium, and a community center.

The sunny days and cool nights are ideal not only for attracting people but also for producing wine. There now more than thirty wineries in the Temecula Valley along with hundreds of antique dealers, specialty shops, and restaurants; nine golf courses; and the largest casino in California. There is hot air ballooning, a car show, a jazz festival, and a film festival. In less than thirty years, this rather small town has evolved into a premiere tourist destination, with seventy thousand people a month staying in Temecula hotels and one-sixth of Temecula's residents involved in the tourist industry.

In 2005, one of the nation's largest mining and construction companies applied for a permit to build a quarry near Temecula—a mega-quarry, really, that would be the equivalent of seventeen football fields long and as deep as the Empire State Building is tall. Rocks would be dislodged from a mountain by daily blasts of 10,000 pounds of explosives and then crushed into gravel and sand (called *aggregate*) that is used for concrete, asphalt, and other construction materials. In addition to the crushing equipment, there would be 2 asphalt plants, a concrete plant, and a rubber recycling plant. Mining and processing would go on 20 hours a day, 6 days a week, producing 5 million tons of aggregate a year. Loading and shipping would be 24 hours a day, 7 days a week, with 1,600 trucks a day entering and leaving the site.

The proposed quarry was in the mountain gap where ocean breezes carry cool air to the Temecula Valley. Residents were understandably alarmed about the effects of this mega-quarry on the city's economy and property values. What would tourists and homeowners do if the sea breeze carried dust, noise, odors, and other pollutants into their beautiful city?

Not to worry, said the mining company. A prominent local economist hired by the company to prepare an economic analysis concluded that the quarry would bring in $172 million in annual benefits with no costs whatsoever for residents. The mining company was Santa Claus in disguise, bringing hundred-million-dollar presents to those who still believe in Santa.

If the company's claims were true, cities would be begging for quarries. Instead of offering tax benefits, low-interest loans, and infrastructure to attract professional sports teams, cities would offer these incentives to mining companies. "Here's one hundred million dollars. Please start mining in our city."

But they don't.

Even the economist that the company hired admitted as much, writing that "aggregate mining operations almost always meet with opposition." Why are people opposed to hundreds of millions of dollars in benefits with no strings attached? Are people simply naive or are the paid consultants' estimates grossly misleading? What's your guess? Let's look at this consultant's estimates of the benefits and costs and see what we find.

The calculations of the economic benefits were presented in several spreadsheets filled with mind-numbing detail about such things as the price of rubble and the amount of flocculent needed to remove fine material from water. All this detail created an illusion of rigorous economic analysis, while disguising the fact that $150 million of the spreadsheet's $172 million bottom line was not actually a local benefit, but the company's annual profits. That's right, the economist counted $150 million of corporate profit as a benefit for local residents simply because the company was selling Temecula's earth. Unless there was some vicarious pleasure from watching a corporation get rich, there was no local benefit whatsoever from such profits.

The remaining $22 million in projected benefits were from ninety-nine jobs at the new quarry, mainly truck drivers transporting aggregate to construction sites. Here, too, there was a problem. The proposed Temecula quarry would be in Riverside County, right next to the border with San Diego County. The company predicted that 60 percent of the aggregate produced at the Temecula quarry would be transported to San Diego County, reducing the need to transport aggregate to San Diego from more distant Riverside County quarries.

The corporate consultants argued that the total production of aggregate would not change. One consultant put it this way: "All that a new quarry can do is substitute for the supply of an existing quarry. New quarries cannot and do not cause additional aggregate to be mined, shipped, or used."

Here, the consultants were correct. The total production of aggregate is determined by demand—how many homes, businesses, and roads are being built. All a new quarry would do is change *where* the aggregate is produced. Five million tons produced in Temecula would mean five million fewer tons produced at quarries in other parts of Riverside County. The company's own argument implies that there would be *no* increase in production or jobs, just a shifting of production and jobs from existing quarries to the new quarry.

So, the claimed $172 million in benefits for local residents turns out to be nothing at all—just $150 million in profits for the construction company and 99 jobs shifted from existing quarries to the new quarry. It is not the costs that are zero, it is the benefits!

What about the economist's claim that there are no costs? Were Temecula residents unnecessarily concerned about property values? Another consultant argued that in the city of Corona, forty miles away, there had been a "direct positive correlation" between mine production and property values. City leaders evidently should be celebrating that their fair city was chosen for this mega-mine—which would have a mega-effect on property values.

This argument is outrageous. When any two things increase over time, there can be a statistical correlation without any causal relationship. Figure 3.1 shows beer sales and the number of married people in the United States. The correlation is a remarkable 0.99. From this strong correlation, can we then conclude that drinking leads to marriage? Or perhaps the other way around, that marriage leads to drinking?

Figure 3.1: Drinking and Marriage

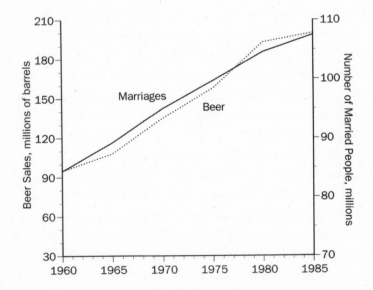

While there are surely a few married folks who would agree with that conclusion, the actual explanation is that as the population has grown over time, so has beer consumption. And so have marriages, babies, automobiles, shoes, college attendance, heart attacks, and many other things. Does wearing shoes increase the number of babies? Does driving cars cause heart disease? There isn't necessarily any relationship between things that increase with the population—other than that they increase with the population.

It's the same with mine production and property values. Both have increased over time and there isn't necessarily a casual relationship between them. The consultants were paid to prove something and when they found superficial evidence, they latched on and wouldn't let go.

We all do this. It is so common that it even has a name: *confirmation bias*. We think we can predict the result of a football game, an election, or a stock pick, and we overestimate our forecasting ability. If our prediction turns out to be correct, this confirms how smart we are. If our prediction does not come true, it was just bad luck—poor officiating, low voter turnout, the irrationality of other investors.

Of course, consultants are often paid to find evidence of things they may not believe. Does anyone really think that living near a quarry increases the value of your home? It doesn't even pass the straight-face test. Try making this claim to a friend without laughing at its absurdity.

Nonetheless, for the right price, some people are willing to look for evidence that confirms the absurd and then pass it off without flinching. They often find confirming evidence in coincidental correlations, and coincidental correlations are the norm with data that grow over time along with the population.

This is exactly what the mining company tried to do, and they even backed it up with misdirecting statistics from surrounding towns. Another consultant (they hired *lots* of consultants) argued that home prices in Corona, California—which has had quarries for decades were —increasing at approximately the same rate as home prices in Temecula, which (so far) has no quarries. Therefore, quarries do not depress property values.

Think about the logic behind this assumption. If the price of steak and the price of potatoes increase at the same rate, does that mean that a steak costs the same as a potato? Suppose that two identical homes are five miles apart in otherwise equally attractive locations. Their market values are the same and have been increasing steadily by 3 percent a year. In 1980, a mine opens next to one home and its value immediately drops 20 percent. After that, both home values continue increasing by 3 percent a year, maintaining a constant 20 percent wedge between their market values, as shown in Figure 3.2.

Figure 3.2: Location, Location, Location

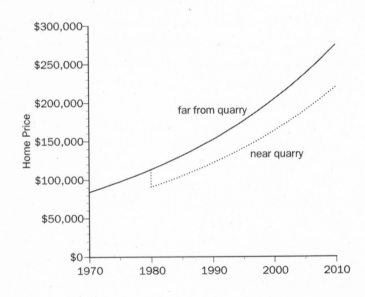

Just as the mining company consultant argued, the value of the home near the mine is increasing at the same rate as the value of the home five miles away. Does this parallel movement tell us whether the mine had a positive effect, a negative effect, or no effect on the value of the home near the quarry? No. The only way to answer this question is to see which home has the higher price!

As any good magician knows, the key to fooling an audience is distraction. By talking about *changes* in home prices, the consultant is trying to distract our attention from the real issue: Are home prices lower near quarries? The answer is a resounding yes.

We will seldom find identical homes, one next to a quarry and one far away, but we can use a statistical model that takes into account home characteristics, such as square footage, the number of bathrooms, proximity to amenities (such as good schools) and proximity to disamenities (such as mines). Using data for many homes—some 1,800 square feet, some 2,400; some with two bathrooms, some with three; some near a mine, some far away—we can estimate what an extra 100 square feet is worth, what an additional bathroom is worth, what proximity to a mine is worth.

A 2006 study of thousands of homes in Ohio did exactly that. Figure 3.3 shows the conclusions. Property values are reduced by 15 percent for homes 1 mile from a quarry, by 9 percent for homes 2 miles away. Surprise, surprise—you can't increase the value of your home by persuading a mining company to put a quarry in your backyard.

Figure 3.3: Living Next to a Quarry

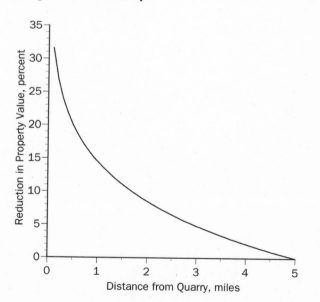

The Temecula Valley Convention & Visitors Bureau and the Chamber of Commerce—two pro-business organizations in a strongly pro-business community—listened to the mining company's arguments and were unpersuaded. Both groups vehemently opposed the quarry.

The corporation spent seven years and millions of dollars trying to get their quarry approved, but after reading thousands of pages of analysis and listening to dozens of hours of testimony from concerned citizens and dueling experts, the Riverside County Planning Commission and Board of Supervisors both rejected the quarry proposal. They evidently don't believe in Santa.

■ **Don't be Fooled:** Comparisons are the lifeblood of empirical studies. We can't determine if a medicine, treatment, policy, or strategy is effective unless we compare it to some alternative. But watch out for superficial comparisons: comparisons of percentage changes in big numbers and small numbers, comparisons of things that have nothing in common except that they increase over time, comparisons of irrelevant data. All of these are like comparing apples to prunes.

4

OOPS!

COMPUTER MAKES CALCULATIONS QUICKLY AND CORRECTLY, BUT doesn't ask if the calculations are meaningful or sensible. A computer just does what it is told.

Sometimes, the answer is wrong because the question is wrong. If I want to know the square root of 169 and I tell the computer to calculate the square root of 196, the computer will report that the answer is 14. This is the correct answer to the question I asked, but it is not the correct answer to the question that I meant to ask. These kinds of mistakes are called *computational errors*, but they are really human errors. Unfortunately, some computational errors have had extremely serious consequences.

In 1998, NASA launched a spacecraft named the Mars Climate Orbiter. The plan was that once the Orbiter neared Mars, it would be sent into orbit more than 100 miles from Mars, where it could safely record weather data. This $300 million space mission failed because the ground-based software measured thrust force in pounds per second and the engineers forgot to convert the numbers into newtons, the metric measurement used by the Orbiter. As the Orbiter neared Mars, the engines were fired to push the spacecraft into orbit around Mars but, because of this miscalculation, the Orbiter was propelled to within 37 miles of Mars and burned up in the atmosphere. Three hundred million dollars fried, all because of a typo.

In 2012 there was a very different and even more expensive mistake. The UK branch of JP Morgan lost between $5 and $10 billion in the "London Whale" debacle, so named for the trader who placed the massive bets. It turned out that the bank's risk had been grossly underestimated because of a silly mistake. Part of the risk measurement involved the calculation of a simple average—for example, the average of 6 and 10 is $(6 + 10)/2 = 8$. The programmer forgot to divide by the number of observations, so the average was incorrectly reported to be $6 + 10 = 16$. The consequence was that the calculated measure of risk was much smaller than the actual risk. JP Morgan thought the whale trades were relatively safe when they were, in fact, quite dangerous and, ultimately, disastrous.

Sometimes, computers are given incorrect data instead of incorrect instructions. The Joint Economic Committee of Congress once reported that the richest one half of 1 percent of US families owned 35 percent of the nation's wealth. This was a staggering increase from the 25 percent figure calculated 20 years earlier. Politicians made speeches (surprise, surprise!). Newspapers reported the story with sensational headlines. The Chairman of the Joint Economic Committee, Wisconsin Democrat David Obey, said that "it is proof that the rich get richer," and noted that the previous record was 32 percent in 1929. Obey concluded that, "This study makes mincemeat of the notion that this country needs more incentives for rich folks." A prominent economist, John Kenneth Galbraith, ominously warned that an intense concentration of wealth in the 1920s had been one of the causes of the Great Depression. Ordinary people could not afford to buy things and companies could not afford to hire people to produce things that people were not buying. David M. Gordon, professor of economics at the New School for Social Research in New York, warned that "democracy in the United States is now in greater jeopardy than at any time in the past 50 years—and probably since the Republic's founding."

Some skeptics in Washington rechecked the calculations and discovered that the reported increase was due almost entirely to the incorrect recording of one family's $2 million wealth as $200 million, an error that raised the average wealth of the handful of rich people who had been surveyed by nearly 50 percent. The corrected numbers showed that the richest one half of 1 percent owned 26.9 percent, not 35 percent of the nation's wealth.

After the mistake was discovered, Obey issued a statement that sounded oddly insincere: "We are gratified to learn that the increased concentration of wealth in the hands of the super rich is not as great as it originally appeared." Other economists hedged their earlier statements but refused to back down from their conclusions.

This error was corrected before it had any effect on economic policies. Another mix-up, though, was not corrected soon enough.

■ THE GOVERNMENT DEBT TIPPING POINT

A 2010 paper by two Harvard professors, Carmen Reinhart and Ken Rogoff, concluded that a nation's economic growth is imperiled when the ratio of federal government debt to the nation's annual output (GDP) exceeds 90 percent. In this case, it would take 90 percent of the nation's output to repay all the money the government had borrowed.

This sounds serious, but it isn't. There is no compelling reason for a government to pay off its debt any time soon. When we buy a home, the mortgage is much larger than our annual income. So what? The relevant question is whether our income is large enough to make our monthly mortgage payments, not whether it is large enough to pay off the loan immediately. It's the same with the government, and their burden is even easier because they can print money if needed. Furthermore, what's special about 90 percent? Why not 80 percent or 100 percent? There is no plausible reason why 90 percent is a magic number, the difference between economic growth and recession.

Nonetheless, the professors argued that a debt/GDP ratio above 90 percent is a tipping point, beyond which nations slip into recession. And people took it seriously because, after all, these are Harvard professors. Their most compelling evidence is in Table 4.1. Reinhart and Rogoff looked at twenty advanced countries (Australia, Austria, Belgium, Canada, Denmark, Finland, France, Germany, Greece, Ireland, Italy, Japan, Netherlands, New Zealand, Norway, Portugal, Spain, Sweden, the United Kingdom, and the United States). For each year, they calculated the nation's debt/GDP ratio (expressed as a percentage) and its rate of growth of inflation-adjusted GDP. These data were divided into four categories based on the debt/GDP ratio.

Table 4.1: Debt and GDP Growth for 20 Advanced Economies, 1946–2009

	Ratio of Government Debt to GDP			
	Below 30%	30% to 60%	60% to 90%	Over 90%
Average GDP Growth	4.1	2.8	2.8	-0.1

Table 4.1 indicates that an increase in the ratio of debt to GDP reduces an economy's growth rate. Past 90 percent, economies are thrown into recession with GDP falling and economies contracting. Reinhart and Rogoff conclude that, "At the very minimum, this would suggest that traditional debt management issues should be at the forefront of public policy concerns."

Their conclusion received worldwide attention as persuasive evidence for austerity. Fiscal hawks in many countries used the Rogoff-Reinhart study as proof that governments should reduce spending and increase taxes in order to balance their budget or, even better, run a surplus so that government debt can be repaid.

In the United States, the Republican Party's 2013 budget proposal stated:

> A well-known study completed by economists Ken Rogoff and Carmen Reinhart confirms this common-sense conclusion. The study found conclusive empirical evidence that gross debt (meaning all debt that a government owes, including debt held in government trust funds) exceeding 90 percent of the economy has a significant negative effect on economic growth.

Who can argue with common sense and conclusive empirical evidence?

Buying into the hype, a 2013 *Washington Post* editorial ominously warned that "debt-to-GDP could keep rising—and stick dangerously near the 90 percent mark that economists regard as a threat to sustainable economic growth." Notice how the *Washington Post* morphed a study by *two* economists into a general opinion by *all* economists.

The reality is that many economists do not think there is a 90 per-

cent tipping point—and they never did. One thing that most economists *do* agree on is that cutting spending and raising taxes in order
to reduce government debt would have been exactly the wrong policies when the economy was still fragile from the Great Recession that
started in December 2007. Many were deeply skeptical of the Rogoff-
Reinhart study, though it was hard to pin down any serious errors.

One concern was that the United States had only four years with
a debt/GDP ratio above 90 percent. The economy had contracted during these four years, but they were very special years: 1946–49, right
after the end of World War II. Government debt was abnormally high
because the government had borrowed heavily to finance the war. The
postwar recession was caused by a drop in government military
spending, not by the debt accumulated during the war. Surely, it was
a mistake to think that these four years were evidence that government debt causes recessions. If anything, these four years were evidence that cutting government spending drastically (as advocated by
the fiscal hawks) actually *causes* recessions.

Nonetheless, the Reinhart-Rogoff study was used by fiscal hawks
throughout the world to bolster support for what British Conservative
Party leader David Cameron called the Age of Austerity. Several European governments tried to reduce their budget deficits by cutting
spending and raising taxes. The average unemployment rate in Europe
rose from 10 percent in 2011 to 11 percent in 2012 and 12 percent in
2013. The International Monetary Fund (IMF), a frequent advocate
of austerity, admitted that European austerity measures had been
much more harmful than they expected.

There is no way of knowing how much output was lost and how
many people lost their jobs because of the Reinhart-Rogoff paper.
Economists sometimes play a game where they name a famous paper
they wish they had written. The Reinhart-Rogoff paper is high on the
list of papers that I am glad I didn't write.

It turns out that the Reinhart-Rogoff study was deeply flawed from
the start. Thomas Herndon, a graduate student at the University of Massachusetts Amherst, took a graduate statistics course in 2012 taught by
Michael Ash and Robert Pollin, and one of his course assignments was
to replicate a famous research paper. Herndon chose Reinhart-Rogoff.

He tried mightily, but he could not replicate their results. He assumed he was doing something wrong, but he couldn't figure out what.

Herndon's professors had seen similar situations before, and it is typically the student's fault. This is one of the goals of this exercise—to teach students to do serious work carefully and correctly. This time, it was different. The famous paper had errors that even the professors couldn't identify.

Herndon gave up trying to make sense of the study and contacted Reinhart and Rogoff, even though he thought it unlikely that famous professors would spend time helping a mere graduate student. When they ignored his initial request, he persisted. And persisted. After all, he needed to figure out what he was doing wrong so that he could pass his class.

Reinhart and Rogoff eventually gave Herndon their data and spreadsheet calculations. He soon discovered the problem, which was actually a series of problems involving inadvertent errors and questionable procedures:

A SPREADSHEET ERROR

The raw data for these twenty countries had been entered in reverse alphabetical order on lines 30 to 49 of a spreadsheet. However, when Reinhart and Rogoff wrote the spreadsheet code for their calculations, they used lines 30 to 44 instead of lines 30 to 49, thereby omitting 5 countries (Australia, Austria, Belgium, Canada, and Denmark). Three of these countries (Australia, Belgium, and Canada) had periods with debt/GDP above 90 percent; all 3 had positive growth rates during those years. All 3 of these counterexamples to the paper's conclusion were omitted from the Reinhart-Rogoff calculations.

SELECTIVE OMISSION OF SOME DATA

The Reinhart-Rogoff spreadsheet calculations omit other data as well. In many cases, this is because there are no data for some countries in some years. However, data for Australia (1946–50), Canada (1946–50), and New Zealand (1946–49) are available, but were inexplicably not included in the calculations.

The New Zealand omission is particularly important because the four omitted years were four of the five years (1951 is the fifth year) when debt/GDP exceeded 90 percent. New Zealand's GDP growth rates in these five years were respectively 7.7, 11.9, -9.9, 10.8, and -7.6 percent. The average growth rate was 2.6 percent. Reinhart and Rogoff excluded the first four years and reported that New Zealand's average growth rate during its high-debt years was -7.6 percent.

UNUSUAL AVERAGING

Reinhart and Rogoff wrote that the calculations in Table 4.1 are based on "1,186 annual observations, [and] there are a significant number in each category, including 96 above 90 percent." One might think that the -0.1 percent average growth rate for the 90-percent category is a straightforward average of 96 annual observations. But one would be wrong.

Reinhart and Rogoff calculated the average growth rate for each country, and then calculated the average of these country growth rates. For example, the United Kingdom had 19 years with a debt/GDP ratio above 90 percent and its average GDP growth rate in these 19 years was 2.4 percent. Because of the 4 omitted years, New Zealand was counted as having had 1 year with a debt/GDP ratio above 90 percent—its GDP growth rate in this year was -7.6 percent. The average growth rate for these 2 countries using 20 annual observations is 1.9 percent. Reinhart and Rogoff instead averaged 2.6 and -7.6, giving an average growth rate of -2.5 percent.

We do not know if this was an inadvertent mistake or if Reinhart and Rogoff intended to make this unusual calculation, giving the same weight to one year of data in one country and nineteen years of data in another country. We do know, however, that their error bolstered their argument.

Table 4.2 shows the effects of these glitches. Ten countries had episodes with debt/GDP ratios above 90 percent. In nine cases, the average growth rate was positive. The only exception was the postwar US, which is irrelevant.

The first two columns show the actual number of high-debt years and the number of years Reinhart and Rogoff include in their calculations. Reinhart and Rogoff omitted the first three countries and four years of New Zealand data. All of these omissions had positive average growth rates.

The next two columns show the average growth rates, with the "correct column" including the three countries and four New Zealand years that Reinhart and Rogoff omitted.

Table 4.2: The Consequences of the Reinhart and Rogoff (RR) Omissions

	Number of Years		GDP Growth	
	Correct	RR	Correct	RR
Australia 1946–50	5	0	3.8	
Belgium 1947, 1984–2005, 2008–09	25	0	2.6	
Canada 1946–50	5	0	3.0	
Greece 1991–2009	19	19	2.9	2.9
Ireland 1983–89	7	7	2.4	2.4
Italy 1993–2001, 2009	10	10	1.0	1.0
Japan 1999–2009	11	11	0.7	0.7
New Zealand 1946–49, 1951	5	1	2.6	-7.6
UK 1946–64	19	19	2.4	2.4
US 1946–49	4	4	-2.0	-2.0

Overall, omitting some data and weighting all countries equally, Reinhart and Rogoff calculate the average GDP growth rate in high-debt years to be -0.1 percent. Including the missing data and taking into account the number of high-debt years, the correct average is 2.2 percent. Herndon, Ash, and Pollin concluded that "contrary to [Reinhart and Rogoff], average GDP growth at public debt/GDP ratios over 90 percent is not dramatically different than when public debt/GDP ratios are lower."

The Reinhart-Rogoff calculations in Table 4.1 tell a clean, compelling story of higher debt inexorably leading to slower growth, with a 90 percent tipping point throwing a nation into recession. In addition to the various errors in their calculations, these summary statistics hide how much variation there is in the data. There is not a simple, close relationship between debt and growth.

Figure 4.1 shows the underlying data, with a vertical line at the 90 percent threshold at which higher debt supposedly plunges a country into recession. There is no persuasive relationship between debt and growth. Many high-debt years were high-growth years. Many low-debt years were low-growth years. The data themselves prove that nothing is special about 90 percent.

Figure 4.1: Debt Equals Recession?

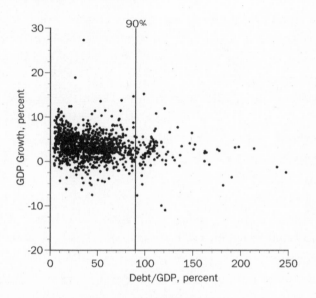

■ CORRELATION EQUALS CAUSATION?

The fiscal-austerity enthusiasts interpret the Reinhart-Rogoff study as evidence that increased government debt reduces economic growth and as a stern warning that increasing the level of government debt past 90 percent of GDP is likely to cause an economic recession.

Perhaps the causation goes the other way, in that economic recessions cause the debt ratio to increase. First, there is a simple arithmetic argument: A drop in GDP directly increases the ratio of debt to GDP. Suppose that debt is 85 and GDP is 100, giving a debt/GDP ratio of 85 percent:

$$\frac{\text{Debt}}{\text{GDP}} = \frac{85}{100} = 0.85$$

If GDP falls to 90, the debt/GDP ratio increases to 94 percent:

$$\frac{\text{Debt}}{\text{GDP}} = \frac{85}{90} = 0.94$$

It is not the debt/GDP ratio that caused GDP to decline. It is declining GDP that caused the debt/GDP ratio to increase.

But wait, there's more. During economic recessions, government tax revenue falls and government spending on unemployment insurance, food stamps, and other safety nets increases. Both of these forces increase government borrowing. An economic recession thus not only causes the denominator of the debt/GDP ratio to fall, it causes the numerator to increase.

If there is a statistical correlation between economic growth and the debt/GDP ratio, it may be mostly—or even entirely—due to the effects of the economy on the debt ratio, rather than the other way around. It is not that a high debt ratio slows growth, it is that slow growth raises the debt ratio.

Another University of Massachusetts–Amherst professor, Arindrajit Dube, looked at this very question. Using the Reinhart-Rogoff data, Dube found that the debt/GDP ratio is more closely correlated with economic growth in the past than with economic growth in the future—which is exactly what we expect if it is economic growth that causes changes in the debt/GDP ratio.

■ DOES ABORTION REDUCE CRIME?

Thirty years ago, mathematical theorists were the gods of economics. Knowing nothing about the real world was almost a badge of honor. When Gerard Debreu was awarded the Nobel Prize in 1983, reporters tried to get him to say something about Ronald Reagan's economic policies. Debreu firmly refused to say anything, and some suspected that he didn't know or care.

The times have changed. Economic theorists are under attack for their unrealistic assumptions and demonstrably incorrect conclusions. The new economic gods are the empiricists who work with data. A sign of the times is the bestselling book *Freakonomics: A*

Rogue Economist Explores the Hidden Side of Everything, coauthored by Chicago economist Steven Levitt and *New York Times* journalist Stephen Dubner.

The title is utterly misleading, chosen exclusively to sell books. There is nothing freakish in the book, Levitt is not a rogue economist, and the book does not explore the hidden side of everything. Far from being a rogue economist, Levitt is the quintessential establishment economist. Levitt has a bachelor's degree from Harvard and a PhD from MIT. He is currently a professor at the University of Chicago. In 2003, the American Economics Association awarded Levitt the John Bates Clark Medal, which is given to the best American economist under the age of forty and is often a precursor to a Nobel Prize. He is one of the empirical gods of economics.

Levitt is justifiably famous for his careful and ingenious use of data to tackle interesting questions—for example, the effects of campaign spending on election outcomes, the effects of imprisonment on the crime rate, and the effects of education incentives on teacher cheating. His conclusions are often provocative: campaign spending doesn't matter much; each prisoner released because of an overcrowding lawsuit leads to fifteen more crimes per year; rewarding teachers for student test scores greatly increases teacher-aided cheating. He once wrote that, "There is nothing we love more than finding things in data that no one else can see."

But even gods make mistakes.

Perhaps Levitt's most famous paper (coauthored with John Donohue) argues that legalized abortion in the United States reduced the overall crime rate. The argument is that the "unwanted" children who were not born because of legalized abortion would have been prone to commit crimes (particularly violent crimes) because of their socioeconomic environment and/or parental neglect (after all, they were unwanted).

It's an interesting theory, and it might even be true. The problem is that there are so many genetic and environmental factors involved that it is hard to sort out the importance of each. Levitt says that he likes to tease results out of the data. It sounds like he's boasting about a valuable skill, but it also sounds like he is fond of ransacking data, which can be treacherous.

Here are the data Levitt relied on. Abortion was legalized in five US states in 1970 and nationwide on January 22, 1973, by *Roe v. Wade*. Figure 4.2 shows that the US murder rate peaked in 1991, eighteen years after *Roe v. Wade*, and then declined, suggesting that the criminal population had indeed been reduced by abortion. After looking at a variety of data for individual states, Donahue and Levitt concluded that, "Legalized abortion appears to account for as much as 50 percent of the recent drop in crime."

Figure 4.2: Murders per One Hundred Thousand People

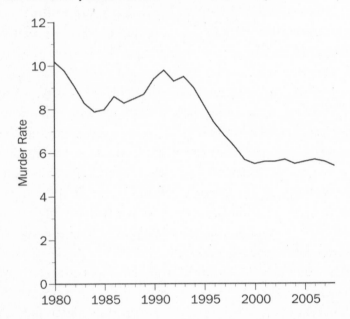

This provocative argument was attacked from a variety of angles. Some argue that the murder rate rose in the 1980s and declined in the 1990s because of the ebb and flow of turf wars between rival cocaine gangs. Another theory is that crime rates dropped in the 1990s because of reduced childhood poisoning from exposure to leaded gasoline and lead-based paint.

Furthermore, some researchers argue that abortion may be more common for women who think clearly about the future consequences of their actions—women who would have been good moms raising law-abiding children. Also, the availability of legalized abortion may have increased sexual activity and out-of-wedlock births, and children growing up in single-parent homes may be more prone to criminal activity. Both these arguments suggest that legalized abortion may actually *increase* crime rates.

Let's look at some data. Figure 4.3 shows the murder rate for 14–17-year-olds. The first legalized abortions under *Roe v. Wade* affected births that would otherwise have occurred in late 1973. These unwanted children would have turned 14 years old in late 1987 and would have turned 18 in late 1991. Thus the first cohort affected by *Roe v. Wade* were in the 14–17 age bracket between late 1987 and late 1991. Figure 4.3 shows that the murder rate continued to increase during these years and did not peak until 1993. The murder rate was three times higher in 1993 than in 1984, even though abortion was legal and readily available when the 1993 cohort was born, and illegal and difficult when the 1984 cohort was born.

Figure 4.3: Murder Rate, 14–17-Year-Olds]

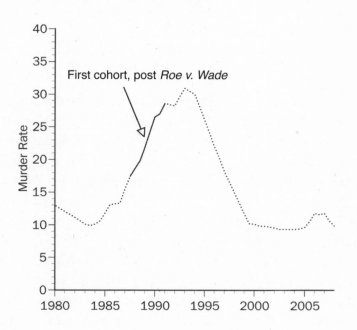

First cohort, post *Roe v. Wade*

Figure 4.4 shows the murder rates for 18–24 and 25–34-year-olds. The murder rate declined for the first 18–24-year-old cohort affected by *Roe v. Wade*, but increased for the first 25–34-year-old cohort affected by *Roe v. Wade*.

Figure 4.4: Murder Rate, 18–24 and 25–34-Year-Olds

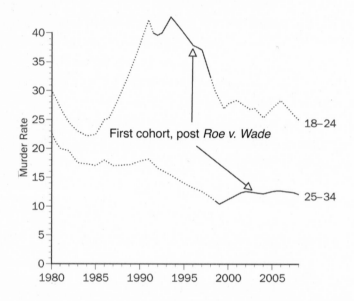

So, murder rates went down for 18–24-year-olds after *Roe v. Wade*, but went up for 14–17 and 25–34-year-olds. These data are not consistent with the theory that *Roe v. Wade* reduced the murder rate. The real consistency in Figures 4.3 and 4.4 is that the murder rate peaked in the early 1990s for all three age groups: 1993 for ages 14–17 and 18–24, 1991 for ages 25–34. The murder rate for the 35+ age group (not shown) peaked in 1990. Put another way, the murder rate peaked in 1990 for the 35+ age group and in 1991 for the 25–34 age group, all of whom were born before *Roe v. Wade*. The murder rate peaked in 1993 for the 18–24 group, some of whom were born before and some after *Roe v. Wade*. Finally, the murder rate peaked in 1993 for the 14–17 group, all of whom were born several years after *Roe v. Wade*.

The real story is that the murder rate peaked for all age groups in the early 1990s. Whatever the explanation, legalized abortion was not the cause.

■ MY BAD

So, how did Donohue and Levitt conclude that legalized abortion reduced crime? Two economists at the Federal Reserve Bank of Boston, Christopher Foote and Christopher Goetz, carefully reexamined the Donohue/Levitt study and found three problems. The first was that Donohue and Levitt use arrest data even though arrests may occur a year or more after the crime is committed. The second problem was that Donohue and Levitt looked at the total number of crimes, rather than the crime rate (number of crimes adjusted for the size of the population). It is not surprising that a smaller population commits fewer crimes, and by its very definition legalized abortion reduced the population.

The third problem was a "programming error," or in reality just a simple human error. Donohue and Levitt said that they used a statistical procedure that controlled for changes from year to year within individual states, but they did not. After correcting for these glitches, Foote and Goetz concluded that abortion most likely increased violent crime rates and had no effect on property crime rates.

Levitt admitted the programming error and remarked, "This is personally quite embarrassing because I pride myself on being careful with data." However, this is not the first such embarrassment for Levitt. An earlier paper on the effect of more police on crime also turned out to have a programming error, which led to this apology: "It is with tremendous personal embarrassment that I acknowledge these mistakes." In both cases, Levitt graciously admitted the mistakes (did he have a choice?), but he continued to argue that other evidence supported his conclusions, though the effects might be smaller than he had originally thought. He may well be right, but it is very hard to live down an oops moment.

■ **Don't be Fooled:** Provocative assertions are provocative precisely because they are counterintuitive—which is a very good reason for skepticism. When you hear such an assertion, don't be easily persuaded that you are wrong. It may well be that the provocative assertion should be dismissed. Think about whether there is some problem with the data, perhaps self-selection bias. Think about whether the causation runs in a different direction. And, oh yes, consider the possibility that there was a mistake—that the computer was told to calculate the square root of 196 instead of the square root of 169. Even the best, and most honest, researchers are human—and humans make mistakes.

The ironic lesson to be learned from the worldwide influence of the Reinhart-Rogoff study and the runaway success of Freakonomics is that it is not true that data are more important than ideas. We are often duped by data.

5

GRAPHICAL GAFFES

G RAPHS CAN HELP US INTERPRET DATA AND DRAW INFERENCES. They can help us see tendencies, patterns, trends, and relationships. A picture can be worth not only a thousand words, but a thousand numbers. However, a graph is essentially descriptive—a picture meant to tell a story. As with any story, bumblers may mangle the punch line and the dishonest may lie.

Data can be distorted and mangled by graphs, either intentionally or unintentionally.

■ OMG

During a routine meeting, an Internet company's analytics group showed the chief executive officer (CEO) the revenue graph in Figure 5.1. The data in this figure are the company's revenue over the previous seven quarters and, frankly, it's a pretty boring figure.

The CEO looked at the figure for a few moments and then she stunned the analytics group by blurted out, "So, why does this chart show revenue is pretty flat and the chart I showed to the board last week showed revenue tanking?" The analytics group hadn't seen the other chart, so they shrugged their shoulders. They honestly didn't know.

The CEO summoned the finance guy who prepared the chart she showed the board, and told him to pass around his chart, which is in Figure 5.2. As soon as analytics people saw the chart, they started laughing because the chart doesn't have a zero on the vertical axis.

Figure 5.1: Revenue is Flat

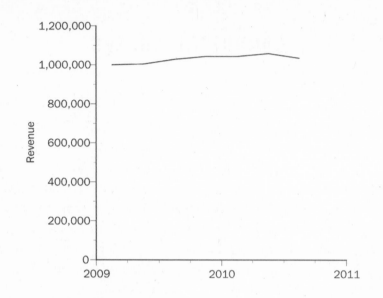

Figure 5.2: Revenue Falls Sharply

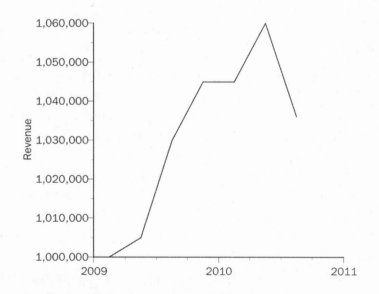

The CEO was not amused. She said that the board kept grilling her, asking her to explain why revenue was down so much. She kept protesting, "It's not!" And the board members kept pointing at that darn chart which showed revenue collapsing.

Figure 5.1 and Figure 5.2 use exactly the same numbers, but Figure 5.1 includes zero on the vertical axis. Figure 5.2 does not. In Figure 5.1, any patterns in the data have been ironed out and we cannot tell when profits peaked. On the other hand, Figure 5.1 does tell us (correctly) that the recent dip was minor.

The omission of zero in Figure 5.2 magnifies the ups and downs in the data, allowing us to detect changes that might otherwise be ambiguous. However, once zero has been omitted, the graph is no longer an accurate guide to the magnitude of the changes. Instead, we need to look at the actual numbers. In Figure 5.2, the height of the line dropped by 40 percent, but the drop in revenue was only 2 percent.

Figure 5.3: The Secret Axis

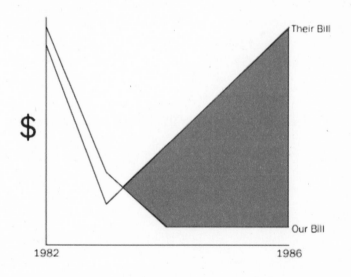

Figure 5.3 shows a graph that is even less transparent because there are no numbers on the vertical axis. President Ronald Reagan used a graph like this on television to compare the taxes a family with $20,000 income would pay with his tax proposal and with a plan drafted by the House Ways and Means Committee. Zero was no doubt omitted from the vertical axis, but the vertical axis doesn't

show any numbers (just a very large dollar sign). Because there are no numbers on the axis, we have no basis for gauging the magnitude of the gap between the lines. It turns out that the 1986 gap is a 9 percent tax reduction, from $2,385 to $2,168. The omission of zero from the vertical axis magnifies this 9 percent difference into 90 percent of the height of the line labeled "their bill," and the omission of numbers from the vertical axis prevents readers from detecting this misleading magnification.

Afterward, David Gergen, a White House spokesman, told reporters, "We tried it with numbers and found it was very hard to read on television, so we took them off. We were just trying to get a point across." Yeah, right.

■ A PHONY CRISIS

In 1976, the National Science Foundation (NSF) constructed Figure 5.4, which apparently shows a shocking decline in the number of Nobel Prizes in science (chemistry, physics, and medicine) awarded to US citizens. What happened to our educational system? Is the pipeline drying up?

Figure 5.4: A Precipitous Decline in US Nobel Prizes in Science?

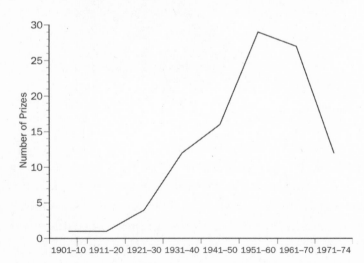

Wait a minute. Look at the time axis. Each of the first seven time periods is for decades; but the eighth is for only a four-year period, 1971–74. Because fewer prizes are awarded during a four-year period than during a ten-year period, the NSF created the illusion of an alarming drop in the number of science prizes awarded to Americans.

Using data for the full decade, Figure 5.5 shows that US citizens ended up winning even more prizes in the 1970s than in the 1960s. Of course, this trend can't continue forever, unless there is an increase in the total number of prizes awarded, but in the 1970s, the US won more than half of the science Nobel Prizes. It was more of the same in the 1980s, 1990s, and 2000s.

Figure 5.5: US Nobel Prizes in Science Keep Increasing

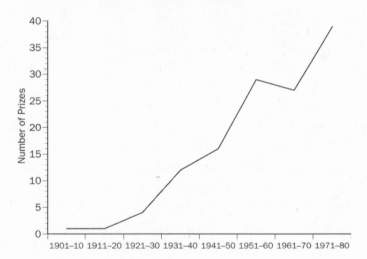

■ LET THEM EAT CAKE

Figure 5.6 is an updated version of a *New York Times* graphic that accompanied an article by neoconservative David Frum titled "Welcome, Nouveaux Riches." Figure 5.6 shows a dramatic acceleration between 1980 and 1990 in the number of households earning more than $100,000 a year. Frum wrote that, "Nothing like this immense crowd of wealthy people has been seen in the history of the planet." Does that seem like a bit of hyperbole?

Figure 5.6: Number of Households Earning More than $100,000 a Year

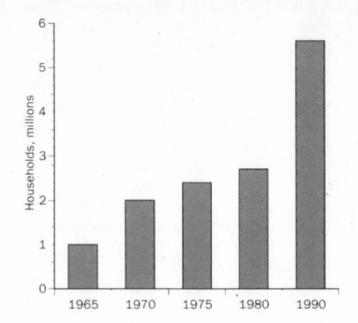

Do you notice anything odd about this figure? There is a five-year difference between each of the first four bars, but a *ten-year difference* between the fourth and fifth bars (1980 and 1990). If the bars had been spaced properly and a 1985 bar inserted, the increase over time would appear gradual, without an abrupt jump between 1980 and 1990.

In addition, $100,000 in 1990 is not the same as $100,000 in 1965. Prices were about four times higher, so that $100,000 in 1990 was roughly equivalent to $25,000 in 1965. Adjusting for inflation, we should compare the number of 1965 families earning $25,000 with the number of 1990 families earning $100,000. We should also take into account the increase in the population between 1965 and 1990. It is not surprising that more people have high incomes when there are more people total.

Figure 5.7 fixes all these problems by showing the percentage of households that earned more than $100,000 in inflation-adjusted dollars, with 1985 inserted. Data for 1995 and 2000 are included to give more historical context. Viewed with appropriately adjusted data, the 1980s are unremarkable. What does stand out is the end of the 1990s, during the Internet bubble.

Figure 5.7: Percent of Households Earning More than $100,000 a Year, Adjusted for Inflation

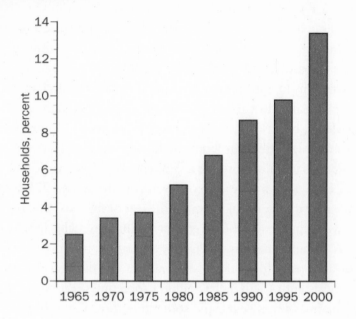

Figure 5.8: Medical Costs March Steadily Upward

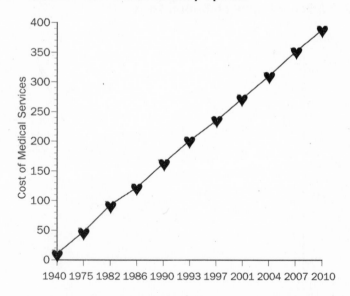

■ ELASTIC AXES

Figure 5.8 is an update of a graph that appeared in the *Washington Post*. This figure indicates that there has been a steady increase in the cost of medical care in the United States from 1940 through 2010. (The costs are scaled to equal one in 1940.)

This straight-line graph is embellished by hearts, perhaps to show that doctors really do care or to suggest Cupid's straight arrow shot through eleven hearts. Or, perhaps, this unnecessary decoration is intended to distract attention from the horizontal axis. The ten equally spaced intervals initially represent a difference of thirty-five years between 1940 and 1975, then a difference of seven years between 1975 and 1982, and then either three or four years for the rest of the axis. These puzzling intervals were apparently chosen so that the line would be approximately straight. A straight line may be visually appealing, but misrepresents the data. For a graph to display the data accurately, the units on each axis must be consistent. A half inch shouldn't sometimes represent thirty-five years, sometimes seven years, and sometimes three years. If the intervals change in mid-graph, the figure will surely distort the data.

Figure 5.9: A Better Picture of Medical Costs

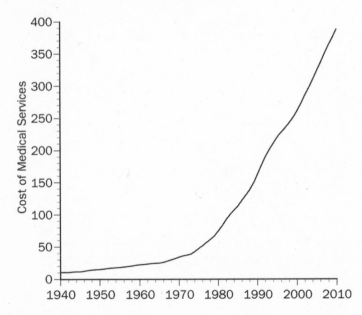

Figure 5.9 uses consistent intervals and shows that medical costs did not increase along a straight line.

Why did costs accelerate after 1970? Perhaps it was the ramping up of Medicare, which began in 1965. Perhaps it was because prices in general were increasing (these graphs should have adjusted medical costs for inflation). We can't tell why from these data alone. What we do know is that changing intervals in mid-graph distorted the data.

■ DOUBLE THE MISCHIEF

In 1786, William Playfair, a Scotsman of many talents (not always employed honestly, despite his name), published *The Commercial and Political Atlas*, a collection of forty-four charts that was a landmark in the graphical presentation of data. Forty-three of these charts showed how wages, prices, and other data had changed over time. This now-commonplace tool was so different from anything seen previously that Playfair felt he had to defend it: "This method has struck several persons as being fallacious, because geometrical measurement has not any relation to money or to time; yet here it is made to represent both."

Figure 5.10: Playfair's Graph of Wages and Prices Over 250 Years

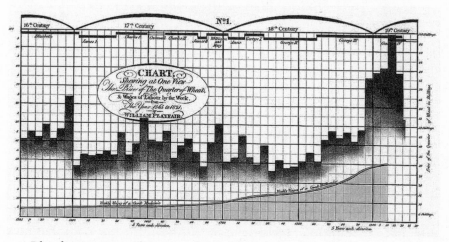

Playfair's most famous graph, published in 1821, shows the weekly wages of a "good mechanic" (the line along the bottom of the figure) and the price of wheat (the black bars) during the years 1565

to 1821. Playfair wrote that, "The main fact deserving of considera-
tion is, that never at any former period was wheat so cheap, in pro-
portion to mechanical labour, as it is at the present time." Although
Playfair drew the correct conclusion, that wages had increased more
than the price of wheat, his graph seems to show exactly the opposite.

I will use US data for 1975 through 2010 on US median household income and the consumer price index (CPI) to show why Playfair's
graph was misleading. It is challenging to put these data on a single
graph because income ranges between $12,000 and $50,000, while
the CPI ranges between 54 and 218. One solution (Playfair's solution)
is to use 2 vertical axes, one for income and the other for the CPI.
Figure 5.11 seems to clearly demonstrate that household income has
increased much more than the consumer price index (CPI). Americans
today are apparently much better off economically.

Figure 5.11: Income Has Gone Up Much More Than Prices]

What Figure 5.11 really demonstrates is that if you double the
axes, you can double the mischief. Using two vertical axes and omitting
zero from either or both opens a statistical beauty parlor with many
cosmetic possibilities. Figure 5.12 shows the very same data, but now
it seems that prices increased much more than income! The gimmick
is the choice of numbers to show on the axes. The ups and downs in
the data can be exaggerated by putting a small range of numbers on

the axis and can be dampened by putting a large range of numbers on the axis. Figure 5.11 uses a narrow range for the income axis and a wide range for the CPI axis to make the growth in income appear larger than increase in prices. Figure 5.12 does the opposite, using a wide range for the income axis and a narrow range for the CPI axis to make the increase in prices appear larger than the increase in income.

Figure 5.12: Prices Have Gone Up Much More Than Income

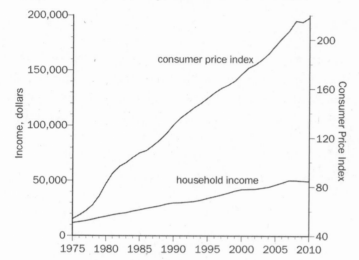

Figure 5.13: Income Adjusted for Prices

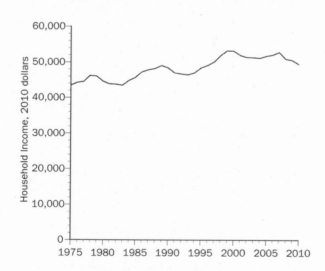

How can we fix it? There is no rule that fits all cases. For this particular case, a good solution is to use the price data to adjust the income data, thereby creating one set of numbers: income adjusted for inflation. Figure 5.13 shows that, adjusted for inflation, the median household income has increased modestly over this thirty-five-year period (income has increased a bit more than prices), but there have been setbacks along the way due to several economic recessions.

■ STUDENT LIES

A student newspaper at a medium-sized college called *Student Life*—affectionately known as "Student Lies" on campus—created Figure 5.14, which plainly shows that during the 1990s, the cost of attending this college (tuition plus room and board) rose dramatically while the college's *U. S. News* ranking fell sharply.

Figure 5.14: The More You Pay, the Less You Get

So many inconsistencies. Where to begin? Figure 5.14 has two vertical axes—one for cost and one for ranking—and zero has been omitted from both axes to exaggerate the changes in costs and ranking. Not only is zero omitted, but the entire axis and the associated numbers have been redacted, so we have no way of gauging whether the changes during the 1990s were large or small. The data behind this graph show that the cost increased from $20,000 in 1990 to $36,000 in 2000, about 6 percent a year, which is not trivial, but similar to the rate of increase at comparable colleges.

The *U.S. News* ranking went from seventeenth to thirteenth, which is a substantial change. But wait. In college rankings, number one is the best! Going from seventeenth to thirteenth is actually an improvement.

Contrary to shocking story told in Figure 5.14, costs went up by 6 percent a year, about the same as at comparable colleges, and the *U.S. News* ranking improved dramatically. Figure 5.14 is an updated and simplified adaptation of an even more bizarre graph published on the front page of the *Ithaca Times* about Cornell University's tuition and ranking. In addition to the distortions in Figure 5.14, the *Times* figure didn't have a horizontal axis because it compared Cornell's tuition and ranking over two different time periods! Tuition was over the thirty-five-year period of 1965–99, while the college ranking was over the twelve-year period of 1988–99.

■ YANKEE TICKETS ARE A BARGAIN

The New York Yankees are baseball's most storied franchise, having played in 40 of the 108 World Series through 2013 and having won 27 times. The St. Louis Cardinals are a distant second with 11 championships. Forty-three Yankees are in the Hall of Fame, including Babe Ruth, Lou Gehrig, Joe DiMaggio, and Mickey Mantle. The Yankees are also one of the most despised teams in professional sports, in part because of the perception that they buy success by taking players from teams in smaller cities that cannot match Yankee salaries. Some baseball fans wear Yankee baseball caps with pride, while others prominently sport "Yankees Suck" T-shirts.

Yankee Stadium opened in 1923 at a cost of more than $30 million in today's dollars and with unprecedented seating for 58,000 people. Babe Ruth was the most popular baseball player in the 1920s and he hit a home run in the first game played at Yankee Stadium. Tickets sold to watch Ruth hit home runs paid for the stadium, giving it the nickname "The House That Ruth Built." Eighty-six years later, in 2009, the Yankees moved across the street to a new Yankee Stadium, built at a cost of over $2 billion. While the new stadium was being built, many fans feared that the Yankees would pay for the stadium by escalating already expensive ticket prices.

Historical data on the price of a box seat at Yankee Stadium were used to create Figure 5.15, which shows that, contrary to perception, ticket prices did not accelerate, but actually slowed down during the years 1995 to 2010.

Figure 5.15: A Slowdown in Yankee Ticket Prices

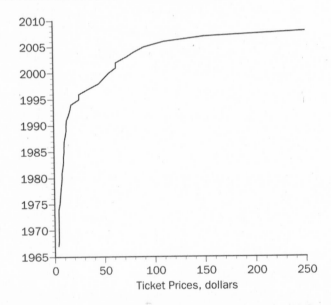

Do you notice anything unusual about Figure 5.15? Inexplicably, time is on the vertical axis. We are so accustomed to seeing time on the horizontal axis that it is very difficult to make sense of Figure 5.15 at first glance. Figure 5.16 shows the same data, with time where it belongs— on the horizontal axis. This reversal of the axes reverses the conclusion, Yankee ticket prices did not slow down, but accelerated, after 1994. The annual rate of increase was 6 percent between 1967 and 1994, and 21 percent between 1994 and 2010. Still look like a bargain to you?

Figure 5.16: An Acceleration in Yankee Ticket Prices

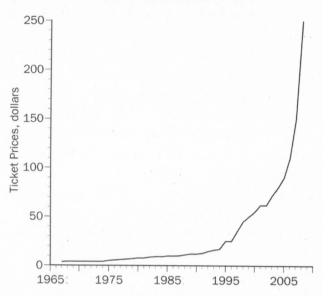

■ THE ART OF GRAPHING

The first full-time graph specialist at *Time* magazine was an art school graduate who asserted that "the challenge is to present statistics as a visual idea rather than a tedious parade of numbers." Numbers are not inherently tedious. They can be illuminating, fascinating, even entertaining. The trouble starts when we decide that it is more important for a graph to be artistic than informative.

IS BIGGER BETTER?

The US rate of inflation was above 13 percent in 1979 when President Jimmy Carter appointed Paul Volcker chair of the Federal Reserve. The Fed increased interest rates to unprecedented levels in an all-out war on inflation. When Volcker was asked if these tight-money policies would cause an economic recession, he replied, "Yes, and the sooner the better." In another conversation, he said that he wouldn't be satisfied "until the last buzz saw is silenced." What Volcker meant was that he wanted to raise interest rates high enough to choke off borrowing and shut down the building industry.

In 1981, interest rates reached 18 percent on home mortgages and were even higher for most other loans. As interest rates rose, households and businesses cut back on their borrowing and on their purchases of automobiles, homes, and office buildings. Construction workers who lost their jobs were soon spending less on food, clothing, and entertainment, sending ripples through the economy. Farmers with expensive loans and declining income drove tractors into downtown Washington, DC, to blockade the Federal Reserve Building. The unemployment rate rose from 5.8 percent in 1979 to above 10 percent in 1982, the highest level since the Great Depression, but the Fed's scorched-earth policy reduced the rate of inflation from above 13 percent in 1979 to below 4 percent in 1982.

Figure 5.17 compares the purchasing power of a $100 bill at the end of three US presidents' terms. By definition, a $100 bill was worth $100 at the end of Gerald Ford's term. By the end of Jimmy Carter's term in 1981, a $100 bill was only worth $67—in that it would only buy as much as $67 bought four years earlier. At the end of Ronald Reagan's term, a $100 bill was only worth $49.

Figure 5.17: The Value of $100 is Going Down, Down, Down!

These shrinking $100 bills seem to show a relatively modest decline in value during Jimmy Carter's term and a much larger decrease during Reagan's term—which is odd since Carter was president during the great inflation in the late 1970s and Reagan became president in January 1981, just as inflation was receding. The numbers—from $100 to $67 to $49—certainly indicate that the value of the dollar fell more during Carter's term than during Reagan's term, but the pictures tell a completely different story. Which story is correct?

One problem with Figure 5.17 is that Carter was in office for four years and Reagan was in office for eight years. Although the years are identified in the figure, this difference in the length of their terms is not obvious because there are no years on the horizontal axis—indeed, there is no axis at all. The invisible vertical axis is also a problem because we cannot tell if zero has been omitted.

Even worse, instead of simple bars, the graph was enlivened with $100 bills. At the end of Reagan's term, prices were twice what they were at the end of Ford's term, and the value of a $100 bill had fallen by half. If the height of the Reagan bill had been reduced by half without changing the width, the picture would have been distorted like a fun house mirror. To avoid this squished image, the width and the height of the Reagan $100 bill were both halved—which creates a different distortion. Now, the area of the Reagan bill is one-fourth the area of the Ford bill, which makes it seem that the value of a $100 bill fell by three-fourths.

This is one of those cases where a few numbers are more informative than a graph. Prices increased at an annual rate of 10.7 percent during Carter years and 3.7 percent during the Reagan years—which is very different from the misinformation conveyed by the well-intentioned but too-cute-by-half Figure 5.17.

OPTICAL DELUSIONS

Native American tribes operate several gambling casinos in Southern California. A consultant was hired by one of the tribes to evaluate the location of these casinos based on driving distances for potential customers. This is a complicated question because it should take into account where households live and also their casino alternatives. The appeal of a casino thirty miles from potential customers is diluted if another casino is only ten miles from these customers.

This consultant developed a proprietary model for estimating "location values." He did not explain his model but he showed the results in Figure 5.18, which doesn't say much, but is a good example of chartjunk. Pictures, lines, blots, and splotches enliven graphs, but too often create unattractive chartjunk that confuses the reader and strains the eyes.

Figure 5.18: An Unhelpful Graph

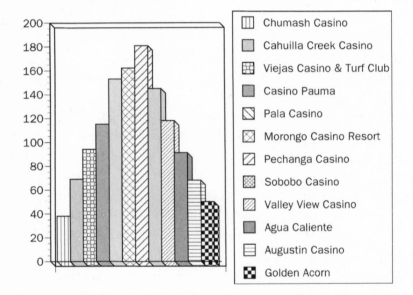

A graph should reveal patterns that would not be evident in a table, and Figure 5.18 does not do this. The bars evidently show the location values for these twelve casinos—I say "evidently" because the vertical axis is unlabeled. We are not told what these numbers mean or how they were calculated. Are these dollars? Percents? Households? The twelve bars are arranged to resemble a bell curve, but there is no reason why the first bar is the Chumash Casino and the last bar is the Golden Acorn. The pattern in the bars—rising to a peak and then falling like a bell curve—reveals no useful information. It would be more sensible to arrange the bars from tallest to smallest.

Moreover, there are no labels on the horizontal axis at all. Instead, we have to look back and forth from the graph to the legend, and the similarity in the bar patterns makes it tedious and difficult to do so. The bar patterns themselves are distracting and the three-dimensional appearance is not helpful. Finally, even if we decipher the bars, it is not easy to line up the bar heights with the numerical values on the vertical axis.

This bar chart is not an improvement over a simple table, such as Table 5.1. Sometimes less is more.

Table 5.1: Sometimes, a Simple Table is Better than a Cluttered Graph

Casino	Location Value
Pechanga Casino	181
Morongo Casino Resort & Spa	162
Pala Casino	153
Sobobo Casino	145
Valley View Casino	118
Casino Pauma	115
Viejas Casino & Turf Club	94
Agua Caliente	91
Cahuilla Creek Casino	69
Augustin Casino	68
Golden Acorn	50
Chumash Casino	38

Computers can also generate *textjunk*—printed documents that look like ransom notes made by pasting together characters in mismatched sizes, styles, and fonts. Just because a word processing program has several style options doesn't mean we have to use them all. I once received a two-page newsletter that used thirty-two different fonts, not counting variations created by letters that were bold, italicized, or different sizes. It was painful to read. Chartjunk, textjunk, it's all junk—worthless clutter that distracts and confuses instead of clarifying and informing. Take out the trash!

■ **Don't be Fooled:** A graph can reveal patterns—for example, how income has changed over time and how income and spending are related to each other. Graphs can also distort and mislead.

Watch out for graphs where zero has been omitted from an axis. This omission lets the graph zoom in on the data and show patterns that might otherwise be too compact to detect. However, this magnification exaggerates variations in the data and can be misleading. Worst of all are graphs with no numbers on the axis, because then there is no way of telling how much the variations have been exaggerated.

Watch out for data that have not been adjusted for the growth of the population and prices. Don't be deceived by graphs that put time on the vertical axis, where we are not used to seeing it, and/or by graphs that use inconsistent spacing—letting a half-inch sometimes be a five-year interval and sometimes be a ten-year interval.

Graphs should not be mere decoration, to amuse the easily bored. A useful graph displays data accurately and coherently, and helps us understand the data. Chartjunk, in contrast, distracts, confuses, and annoys. Chartjunk may be well-intentioned, but it is misguided. It may also be a deliberate attempt to mystify.

6

COMMON NONSENSE

THE GREAT FRENCH MATHEMATICIAN PIERRE-SIMON LAPLACE observed that probabilities are "nothing but common sense reduced to calculation." We should be cautious about calculating without thinking. Calculations are the easy part. The more important question is whether they make sense.

■ THE MONTY HALL PROBLEM

Statistical puzzles and paradoxes can be entertaining and challenging mental workouts. They also illustrate the value of thinking before calculating. A wonderful example is the Monty Hall problem: On the television show *Let's Make a Deal*, you are offered a choice of what is behind one of three doors, one a grand prize and the other two goats. After you pick a door, the host, Monty Hall, does what he always does by showing you a goat behind a door you did not choose and asking if you want to switch doors.

Most people think that, because there are two doors left, your chances are now 50–50. But use your common sense. You already knew that one of the doors you didn't choose had a goat behind it. Does it matter if Monty Hall reminds you that there is a goat behind one of these doors, or if he proves it by showing you a goat? You haven't learned anything useful about the door you did choose. There is still a one-third chance that it is the winning door, and therefore, the probability that the last door is the winner has risen to two-thirds. You should switch.

Table 6.1 shows the consequences of 300 plays of this game, each time with Door 1 being your initial choice. In the 100 cases where the prize is behind Door 1, the host shows Door 2 half the time and Door 3 half the time. When Door 2 or Door 3 has the prize, the host must show the other door.

Door 2 is shown 150 times; Door 3 is shown 150 times. No matter whether Door 2 or 3 is shown, the prize is behind Door 1 one-third of the time.

Table 6.1: The Monty Hall Problem

	Door 1 Has Prize	Door 2 Has Prize	Door 3 Has Prize	Total
Door 2 is shown	50	0	100	150
Door 3 is shown	50	100	0	150
Total	100	100	100	300

Another way to think about this puzzle is to suppose that you faint after you choose Door 1. You do not see Monty open a door and you do not hear his offer to switch. When you are revived, Monty shows you what is behind the door you chose. Surely, your chances of winning are still one-third.

Skeptics are sometimes persuaded by the extreme case of one million doors. Suppose that you play this game over and over. Each time, Monty shows you goats behind all but one of the remaining doors. Do you think that you will win the grand prize half the time?

Marilyn vos Savant, listed in the Guinness Book of World Records Hall of Fame for "Highest IQ," set off a nationwide furor when she discussed the Monty Hall problem in her syndicated column "Ask Marilyn." She gave the correct answer and then received more than ten thousand letters, many from college professors, most saying that she was wrong. A math professor at George Mason University was incensed:

You blew it! Let me explain: If one door is shown to be a loser, that information changes the probability of either remaining choice—

neither of which has any reason to be more likely—to 1/2. As a professional mathematician, I'm very concerned with the general public's lack of mathematical skills. Please help by confessing your error and, in the future, being more careful.

Marilyn stuck to her answer and invited people to play the game at home. Tens of thousands of students tried it in classrooms all over the country. Computer simulations were run at the Los Alamos National Laboratory in New Mexico. Slowly, public opinion shifted. Marilyn was right. The George Mason professor said that he "wrote her another letter, telling her that after removing my foot from my mouth I'm now eating humble pie. I vowed as penance to answer all the people who wrote to castigate me. It's been an intense professional embarrassment."

The New York Times published a story on this saga, including an interview with the real Monty Hall, who played a version of this game at the conclusion of thousands of episodes of the television show *Let's Make a Deal*. Hall knew that the contestant's initial choice still had a one-third chance of being correct, and he also knew that opening one door made contestants think that their chances had just increased to one-half. He called this the Henry James Treatment, or "The Turn of the Screw." Once the contestant's mindset was 50–50, Hall could psychologically push them one way or another by offering them thousands of dollars to switch or not switch. Hall also noted that he didn't have to play by Marilyn's rules. If the contestant's initial choice was a door with a goat behind it, Hall could simply open the door without offering the contestant a chance to switch. Hall played the game with the *Times* writer ten times, and the writer ended up with a goat every time.

▪ A GIRL NAMED FLORIDA

Another paradox involves a man named Smith who is walking with his daughter and says that he has another child at home. What is the probability that the absent child is a girl? At first blush, it seems to be one-half, but some experts dismiss this answer as naive. These experts say the correct answer is one-third. They also say that the probability changes from one-third to one-half if we find out that the girl with Smith is his older child. But how can that be true?

This paradox has appeared in many different forms, involving boys, girls, bears, and beagles, and in many different places, including a Martin Gardner 1959 column in *Scientific American*, John Paulos's 1988 book *Innumeracy*, and Leonard Mlodinow's 2008 book *The Drunkard's Walk*. The traditional assumptions undergirding the problem are that one-fourth of all two-child families have two boys (BB), one-fourth have two girls (GG), and one-half have one boy and one girl (BG if the boy is born first, GB if the girl is born first). These assumptions are not exactly correct empirically, but this puzzle is about logic, not data.

The "expert" argument is that once we learn that one of Smith's children is female, there are only three possibilities left: BG, GB, and GG. Therefore, the probability of two girls (GG) is one-third and the probability of one boy and one girl (BG or GB) is two-thirds. Sounds reasonable. But before you agree, consider this: if this logic is correct, it would also apply if Smith happened to be walking with a boy. Then, we could rule out GG and conclude that there is a two-thirds probability that Smith has one boy and one girl.

If this argument is correct, it doesn't matter whether Mr. Smith is walking with a girl or a boy! Either way, there would be a two-thirds probability that he has one boy and one girl. Therefore, we don't need to know the gender of the child with Smith. The child could be of indeterminate gender, hiding behind Smith, or playing in the park with dozens of other children. No matter what, there is a two-thirds probability that Smith has one boy and one girl. This is nonsense. Only half of all two-child families have one boy and one girl. Common sense must be correct and the expert reasoning must be flawed.

Step back and consider how Smith happens to be walking with one of his children. Table 6.2 shows 400 families evenly divided among BB, BG, GB, and GG. In the 100 cases where Smith has two boys (BB), he always walks with a boy. In the 100 cases where Smith has two girls (GG), he always walks with a girl. In the cases where he has a daughter and son (BG or GB), a plausible assumption is that he is equally likely to walk with either child.

Table 6.2: Smith's Other Child is Equally Likely to be a Boy or a Girl

	BB	BG	GB	GG	Total
Walks with girl	0	50	50	100	200
Walks with boy	100	50	50	0	200
Total	100	100	100	100	400

Now look at the first row—the 200 cases where Smith is walking with a girl. The absent child is a girl in 100 cases (GG) and a boy in the other 100 cases (BG or GB). In the second row, the 200 cases where Smith is walking with a boy, the absent child is a boy in 100 cases (BB) and a girl in the other 100 cases (BG or GB). No matter whether Smith walks with a girl or boy, his other child is equally likely to be a boy or a girl. The experts are wrong and common sense is correct.

The experts continue their flawed logic by arguing that if we learn that the girl walking with Smith is older than her sibling, the probability that her sibling is female increases from one-third to one-half. The expert argument is that after we learn that the daughter accompanying Smith is the older child, we can rule out BB and BG, leaving only GB and GG. Therefore, the probability of two daughters increases from one-third to one-half. But let's use our common sense to consider the logical implications. If learning that the daughter is older increases the probability of two daughters from one-third to one-half, then learning that the daughter is younger would also increase the probability of two daughters from one-third to one-half. But the girl *must* be either older or younger and, according to the expert argument, the probability increases from one-third to one-half either way. Therefore, we know the probability is one-half even if we do not know whether this girl is older or younger! Common sense is right and the experts are wrong once again.

Mlodinow recently enhanced the two-child paradox by arguing that if the girl reveals that she has an unusual name, like Florida, this, too, increases the probability of two girls from one-third to one-half. His argument is again counterintuitive and ultimately incorrect. If Mlodinow's argument were correct, it would apply to every name, since every name is unusual. (If the first name is not sufficiently unusual, make it the first and middle names or the first name, middle name, and birth date.) If the argument applies to every name, then it doesn't matter what the name is, or whether we even know the name. There is no paradox, just tortured logic.

In 2010, at Gathering for Gardner, a biennial conference honoring Martin Gardner, Gary Foshee presented yet another variation. He walked to the stage and said, "I have two children. One is a boy born on a Tuesday. What is the probability I have two boys?" After a few moments, Foshee continued: "The first thing you think is, 'What has Tuesday got to do with it?' Well, it has everything to do with it." And then he stepped down from the stage. This ignited a storm of debate at the conference and on the Internet.

My answer is that, well, Tuesday does have nothing to do with it. If Tuesday changed the probability, then so would Wednesday, Thursday, or any other day of the week. But the child must be born on some day. Therefore, if Foshee's argument is correct, we can change the probability without knowing the day of the week. Foshee is wrong. The day of the week doesn't matter.

■ WHAT IF?

An impatient relative—let's call him Bob—went to a big-box store to buy a smartphone. So many choices! He asked a store employee for help and was increasingly frustrated by the employee's incomprehensible answers. Bluetooth, geotagging, megapixels, HDML, IOS, LCD, RAM, ROM, blah, blah, blah. Finally, Bob blurted out, "Are you on drugs?" and stormed out of the store.

During his drive home, Bob had a great idea. Businesses should use drug tests to screen job applicants and monitor employees. They do it in the Olympics. They do it in cycling. They do it in greyhound racing. Why not do it for something important, like customer service?

Bob did a little research and found that a simple urine test for marijuana usage is 95 percent accurate. That is certainly good enough! If 95 percent accurate is good enough for statistical tests, it is good enough for weeding out weed users.

But if Bob's idea were put into practice, America's unemployment rates might go through the roof, and not because we are a nation of stoners. Bob's mistake, which is very common, is that he confused two conditional probabilities.

Several years ago, a black college professor asked a group of black military veterans how many African American professional athletes there are in the United States. The guesses ranged from 50,000 to 500,000. The correct answer was 1,200. There were twelve times that many black lawyers and fifteen times that many black doctors in the United States. No one in the audience believed him, but he was right.

The underlying problem is a confusion of conditional probabilities. We see that a large percentage of professional athletes are black and subconsciously think that a large percentage of blacks are professional athletes. The error is even more obvious if we change it from race to gender. One hundred percent of the players in the NBA are male, but only a minuscule fraction of all males play in the NBA.

At the time, many (maybe most) African American children wanted to be the next Michael Jordan or Magic Johnson. Today, they want to be LeBron James or Kevin Durant. The tragedy is that they almost surely won't. It is great to have dreams and ambitions, but it is also important to be realistic. Academics and athletics are both important, and the scholar-athlete should be revered. But the scholar is more likely to end up with a good job than is the athlete.

In 2012, the third-string quarterback at Ohio State University tweeted, "Why should we have to go to class if we came here to play FOOTBALL, we ain't come to play SCHOOL classes are POINTLESS." Well, a few years from now, we will see how that worked out.

THE FALSE-POSITIVE PROBLEM

The same confusion arises in drug testing. Ninety-five percent accuracy for a marijuana test means that of those who use marijuana,

95 percent test positive. A very different question is: Of those who test positive, what fraction are marijuana users?

If an employee is given a drug test, two kinds or errors can happen. A false-positive occurs if the test incorrectly indicates the presence of a drug; a false-negative occurs if the test fails to detect the presence of drugs. To illustrate the potential seriousness of the false-positive problem, consider a test administered to 10,000 employees, of whom 500 (5 percent) use marijuana and 9,500 (95 percent) do not. Suppose, further, that the test is 95 percent accurate: 95 percent of marijuana users test positive and 95 percent of those who do not use marijuana test negative.

Table 6.3 shows that, of the 500 people who use marijuana, 475 (95 percent) have a positive test result and 25 (5 percent) do not. Of the 9,500 who do not use marijuana, 475 (5 percent) have a positive result and 9,025 (95 percent) do not. So far, so good.

Table 6.3: The False-Positive Problem

	Test Positive	Test Negative	Total
Marijuana user	475	25	500
Not marijuana user	475	9,025	9,500
Total	950	9,050	10,000

However, Table 6.3 also shows that of the 950 positive test results 475 are false positives. An astounding 50 percent of those who test positive do not use marijuana. This is why we need to be careful with conditional probabilities. Although 95 percent of all marijuana users test positive, only 50 percent of those who test positive are marijuana users.

In *Chandler v. Miller* (1997), the US Supreme Court ruled 8–1 that a Georgia law requiring candidates for certain state offices to pass a drug test violated the Fourth Amendment's protection against unreasonable searches. The court ruled that searches are permissible in some "closely guarded" cases where a specific individual is not suspected of a crime but a special need overrides the right to privacy—for example, drug testing of airline pilots. However, the court concluded that the possibility that a state's elected officials use drugs does not jeopardize public safety. (That's an invitation to supply your own punch line.)

THE RARE DISEASE PROBLEM

The false-positive problem also arises in medical tests for a disease. As with the marijuana test, even though a test might be very accurate in detecting a disease, it may still be the case that many (even most) people who test positive do not actually have the disease.

Here is a very specific example. One hundred doctors were asked this hypothetical question:

> In a routine examination, you find a lump in a female patient's breast. In your experience, only 1 out of 100 such lumps turns out to be malignant, but, to be safe, you order a mammogram X-ray. If the lump is malignant, there is a 0.80 probability that the mammogram will identify it as malignant; if the lump is benign, there is a 0.90 probability that the mammogram will identify it as benign. In this particular case, the mammogram identifies the lump as malignant. In light of these mammogram results, what is your estimate of the probability that this lump is malignant?

Of the 100 doctors surveyed, 95 gave probabilities of around 0.75. However, the correct probability is actually one-tenth of that: 0.075!

Table 6.4 shows the calculations for 1,000 patients. The lumps are malignant in 10 cases (1 percent of 1,000) and the test gives a correct positive result in 8 of the malignant cases (80 percent). Of the 990 benign cases, the test gives a correct negative result in 891 cases (90 percent).

Table 6.4: False Positives for the Mammogram X-Ray Test

	Test Positive	Test Negative	Total
Malignant	8	2	10
Benign	99	891	990
Total	107	893	1,000

Looking at the first numerical *row*, for those ten patients with malignant tumors, the test gives a positive result 80 percent of the time, 8/10 = 0.80. Yet, looking at the first numerical *column*, of the 107 patients with positive test results, only 7.5 percent actually have malignant tumors: 8/107 = 0.075. Even though 80 percent of the 10 malignant tumors are correctly identified as malignant, these positive test results are far outnumbered by the false positives—the 10 percent of 990 benign lumps that are identified incorrectly. Sometimes, as here, a small percentage of a large number is bigger than a large percentage of a small number.

It is very easy to misinterpret conditional probabilities, and these doctors evidently did so. According to the researcher who conducted this survey,

> The erring physicians usually report that they assumed that the probability of cancer given that the patient has a positive X-ray . . . was approximately equal to the probability of a positive X-ray in a patient with cancer . . . The latter probability is the one measured in clinical research programs and is very familiar, but it is the former probability that is needed for clinical decision making. It seems that many if not most physicians confuse the two.

Most doctors evidently confused the following conditional statements. If the lump is malignant, what is the probability that the test result will be positive? (Answer: 80 percent.) If the test result is positive, what is the probability that the lump is malignant? (Answer: 7.5 percent.) Their misinterpretation of medical data could have tragic consequences.

■ THE DARTMOUTH SALMON STUDY

False positives are inevitable when there are a large number of tests. For example, suppose that a seemingly healthy woman has a physical checkup which involves several independent tests of risk factors (such as cholesterol and blood pressure) that might indicate a health problem. For each test, the result is flagged as abnormal if the reading is outside a range that encompasses 95 percent of the readings for healthy women. On any single test, there is a 5 percent chance of a false positive. For 10 tests, there is a 40 percent chance of a false positive. For 100 tests, the probability of a false positive result is above 99 percent. As the number of tests increases, the chances of a false positive approaches 100 percent.

Here's an example with a standard neuroscience experiment that involves a very large number of tests. A volunteer is put in an MRI machine and shown various images and asked questions about the images. Instead of using electrodes implanted in the brain to track brain activity, functional magnetic resonance imaging (fMRI) is used to measure magnetic disruption, which happens as oxygenated and deoxygenated blood flows through the brain. After the test, the researchers look at up to 130,000 voxels (3-D data) to see which parts of the brain were stimulated by the images and questions.

The fMRI measurements are very noisy, picking up all sorts of magnetic signals from the environment and from variations in the density of fatty tissue in different parts of the brain. Sometimes the voxels miss brain activity (a false negative). Sometimes they suggest activity where there is none (a false positive).

A student named Craig Bennett did an unusual variation on this experiment in a Dartmouth laboratory. He used an MRI machine to study the brain activity of a salmon as it was shown a series of fifteen photographs. Here is part of his report:

> *Subject.* One mature Atlantic Salmon (*Salmo salar*) participated in the fMRI study. The salmon was approximately 18 inches long, weighed 3.8 lbs, and was not alive at the time of scanning.
>
> *Task.* The task administered to the salmon involved completing an open-ended mentalizing task. The salmon was shown a series of photographs depicting human individuals in social situations with a specified emotional valence. The salmon was asked to determine what emotion the individual in the photo must have been experiencing.
>
> *Design.* Stimuli were presented in a block design with each photo presented for 10 seconds followed by 12 seconds of rest. A total of 15 photos were displayed. Total scan time was 5.5 minutes.

Analysis. Voxelwise statistics on the salmon data were calculated through an ordinary least-squares estimation of the general linear model (GLM). Predictors of the hemodynamic response were modeled by a boxcar function convolved with a canonical hemodynamic response. A temporal high pass filter of 128 seconds was include to account for low frequency drift. No autocorrelation correction was applied.

The Analysis section sounds pretty professional, right? But did you notice in the Subject section that the salmon "was not alive at the time of scanning"? Yep, Craig put a dead salmon he purchased at a local market into the MRI machine, showed it photographs, and asked it questions. Nonetheless, with so many voxels, some false positives showed up, which might be interpreted as the salmon's reaction to the photos and questions. Except that the salmon was dead.

Figure 6.1: fMRI of Tested Salmon

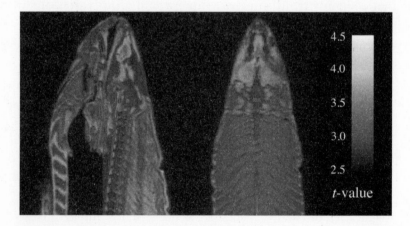

Bennett and his professor, Abigail Baird, use this experiment to argue forcefully that fMRI research needs to take into account the false positive problem, which up to 40 percent of published papers had not done.

This dead-salmon study got more press than most fMRI studies, even winning one of the Ig Nobel Prizes awarded annually at a hilarious Harvard ceremony for "achievements that first make people laugh, and then make them think."

■ **Don't be Fooled:** The Monty Hall problem is a great paradox because our intuition is wrong and can be improved by using common sense. The two-child paradox is also wonderful, but for a very different reason. Here, our intuition is correct and can be confirmed by using common sense.

Don't just do the calculations. Use common sense to see whether you are answering the correct question, the assumptions are reasonable, and the results are plausible. If a statistical argument doesn't make sense, think about it carefully—you may discover that the argument is nonsense.

The false-positive problem is related to a confusion of conditional probabilities. A test may be very likely to show a positive result in certain situations (for example, if a disease is present), yet a positive test result does not insure that the condition is present. It may be a false positive. False positive are more common when the condition is rare (like a malignant tumor) or when there are a large number of readings (like the dead-salmon MRI).

7

CONFOUND IT!

CHOLERA IS AN OFTEN FATAL INTESTINAL DISEASE MARKED BY diarrhea and vomiting. Originally confined to the Indian sub-continent, the development of overland and oceanic trade routes spread the disease throughout the world in the nineteenth century, killing tens of millions of people.

Cholera hit London in 1832 and killed 6,500 people. The medical establishment at the time believed that cholera, like other diseases, was caused by breathing "miasma," or noxious air. London stank from rotting garbage, human and animal feces in the streets, and foul smells coming from the polluted Thames River. The air was particularly offensive during the dank foggy nights. Many people feared "night air" and stayed indoors with their windows shut or covered their faces if they had to go outside. The miasma theory was supported by the fact that cholera was more commonplace in poor neighborhoods that lacked proper sanitation services and smelled awful.

The miasma theory could not be proven definitively because other confounding factors needed to be taken into account. For instance, the people living in poor neighborhoods tended to be older than in other neighborhoods. Some people ate different foods or had different occupations or had little or no heat. Was it one of those factors, or all of them together?

Sometimes scientists can isolate the effects of one factor by doing an experiment under controlled conditions, holding constant the confounding factors. If all other relevant factors are held constant, then the factor that does vary is evidently causing the observed outcome.

However, it is often not practical or ethical to do controlled laboratory experiments, so researchers must draw conclusions from what they observe and cannot control. That was the case with cholera. Doctors certainly could not force randomly selected people to breathe poisonous air while other randomly selected people lived and worked in a clean-air environment. However, a natural experiment occurred that revealed the cause once and for all.

For centuries, houses in London and other large cities had basement cesspits that collected human waste. These cesspits were periodically emptied by tradesmen who carted the waste away in horse-drawn wagons. The waste was called "night-soil" because it was hauled away at night when the city streets were less crowded and it was often taken to nearby farms where the waste was used as fertilizer.

An 1848 law required Londoners to stop using cesspits and instead connect their homes to the sewer lines being built throughout London. While this law reduced the stench and hazards created by cesspits and the transport of night-soil, it created another problem. The sewer lines deposited the raw sewage into the Thames River which, directly or indirectly, was the source of drinking water for many Londoners.

In 1849 a thirty-six-year-old doctor named John Snow published an essay titled *On the Mode of Communication of Cholera* arguing that cholera was not caused by breathing foul air, but by "a poison extracted from a diseased body and passed on through the drinking water which had become polluted by sewage." It is not clear how Snow came up with this theory. He may have reasoned that breathing bad air should affect the lungs, and the fact that cholera affects the intestines suggested it had something to do with what people were eating or drinking. Snow also saw that the 1848 law banning cesspits was followed shortly thereafter by the 1848–49 cholera epidemic. Of course, this sort of reasoning is a logical fallacy known as *post hoc ergo propter hoc* ("after this, therefore because of this")—the fact that one event happened shortly after another doesn't mean that the former necessarily caused the latter.

Snow's theory was dismissed by Florence Nightingale and other leading public health authorities as naive and ill-informed. The miasma theory was too well-established to be upended by fanciful speculation by a young doctor. Snow could not test his theory by holding constant all potentially confounding factors, including miasma, and forcing some people to drink contaminated water while others drank clean water. But, in 1854, another cholera epidemic hit London and Snow figured out two different ways to test his theory.

For several years, two water companies, the Southwark and Vauxhall Water Company and the Lambeth Company, supplied water to the same London neighborhoods through separate pipes using water drawn from the same polluted part of the Thames River. In the 1848–49 cholera epidemic, their customers had similar death rates. After the 1848 law banning cesspools, Arthur Hassall, a British microbiologist, did a careful, thorough study of the relationship between London's water and sewage systems. His shocking conclusions were published in 1850 in the prestigious British medical journal *The Lancet* and in a book titled *A Microscopical Examination of the Water Supplied to the Inhabitants of London and the Suburban Districts*. He wrote:

> I have shown that various matters, animal and vegetable, connected with sewage, including some of those of the feces, are at all times to be detected in Thames water; and further, that the same substances exist in the waters of several of the companies as supplied to the public; the chain of evidence is complete and conclusive; thus the muscular fibre of the meat, as well as the more indestructible parts of the vegetable tissues consumed, have been repeatedly traced from the [water] closet to the sewer, from the sewer to the Thames, from this to the companies' reservoirs, and from these back again to the public.
>
> It is thus beyond dispute that, according to the present system of London water supply, a portion of the inhabitants of the metropolis are made to consume, in some form or another, a portion of their own excrement, and, moreover, to pay for the privilege.

Influenced by Hassall's careful but distressing conclusions, the Metropolitan Water Act of 1852 mandated that London water companies stop taking water from the heavily polluted part of the Thames River by August 31, 1855. Lambeth had already acquired land twenty-two miles upriver and made the move in 1852, so that it was now drawing water from the Thames before it became polluted by London sewage. Southwark and Vauxhall did not relocate until 1855.

Snow realized that this was a perfect opportunity to test his theory. The fact that people living in adjacent houses happened to be served by different water companies naturally controlled for a variety of potentially confounding factors. Snow wrote:

> The experiment, too, was on the grandest scale. No fewer than three hundred thousand people of both sexes, of every age and occupation, and of every rank and station, from gentlefolks down to the very poor, were divided into two groups without their choice, and, in most cases, without their knowledge; one group being supplied with water containing the sewage of London, and, amongst it, whatever might have come from the cholera patients, the other group having water quite free from such impurity.

Snow examined all recorded cholera deaths during the first seven weeks of the 1854 epidemic and determined which homes received their water from these two water companies. He found that the number of deaths per 10,000 houses was nearly nine times higher for Southwark and Vauxhall customers:

Table 7.1

	Number of Houses	Deaths from Cholera	Deaths per 10,000 Houses
Southwark and Vauxhall Company	40,046	1,263	315
Lambeth Company	26,107	98	37
Rest of London	256,423	1,422	59

These data provided convincing evidence of a relationship between drinking contaminated water and the incidence of cholera.

Snow found other strong evidence in support of his theory. The 1854 epidemic hit the Soho district, close to where Snow lived, especially hard, killing more than five hundred people in ten days. Three-fourths of the residents fled, evidently trying to escape the miasma, but Snow stayed to investigate his theory.

At the time, London had dozens of public wells throughout the city that allowed people to pump water to drink or bring home. The Soho district was not yet connected to the London sewer system and Snow suspected that Soho's cesspits were contaminating the water being pumped from Soho's public wells. Snow drew a map showing the location of 13 public water pumps and the homes of 578 cholera victims. It soon became apparent that many of the victims lived near a pump on Broad Street. Figure 1 shows part of his map. The pump is at the intersection of Broad Street and Cambridge Street. The stacked lines drawn on the map show the residences of cholera victims, and there is a clear concentration near the pump, presumably because they drank from this well.

Figure 7.1: Cholera deaths near the Broad Street pump, shown by lines in front of their residence

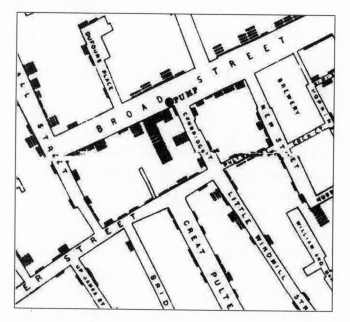

Snow personally visited the homes of cholera victims who lived closer to other public water pumps and found that they often drank from the Broad Street pump as they walked past the well on their way to work, shop, or attend school. Snow also found that some families used the Broad Street pump because the water smelled better.

Even more damning for the miasma theory, many people who lived near the Broad Street pump but did not drink the water had not been affected by cholera. The people in this neighborhood breathed the same air, but the only ones who died of cholera were those who drank water from the Broad Street pump.

The Board of Guardians of St James's parish were responsible for the Broad Street well and desperate to try anything to end the epidemic. Snow was able to persuade them to remove the pump handle so that no one could drink from the well. The epidemic ended soon afterward. Nonetheless, after the epidemic ended, the pump handle was reattached. The miasma theory was too strongly entrenched to be demolished by this upstart doctor.

Later, it was discovered why the Broad Street pump was spreading cholera. The well had been dug three feet from an old cesspit that had been abandoned when the house over the cesspit burned down and the street had been widened. The diapers from a baby with cholera had gone into this cesspit, which leaked and contaminated the Broad Street well.

Snow suffered a stroke and died in 1858, before he could see his theory accepted and the cholera epidemics end. London began building a modern sewer system in 1859, ironically with the intent of reducing miasma by getting sewage underground where it wouldn't be smelled. The unintended benefit was that sewage no longer contaminated the water supply. Another cholera epidemic hit London in 1866, but spared those parts of town that were connected to the new sewer system. When the system was fully completed, London was safe.

Modern scientists eventually confirmed that Snow's theory was correct. Cholera is transmitted by ingesting food or water contaminated by fecal matter. Throughout the developed world, cities have eradicated cholera epidemics by constructing effective sewage treatment systems and clean water supplies. Today, John Snow is recognized and celebrated for his ingenious use of data to study a critical public health issue. He is considered the father of epidemiology, the study of the patterns, causes, and effects of disease.

Confounding factors are often present in studies using observational data, simply because there is no practical way to hold these factors constant. However, sometimes nature is kind to researchers. In his cholera study, Snow was fortunate to be able to study an area of London in which adjacent houses were served by different water companies, thereby reducing the confounding effects of socioeconomic factors. Snow reasoned that families living in adjacent homes were likely to be of the same socioeconomic class. This would not have been the case if Snow had been forced to compare neighborhoods or cities served by different water companies.

Sometimes, observational data can be subdivided in order to deal with confounding factors. In a study of the effects of smoking on health, gender may be a confounding factor. A well-designed study might control for gender by analyzing male and female data separately. In a study of the effects of income on child-bearing, age and religious beliefs might be confounding factors. A well-designed study might separate the data into groups of the same age with similar religious beliefs.

The important lesson is that we should always think about whether a study's conclusions are muddled by confounding factors.

■ SOMEBODY'S PARADOX

In 2010 an Internet company collected data for two different web page layouts. In the "one-click" format, advertisements appear on the web site's first page. In the "two-click" format, there are keywords on the first page—if the user clicks on a keyword, the user is sent to another page with ads that are targeted to the keyword. Either way, the company receives revenue if the user clicks on an ad. The two-click format requires more user effort, but the targeted ads are more likely to be effective. The company consequently gets more revenue when a user selects a two-click ad.

The company's CEO was shown the data in Table 7.2. (Revenue and users are both in millions.) RPM (revenue per thousand users) was higher with the two-click format ($12.14 versus $11.60) and the course of action seemed clear: revenue would increase if they went with the two-click format on all their web sites.

Table 7.2: Revenue, Users, and Revenue per Thousand Users (RPM)

	1-Click			2-Clicks	
Revenue	Users	RPM	Revenue	Users	RPM
$2.9	250	$11.60	$1.7	140	$12.14

This conclusion might be an expensive mistake. These are observational data and there may be self-selection bias in that users who go to sites with the one-click format may be systematically different from users who go to sites with the two-click format. For a valid comparison, the company could do a controlled experiment. For each web site, users could be randomly directed to one of the two formats. The company could then legitimately compare the success of each format.

There is also a less obvious problem. A pesky statistician passed around Table 7.3, with the data grouped by whether the user was inside or outside the United States. The one-click format had the higher RPM for both types of users. This certainly shook up the discussion! The CEO threw up her hands and asked how the one-click format could be superior both inside and outside the United States, and yet inferior overall. Some staff members suggested checking the math. Others stared blankly, hoping someone else would figure out this paradox.

Then the lightbulbs went on.

Table 7.3: The Separation of US and International Users

	1-Click			2-Clicks		
	Revenue	Users	RPM	Revenue	Users	RPM
United States	$1.8	70	$25.71	$1.2	50	$24.00
International	$1.1	180	$6.11	$0.5	90	$5.56
Total	$2.9	250	$11.60	$1.7	140	$12.14

This is an example of Simpson's Paradox, which was described by Edward Simpson in a 1951 paper, but was actually discovered by two other statisticians fifty years earlier, making Simpson's Paradox an example of Stigler's law: "No scientific discovery is named after its original discoverer" (which Stigler himself illustrated by identifying Robert K. Merton as the discoverer of Stigler's law). Simpson's Paradox occurs if a pattern in aggregated data is reversed when the data are disaggregated. Here, for the aggregated data, two-click is superior. When the data are separated into US and international, one-click is superior.

To understand this reversal, start with the aggregated data—which indicate that two-click sites have a higher RPM. The type of user—US or international—is a confounding factor in that RPM is related not only to the click format, but also to the type of user. US users have a higher RPM than do international users and US users happened to be more likely to go to two-click pages, which boosts the overall RPM for two-clicks. If we take this confounding factor into account—by separating the data into US and international users—we see that the one-click RPM is higher for both types of users.

Contrary to their initial impression, the company could expect its overall revenue to increase if it used a one-click format for all its web pages. Fortunately, this company's data wonks were smart enough to: (a) recognize Simpson's Paradox; and (b) do the controlled experiment described earlier. Their conclusion: the one-click format worked better on most of their web sites, but some sites benefitted from the two-click format.

The key to being alert to a possible Simpson's Paradox is to think about whether a confounding factor has been ignored. Here is another example. In the 1970s, a lawsuit accused the graduate school at the University of California at Berkeley of discriminating against female applicants. As evidence, the data in Table 7.4 showed that 44 percent of the men who applied were accepted while only 35 percent of the female applicants were accepted.

Table 7.4: Men Are More Likely to be Accepted

	Applicants	Admitted
Men	8,442	44%
Women	4,321	35%

An investigation was launched to determine which departments were most at fault. However, an examination of admission rates in the school's eighty-five departments found little, if any, evidence that women were being discriminated against. If anything, the reverse was true, in that several departments had higher acceptance rates for women than for men.

Table 7.5 shows the acceptance rates for the six largest departments. Department 1 had the highest acceptance rate, Department 2 the second highest, and so on. Overall, 45 percent of the male applicants were accepted and only 30 percent of the female applicants—seemingly clear evidence of discrimination against women. Yet, when we look at the individual departments, only 2 departments (3 and 5) had higher acceptance rates for men, and the differences were small and not statistically significant. The only statistically significant difference in acceptance rates was for Department 1, where women were substantially *more likely* than men to be admitted (82 percent versus 62 percent).

Table 7.5: Acceptance Rates for the Six Largest Departments

	Total		Men		Women	
Department	Applicants	Admitted	Applicants	Admitted	Applicants	Admitted
1	933	64%	825	62%	108	82%
2	585	63%	560	63%	25	68%
3	918	35%	325	37%	593	34%
4	792	34%	417	33%	375	35%
5	584	25%	191	28%	393	24%
6	714	6%	373	6%	341	7%
Total	4,526	39%	2,691	45%	1,835	30%

Simpson's Paradox again. A pattern in the aggregated data is reversed when the data are disaggregated. Here, the confounding factor
is that some departments have much higher acceptance rates than others. Department 1 accepted 64 percent of all applicants; Department
6 had a 6 percent acceptance rate. Now, look at how men were more
likely to apply to Department 1 than Department 6, while it was the
other way around for women.

Figure 7.2: Women Were More Likely to Apply to Departments With Low Acceptance Rates

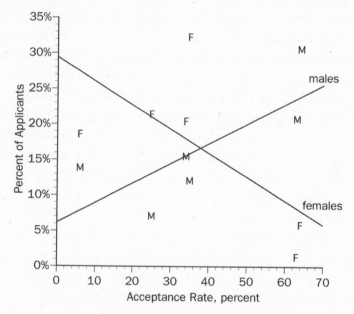

Figure 7.2 visually confirms what the data in Table 7.3 show. The
horizontal axis is the department's acceptance rate. The vertical axis
is the fraction of applicants of each gender who applied to that department, with the letter F denoting female applicants and M male
applicants. For example, the two leftmost dots are for Department 6,
which had a 6 percent acceptance rate. Fourteen percent of the male
applicants and 19 percent of the female applicants applied to Department 6. The fitted lines show that, overall, women tended to apply to
departments with low acceptance rates, while the reverse was true of
males applicants. Men had a higher overall acceptance rate because

they applied in disproportionate numbers to the departments that were the easiest to get into. Looking at all 85 departments and taking into account this confounding factor, a careful study concluded that there was a "small but statistically significant bias in favor of women."

It is not always easy to identify confounding factors. The point is that we should be alert to whether there are any possible confounding factors that, if taken into account, would change our conclusions. Let's try a few.

Alaska Airlines had a better on-time performance record than another airline in the five major airports they competed in, but a worse overall on-time record. Why? Because Alaska Air had many more flights into Seattle where weather problems frequently cause delays. Female mortality rates are lower in Sweden that in Costa Rica for every age group, but the overall female mortality rate is higher in Sweden. Why? Because Sweden has more elderly women (and the elderly have a relatively high death rate). A medical study found that one kind of surgery was more successful than another kind in treating small and large kidney stones, yet less successful overall. Why? Because it was more often used for large stones (which have a relatively low success rate).

In all these examples, and many more, Simpson's Paradox emerges because a confounding factor affects aggregated data. Still, this doesn't mean that disaggregated data are always better than aggregated data. Table 7.6 compares two hypothetical baseball players, with the data disaggregated into even-numbered and odd-numbered days of the month. For example, Cory had 20 base hits in 100 times at bat on even-numbered days, a batting average of 20/100 = 0.200. In these made-up data, both players happened to do better on odd-numbered days, and Cory happened to have more times at bat on odd-numbered days. As a result, even though Jimmy had the higher batting average on both even-numbered and odd-numbered days, Cory had the higher batting average for the season as a whole.

Table 7.6: Who Is the Better Batter?

	Even-Numbered Days	Odd-Numbered Days	All Days
Cory	20/100 = 0.200	90/300 = 0.300	110/400 = 0.275
Jimmy	61/300 = 0.203	31/100 = 0.310	92/400 = 0.230

Based on these data, who would you say is the better hitter? I would say Cory, because there is no logical reason to think that even or odd is a relevant confounding factor. It is just a fluke in the data. The same thing might happen if we split the data by the number of letters in each day or if we put the days in alphabetical order. In these cases, the patterns in the disaggregated data are a coincidence that can be safely ignored. The aggregated data give a more accurate measure of who is the better batter. In other cases, confounding factors are real and it is perilous to neglect them.

■ I'LL HAVE ANOTHER COFFEE

Coffee has had a long and controversial history. Coffee shrubs originated centuries ago in African tropical forests. Originally, crushed beans were mixed with fruit and then eaten, grounds and all. Drinking liquid coffee after discarding the grounds seems to have originated in the fifteenth century in Yemen, and then spread everywhere. In Turkey, coffee became such an important part of everyday life that prospective brides were evaluated on their ability to make a good cup of coffee. Once married, a woman could divorce her husband if he did not provide a daily supply of coffee.

Coffee is now one of the most popular beverages in the world. While many people love coffee, others believe it is addictive and unhealthy. It has even been called the most abused drug in the world. What is the truth? The first statistical study of coffee was an interesting experiment in Sweden in the 1700s.

Coffee was introduced to Sweden in the seventeenth century and became increasingly popular over time—although many viewed coffee as a Satanic brew that addicted the rich and incited the masses. For many years, coffee was taxed heavily or banned completely. Then,

King Gustav III performed a curious experiment, said to be Sweden's first clinical trial.

Gustav was an often enlightened dictator. He enacted many economic and social reforms, granted religious freedoms to Catholics and Jews, curtailed capital punishment and torture, and supported the arts generously. Some ventures were less successful. He once tried to unite the people by initiating a war with Russia. The tailors at the Royal Swedish Opera prepared Russian military uniforms for a small group of Swedes who crossed the Russian border and fired shots at a Swedish border outpost. After this staged provocation, Gustav launched a "defensive" attack on Russia. It was an expensive war with both sides losing soldiers, ships, munitions, and equipment, and no land gained or lost. Instead of uniting the Swedes against a common enemy, the casualties and economic costs fueled popular disillusionment with King Gustav.

Equally unsuccessful were Gustav's wars on alcohol and coffee. To raise revenue for his military misadventures, Gustav made the production and sale of alcohol a government monopoly. This worked about as well as Prohibition in the United States. Farmers continued to make alcohol and drinking went up, not down. As for coffee, some prominent Swedish scientists believed that coffee was a healthful tonic, while others believed the opposite. Gustav was convinced that coffee was a poison and determined to prove it. He found identical male twins who had been convicted of murder and were waiting to be beheaded. Gustav changed their sentences to life imprisonment, with one condition. One man had to drink three pots of coffee every day, the other drank three pots of tea. Two court-appointed doctors would ensure that the conditions were carried out and let the king know when the twins died. Gustav was certain that he had condemned the coffee-drinking twin to death as surely as if he were to be beheaded—and that the death would demonstrate once and for all that coffee was poison.

Instead, both twins outlived the doctors and Gustav (who was assassinated). The tea-drinking twin finally died at age eighty-three, with the coffee-drinking twin still going strong. Despite this unexpected outcome, the Swedish government continued to outlaw coffee until the 1820s, when it finally decided to let the Swedish people legally do what they wanted to do all along—drink coffee, lots of coffee.

Gustav's experiment was noteworthy for his clever choice of identical male twins, which eliminated the confounding effects of gender, age, and genes. The most glaring weakness was the small sample size. Nothing statistically persuasive—for coffee or against coffee—can come from such a small sample.

Many years later, some much larger studies concluded that Gustav was right about the evils of coffee. But fatal flaws hamper each of these studies. A recurring problem is that there is no practical way to do randomized long-term experiments. Gustov was king and he could do what he wanted with a pair of soon-to-be-headless twins. We can't make people drink coffee or not drink coffee. Instead, we have to make do with observational data. We observe some people drinking coffee, we observe other people not drinking coffee, and we compare the two groups. The problem is that there may be systematic differences between the people who choose to drink coffee and those who do not.

For example, a 1971 study found that people with bladder cancer were more likely to be coffee drinkers than were people who did not have bladder cancer—suggesting that coffee causes bladder cancer. However, a confounding factor was that coffee drinkers were also more likely to be cigarette smokers. Was it the coffee or the cigarettes that was responsible for the bladder cancer? In 1993, a rigorous analysis of thirty-five studies placed the blame on cigarettes and exonerated coffee, concluding that there is "no evidence of an increase in risk of [lower urinary track cancer] in men or women after adjustment for the effects of cigarette smoking." A 2001 study confirmed that tobacco increases the risk of bladder cancer and coffee does not, but added a new twist: smokers who drank coffee were less likely to develop bladder cancer than were smokers who did not drink coffee. Coffee seemed to partly offset the ill effects of tobacco.

Here's another example. In the early 1980s, a group led by Brian MacMahon, a widely respected researcher and chair of the Harvard

School of Public Health, found a strong relationship between coffee drinking and pancreatic cancer. This study was published in *The New England Journal of Medicine*, one of the world's premier medical journals, and reported nationwide. The Harvard group advised that pancreatic cancer could be reduced substantially if people stopped drinking coffee. MacMahon followed his own advice. Before the study, he drank three cups a day. After the study, he stopped drinking coffee.

MacMahon's study compared hospitalized patients with pancreatic cancer to patients with other diseases who had been hospitalized by the same doctors. This was a convenient sample with observational data, and that was a problem. The doctors were often gastrointestinal specialists, and many of the hospitalized patients who did not have cancer had given up coffee because of fears that it would exacerbate their ulcers and other gastrointestinal problems. The patients with pancreatic cancer had not stopped drinking coffee. This virtually guaranteed that there were more coffee drinkers among the patients with pancreatic cancer. It wasn't that coffee caused pancreatic cancer, but that other illnesses caused other people to stop drinking coffee.

Another problem was that MacMahon did the study because he thought there might be a link between alcohol or tobacco and pancreatic cancer. He looked at alcohol. He looked at cigarettes. He looked at cigars. He looked at pipes. When he didn't find anything, he kept looking. He tried tea. He tried coffee and finally found something: patients with pancreatic cancer drank more coffee.

When a theory is generated by ransacking data, we can't use these pillaged data to test the theory. Suppose I flip a coin one hundred times and, after examining the data from all possible angles, I notice that a sequence of two heads and a tail is followed by another head more than half the time. This wacky theory came from scrutinizing my own data, so of course it is confirmed by the data. For a fair test, I need to state the theory in advance and test it with fresh coin flips.

Subsequent studies, including one by MacMahon's group, failed to confirm the initial conclusion: "In contrast to the earlier study, no trend in risk was observed for men or women." The American

Cancer Society agreed: "The most recent scientific studies have found no relationship at all between coffee and the risk of pancreatic, breast, or any other type of cancer." Not only has subsequent research not confirmed MacMahon's initial theory, it now appears—at least for men—that drinking coffee reduces the risk of pancreatic cancer!

Coffee seems to have many health benefits, including reduced risk of many types of cancer, cirrhosis of the liver, gallbladder disease, cardiovascular disease, Alzheimer's, Parkinson's, plaque disease, and gout. The biggest risk seems to be to the lining of the gastrointestinal organs. This is why people with ulcers and other gastrointestinal problems are urged to stop drinking coffee—and is one of the reasons why the original pancreatic cancer study was flawed.

The results of the largest study to date, of 400,000 people over a 13-year period, was published in 2012 in *The New England Journal of Medicine*, the same prestigious journal that published the flawed pancreatic cancer study. The 2012 study found that, compared to people who don't drink coffee (and taking into account the confounding effects of smoking, drinking, and exercise), people who drank 1 cup of coffee daily were 5–6 percent less likely to die at every age. For those who drank 2 or 3 cups a day, the risk fell by 10 percent for men and 13 percent for women.

Why do researchers keep changing their minds? Chocolate was bad, now chocolate is good. Wine was bad, now wine is good. Coffee was bad, now coffee is good. Sunshine was bad, now sunshine is good. Good turns into bad, and bad into good, because the initial research was flawed—usually because confounding factors were ignored or the data were ransacked to find something publishable.

■ **Don't be Fooled:** If a study supports your beliefs, there is a natural inclination to nod knowingly and conclude that your beliefs are confirmed. It would be smarter to look closely and think about confounding factors. You should do the same when a study doesn't make sense.

For example, it seemed plausible that Berkeley's graduate admissions policies discriminated against women. However, a deeper investigation intended to identify the departments that were the worst offenders found something unexpected—if anything, departments tended to favor female applicants. Women had a lower overall acceptance rate because they were more likely to apply to programs with low acceptance rates.

Observational studies are inherently challenging because of the potential for self-selection bias and confounding factors. Always be wary of studies that use the data to discover the theory.

8

WHEN YOU'RE HOT, YOU'RE NOT

N THE SECOND GAME OF THE 2010 NATIONAL BASKETBALL ASSOCIA-
tion (NBA) finals between long-time rivals the Boston Celtics
and the Los Angeles Lakers, Celtic guard Ray Allen made seven
three-point shots in a row. One teammate said it was "incredible."
Another called it "unbelievable." One sportswriter wrote that "Allen
got hot." Another wrote that Allen had "slipped into that shooting
zone only visited by real-life superstars and movie characters."

Ray Allen isn't alone. Hot and cold streaks are commonplace in
sports. Many basketball players have made (or missed) several shots
in a row. Many football quarterbacks have thrown several consecutive
complete (or incomplete) passes. Many baseball players have made
several hits (or outs) in a row. Fans and players alike see these streaks
and conclude that the player has gotten hot or cold. Purvis Short, who
averaged seventeen points a game over his twelve-year NBA career and
once scored fifty-nine points in a single game, expressed the common
perception: "You're in a world all your own. It's hard to describe. But
the basket seems to be so wide. No matter what you do, you know the
ball is going to go in."

Once again, we see a pattern and make up a theory that fits the
pattern. If a basketball player makes several shots in a row, it must
be because he has gotten hot, with an increased probability of making
shots. If a player misses several shots in a row, it must be because he
is cold, with a reduced probability of making shots. What most people
—fans and players—do not appreciate is that even if each shot, pass,
or swing is independent of previous shots, passes, and swings, coincidental streaks can happen by chance alone.

For example, I flipped a coin twenty times, and we can pretend that each flip represents a basketball shot. Heads counts as making a basket, and tails counts as a miss. A string of consecutive heads is a hot streak, a string of tails is a cold streak. Here are my results:

H   H   H   T   T   T   T   H   H   T

H   H   H   H   T   H   H   T   T   H

Beginning with the fourth flip, there was a streak of four tails in a row. Beginning with the eleventh flip, there was a streak of four heads in a row. I had a cold streak and, a little later, a hot streak, even though every coin flip was independent!

I did this experiment ten times. In seven of my ten experiments, I had a streak of at least four heads or tails in a row. I had two streaks of four in a row, four streaks of five in a row, and one streak of ten in a row. Table 8.1 shows the theoretical probability of streaks of various lengths when a coin is flipped twenty times. There is a 0.768 probability of a streak of four or more, and seven of my ten experiments had such streaks. My streak of ten is a row is unusual, but has about an 11 percent chance if, as here, the experiment is repeated ten times.

Table 8.1: Streak Probabilities for Twenty Coin Flips

| | Probability of a Streak | |
Length of Streak	Exactly this Long	At Least This Long
< 3	0.021	1.000
3	0.211	0.979
4	0.310	0.768
5	0.222	0.458
6	0.121	0.236
7	0.061	0.115
8	0.029	0.054
9	0.013	0.025
> 9	0.012	0.012

Of course, these were coin flips, not real basketball shots. But that is exactly the point! Hot and cold streaks often appear, simply by coincidence, in completely random coin flips. This fact does not prove that athletic hot and cold streaks are just coincidences, but it does caution that a hot streak does not ensure continued success, and a cold streak does not guarantee continued failure. Hot and cold streaks may be nothing more than luck.

Ray Allen took more than 7,000 three-point shots in his NBA career and made 40 percent of them. Imagine a coin with a 40 percent chance of heads being flipped 7,000 times. It is, in fact, almost certain that there will be a streak of seven heads in a row at some point in those 7,000 flips. Ray Allen's streak may be no more meaningful than seven heads in a row.

■ THE LAW OF SMALL NUMBERS

Daniel Kahneman and Amos Tversky collaborated on many papers, including pioneering research identifying ways in which our judgment is affected by systematic biases and errors, and in 2002, Kahneman was awarded the Nobel Prize in Economics. Tversky could not share the prize because he was deceased, but Kahneman said that, "I feel it is a joint prize. We were twinned for more than a decade."

One of the cognitive errors Kahneman and Tversky observed is a belief in the law of small numbers. Imagine that we draw ten balls from a giant container filled with red and blue balls. The law of small numbers is the erroneous belief that if 50 percent of the balls in the container are red, then five of the ten balls we draw will be red. Not so. There is only about a 25 percent chance of five reds and five blues. Most of the time, there will be an unequal number of red and blue balls.

The mistaken law of small numbers causes two related errors. The first is called the gambler's fallacy. If the first three balls we draw are red, then we are tempted to reason (incorrectly) that the next ball will most likely be blue because we must end up with five red balls and five blue balls. Similarly, if a coin is flipped ten times and lands heads on the first three flips, the next flip will most likely be tails because we have to end up with five heads and five tails. This fallacy is discussed in more detail in Chapter 10.

The second error occurs when we don't know how many red and blue balls are in the container. If we draw five balls and four are red, we reason (incorrectly) that 80 percent of the balls in the container must be red. So, there is an 80 percent chance that the next ball will be red, too.

Similarly, if a basketball player makes four out of five shots, we might think he has an 80 percent chance of making his next shot. If this player misses four of five shots, he has only a 20 percent chance of making his next shot. Based on a small number of shots, we think that players swing from being hot to being cold, from being 80-percent shooters to being 20-percent shooters. We don't realize that even if the player has a constant 50 percent chance of making a shot, he will sometimes make four of five and sometimes miss four of five. Doing so means nothing at all.

These misperceptions are part of our natural tendency to look for patterns and believe that there must be a logical explanation for the patterns we see. The Zenith Radio Corporation broadcast a series of weekly ESP experiments in 1937 and 1938. This radio program invited listeners to mail in their guesses about the symbols that were being looked at by "senders" in the radio studio. An experiment involved five random selections of one of two possibilities (such as a circle or square), similar to five coin flips.

This nationwide experiment did not demonstrate that ESP was real. Instead, the main conclusion was that people underestimate how frequently patterns appear in random data. The listeners chose sequences that seemed random and they avoided sequences that did not. For example, in one experiment, 121 listeners chose this sequence,

while only 35 chose

and only one chose

If squares and circles were randomly chosen, like five coin flips, each of these sequences has exactly the same probability of occurring. However, listeners felt that squares and circles should balance out (the fallacious law of averages discussed in Chapter 10), so that there won't be all squares or all circles. They also felt that a perfect balancing of alternating squares and circles was unlikely because it doesn't look random. Listeners were reluctant to guess five squares in a row or a perfectly alternating sequence of squares and circles because they didn't believe these would happen by chance.

Now look at it the other way around. Instead of guessing how a circle-square sequence will turn out, imagine your reaction to seeing one of these patterns. The first pattern is nothing special. The second pattern is striking, and the third pattern even more so. Even though we are told that circles and squares are equally likely, we discount the possibility that five squares in a row or a perfectly alternating sequence could have happened by luck alone. Instead, we think something special must be going on. Perhaps the radio people aren't really choosing circles and squares randomly?

In the same way, when a basketball player who generally makes 50 percent of his shots makes 5 in a row, we think something special is happening. The player is hot, and is very likely to make his next shot. A quarterback who completes 5 passes in a row is hot, and is very likely to complete his next pass. A card player who is dealt 5 good hands in a row is hot, and it is likely that the next deal will be a good hand, too.

We consistently underestimate the role of chance in our lives, failing to recognize that randomness can generate patterns that appear to be meaningful, but are, in fact, meaningless. We are too easily seduced by explanations for the inexplicable.

■ A BASKETBALL STUDY

Three prominent psychologists—Thomas Gilovich at Cornell and Robert Vallone and Amos Tversky at Stanford—did an interesting study of the hot hands phenomenon. They surveyed one hundred basketball fans and found that 91 percent agreed with the statement that a player has "a better chance of making a shot after having just made his last two or three shots than he does after having just missed his last two or three shots." These fans were also asked to estimate the probability that a hypothetical player who makes 50 percent of his shots would make a shot if he: (a) made his last shot; and (b) missed his last shot. The average estimates were 61 percent and 42 percent, respectively.

Players, too, believe in hot and cold hands. Five of seven pros they surveyed (71 percent) agreed that a player is more likely to make a shot after making his last two or three shots. For the hypothetical player who makes 50 percent of his shots, the pros' average estimate of his chances of making a shot were 62.5 percent if he made his last shot and 49.5 percent if he missed his last shot.

Gilovich, Vallone, and Tversky looked at a variety of basketball data and concluded that this common perception is incorrect. Their most persuasive data were for the Philadelphia 76ers NBA team during the 1980–81 season. The professors compared how frequently each player made a shot after making one, two, or three shots in a row with how frequently the player made a shot after missing one, two, or three shots in a row. They found that, if anything, players tended to do slightly *worse* after making shots than after missing them.

One weakness in their analysis is that their data do not identify how much time passed between shots. A player's two successive shots might be taken thirty seconds apart, five minutes apart, in different halves of a game, or even in different games. Fans and players do not claim that making a shot Tuesday in Philadelphia will affect the probability of making a shot Thursday in Boston. Another problem is that a player who makes several shots may be tempted to take more difficult shots. That would explain the fact that players tend to do worse after making shots.

In addition, the opposing team may guard a player differently when he is perceived to be hot or cold. Shot selection may also be affected by the score, the time remaining in the game, and the number of fouls accumulated by players on both teams. There are lots of confounding factors.

The average NBA starter takes ten to twenty shots a game, five to ten in each half. If the hot hand is a relatively modest phenomenon, a statistical test based on five to ten shots is unlikely to detect it, especially if the hot hand is hidden in data that combine shots of varying difficulty, separated by varying periods of time, and subject to other confounding influences.

Gilovich, Vallone, and Tversky's conclusion not only contradicts the beliefs of fans and players, but also contradicts substantial evidence from a wide variety of sports that athletes perform better when they are confident. In one arm-wrestling study, the competitors were told beforehand whether they were stronger or weaker than their opponent. When they were given misinformation, so that both people incorrectly believed the weaker person was stronger, the weaker person won ten of twelve matches. When the competitors had correct information about who was the stronger, the stronger person won all twelve matches.

It seems reasonable that a basketball player who makes several shots in a row will become more confident and that this confidence will help him perform better. Maybe the hot hand is real, but hard to detect in basketball games because of such confounding factors as shot selection, lengthy spells between shots, and defensive adjustments.

What about evidence from other sports? There is some experimental evidence of hot and cold hands in golf putting and dart throwing. However, these studies involved volunteers putting and throwing over and over for meager compensation. (Would you believe five dollars per day?) With so many trials and so little reason to take them seriously, the observed hot and cold streaks might be due to ups and downs in the attentiveness of poorly motivated volunteers. If success is more likely when the volunteers are focused and less likely when they are bored, hits and misses will cluster in the data into hot and cold streaks. But it is not their ability that swings back and forth between hot and cold. It is whether they care.

To get around these problems with the basketball study and the artificial experiments, I tried to think of sports in which highly skilled and motivated athletes compete for meaningful stakes without confounding influences. Ideally, every attempt would be under identical conditions, of equal difficulty, and with little time between attempts. I thought of two sports: professional horseshoes and bowling. They are not glamor sports, but they do have the characteristics I needed.

■ WALTER RAY WILLIAMS, JR.

By luck, it turns out that a remarkable athlete named Walter Ray Williams, Jr., excels in both sports. Williams started out throwing horseshoes right-handed, and earned the nickname Deadeye when he was ten years old after throwing forty-five ringers in fifty throws in a tournament. When he was thirteen, he broke a finger on his right hand and learned how to throw left-handed. When he was eighteen, he broke his right wrist and switched to his left hand, throwing about 50 percent ringers compared to 85 percent with his right hand. Yes, that's right—he threw better with his weaker hand then you or I could do with our stronger hand.

Throwing right-handed, Williams won 6 world championships. When his ringer percentage dropped to 70 percent, he switched to his left hand and, at age 46, finished second in the world championships throwing southpaw. Williams says that he now pitches shoes equally well with either hand, but enjoys throwing left-handed more.

His bowling accomplishments are perhaps even more impressive, and certainly more financially rewarding. (You can't make a living pitching horseshoes, but you can become a millionaire rolling balls.) Williams is seven-times Professional Bowlers Association (PBA) player of the year and has won nearly $5 million in PBA tournament prize money. Still, his first love is horseshoes and he drives a motorhome all over the country, from one horseshoe or bowling event to the next, squeezing in golf when he can (he has a three handicap). Asked how he does it, his answer is simply, "I've been doing this so long, that it seems normal to me."

Williams has had many great streaks. In 1991, when he was thirty-two years old, he threw fifty-six ringers in a row in horseshoes. He has bowled eighty perfect games (twelve strikes in a row) in PBA competition. But then, again, he is a world champion in both sports and has pitched a lot of shoes and rolled a lot of balls. Perhaps these streaks were just lucky coincidences.

Williams is a smart jock. He recalls taking a computer class at a local college while he was still in high school: "At first I was a bit scared of them as are a lot of people who don't know anything about computers because they think computers are smart. It turns out computers are really stupid. They do what you tell them. If you don't tell them the right thing they will do the wrong thing." As I said, he is a smart jock.

Williams was a physics major at Cal Poly, Pomona, with a minor in mathematics. In the fascinating bowling documentary *A League of Ordinary Gentlemen* Williams says that if bowling hadn't worked out he "probably would either be a teacher or maybe working for NASA." For his senior thesis at Cal Poly, he wrote a computer program for predicting the trajectory of a bowling ball. He has also written a software program for keeping detailed records of horseshoe tournament results. When I was stumbling around looking for horseshoe data, I found Williams and the data he had collected. He was interested in hot hands too and gladly shared his data with me.

■ HORSESHOE PITCHING

A horseshoe court has two stakes, forty feet apart. In each inning, each player pitches two shoes at the same stake, with the score tallied after all four shoes have been pitched. A shoe that encircles the stake is a ringer worth three points, a nonringer within six inches of the stake is worth one point. In conventional cancellation scoring, ringers thrown by both players cancel each other, as do shoes that are equidistant from the stake. If one player throws double ringers and the opponent throws one ringer, the first player scores three points. If both players throw double ringers, no points are scored. The first player to reach forty points is the winner.

At the World Championships, sixteen players qualify for the championship matches and each player pitches against each of the fifteen other players. The final standings are determined by the players' overall win-loss records.

In top competition, players typically throw 60 to 80 percent ringers and games last 20 to 30 innings. One of the greatest games of all time occurred at the 1965 World Championships when Ray Martin threw 89.7 percent ringers and lost a 2 1/2hour, 97-inning marathon to Glen "Red" Henton, who pitched 90.2 percent ringers.

The hot-hands question is whether the number of ringers a player pitches in an inning depends on the number of ringers pitched in previous innings. Because double misses are unusual for world-class pitchers, I characterized each player's inning as a double ringer or not a double ringer. The top players throw doubles roughly half the time, making a nice analogy to coin flips.

Using the 2000 and 2001 World Championship data Williams gave me, Table 8.1 shows that players were more likely to throw a double after a double than after a non-double (0.548 versus 0.501). They were also more likely to throw a double after two doubles in a row than after two non-doubles (0.545 versus 0.490). These hot-hand patterns imply analogous cold hands: non-doubles are more likely after throwing a non-double than after throwing a double (0.499 versus 0.452).

The empirical differences in Table 8.1 may seem modest, but they are the difference between being a champion and an also-ran.

Table 8.2: Frequency of Doubles and Non-Doubles After Doubles or Non-Doubles

	Frequency of Doubles	Frequency of Non-Doubles
After 2 Doubles	0.545	0.455
After 1 Double	0.548	0.452
After 1 Non-Double	0.501	0.499
After 2 Non-Doubles	0.490	0.510

Fifty-one of the sixty-four players were more likely to throw a double after a double than after a non-double. Forty-eight of sixty-three were more likely to throw a double after two doubles than after two non-doubles (one player was equally likely). Each of these differences is highly statistically significant. Horseshoe pitches are not as random as coin flips. Players do get hot and cold hands.

■ BOWLING

In bowling, ten target pins are arranged in a pyramid shape sixty feet from the beginning of the lane. Each game has ten frames. If a bowler knocks down all ten pins on the first roll in a frame, this is a strike. If the bowler doesn't roll a strike, the fallen pins are cleared away and the bowler is given a second chance to hit the remaining pins. If the remaining pins are knocked down on the second roll, this is a spare.

The bowler's base score in each frame is equal to the number of pins knocked down. If there is a spare, the score is 10 plus the number of pins knocked down on the next roll; if there is a strike, the score is 10 plus the number of pins knocked down on the next 2 rolls. If a spare or strike is rolled in the 10th frame, the bowler gets bonus rolls (1 for a spare and 2 for a strike). A perfect game consists of 12 strikes (10 frames plus 2 bonus rolls), which gives a score of 300. Professional bowlers roll strikes around 60 percent of the time and average more than 200 points per game.

PBA tournaments start with all players bowling nine games. The top sixty-four bowlers from this round advance to the next round and again bowl nine games. The top thirty-two advance to the match-play rounds between pairs of bowlers who are seeded based on their performance in the first eighteen games. The first seed goes against the thirty-two seed, two against thirty-one, and so on.

Using the data for the 2002–2003 PBA match-play rounds, Table 8.3 shows that players were more likely to roll a strike after rolling a strike than after rolling a non-strike the previous frame (0.571 versus 0.560). They were also more likely to roll a strike after rolling strikes in the 2 previous frames than after rolling 2 non-strikes (0.582 versus 0.546).

As with horseshoes, the differences in Table 8.3 may seem modest, but they are the difference between winning and losing.

Table 8.3: Frequency of Strikes Following Strikes or Non-Strikes

	Frequency of Strikes	Frequency of Non-Strikes
After 2 Strikes	0.582	0.418
After 1 Strike	0.571	0.429
After 1 Non-Strike	0.560	0.440
After 2 Non-Strikes	0.546	0.454

Eighty of 134 bowlers were more likely to roll a strike after a strike than after a non-strike. In addition, 77 of 110 bowlers were more likely to roll a strike after 2 strikes than after 2 non-strikes (24 bowlers did not have enough data for a valid comparison). As with horseshoes, these bowling differences are highly statistically significant.

A perfect game of twelve consecutive strikes might be considered the ultimate hot hand. During match play on the 2002–2003 PBA tour, there were nineteen perfect games, which is nearly double the number that would be expected if the hot hand were a myth. It is also nearly double what would be expected for the forty-two players who rolled all strikes in the first ten frames and needed strikes in their two bonus rolls to complete a perfect game. Both of these are statistically significant.

Our conclusion is complicated. We are seduced by patterns and we want explanations for these patterns. When we see a string of successes, we think that a hot hand has made success more likely. If we see a string of failures, we think a cold hand has made failure more likely. It is easy to dismiss such theories when they involve coin flips, but it is not so easy with humans. We surely have emotions and ailments that can cause our abilities to go up and down. The question is whether these fluctuations are important or trivial.

Most empirical studies of the hot hand do not give convincing answers because the data are muddled by confounding influences. For example, basketball shots are taken from different locations with different defensive pressure. So, it is hard to say whether the observed ups and downs in a player's success are because his ability fluctuated between hot and cold or because he took different shots or was guarded differently.

Data for horseshoes and bowling, which do not have these confounding influences, show evidence of hot and cold hands. The observed fluctuations in performance are large enough to be the difference between victory and defeat—but not nearly as large as people think.

■ **Don't be Fooled:** We inexorably look for patterns in data and invent explanations for the patterns we see. This is why it is so easy to be persuaded that hot and cold hands are real, with the probability of success fluctuating dramatically. Remember that eye-catching hot and cold streaks can happen by chance, even in random coin flips.

Hot and cold hands probably do exist, but they are much smaller than we imagine.

9

REGRESSION

HORACE SECRIST HAD A DISTINGUISHED CAREER AS A PROFESSOR OF economics at Northwestern University. He wrote thirteen textbooks and was director of Northwestern's Bureau of Economic Research. In 1933, in the depths of the national economic tragedy that became known as the Great Depression, he published a book that he hoped would explain the causes, provide solutions, and secure his legacy. Instead, it made him infamous.

At the time, the conventional economic wisdom was that, for the nation as a whole, supply creates its own demand. There could be no such thing as inadequate aggregate demand since, by paying workers to produce goods and services, firms simultaneously guarantee that a nation's citizens have the means to buy these goods and services. There could be no such thing as an unemployment problem because, by equating demand and supply, labor markets assured that everyone who wants a job has one. That's what demand equals supply means: firms hire the number of people they want to hire and people who want jobs have jobs.

British economist John Maynard Keynes surveyed the worldwide economic carnage and concluded that the conventional wisdom was mistaken. Between 1929 and 1933, US production fell by half and the unemployment rate rose from 3 percent to 25 percent. Farm income fell by a third and more than a hundred thousand businesses failed, including more than a third of the nation's banks. Desperate people begged for money on street corners and scavenged for food in dumps. In Britain, output fell by a third and the unemployment rate hit 20 percent.

Keynes concluded that:

> Professional economists, after Malthus, were apparently unmoved by
> the lack of correspondence between the results of their theory and the
> facts of observation . . . which has led to economists being looked upon
> as Candides, who, having left this world for the cultivation of their gar-
> dens, teach that all is for the best in the best of all possible worlds pro-
> vided we will let well alone. . . . It may well be that the classical theory
> represents the way in which we should like our economy to behave.
> But to assume that it actually does so is to assume our difficulties away.

Keynes argued that not only was inadequate demand possible, it was
the cause of the Great Depression. One only had to open one's eyes
to see it. Instead of supply automatically creating demand, he argued
that demand often creates supply. If people reduce their spending on
furniture, businesses will manufacture less furniture and let go some
of the people they were paying to make furniture. The furniture-makers
who lose their jobs and income will cut back on their purchases of
food, clothing, and entertainment, leading firms in these industries to
reduce production and employment. The effects ripple through the
economy because every person's spending provides income to others,
and every drop in spending diminishes other people's income and ability to spend. Unemployment can cumulate and last for years.

Keynes's classic treatise, *The General Theory of Employment, Interest and Money*, was published in 1936 and revolutionized economic theory. Indeed, it created a whole branch of economics called
macroeconomics.

Horace Secrist, writing years before Keynes and straightjacketed
by classical economics, believed that the causes of the Great Depression must be on the supply side. So he studied business practices.
Secrist and his assistants spent 10 years collecting and analyzing data
for 73 different industries in the United States, including department
stores, clothing stores, hardware stores, railroads, and banks. He
compiled annual data for the years 1920 to 1930 on several metrics
of business success, including the ratios of profits to sales, profits to
assets, expenses to sales, expenses to assets. For each ratio, he di-

vided the companies in an industry into quartiles based on the 1920 values of the ratio: the top 25 percent, the second 25 percent, the third 25 percent, and the bottom 25 percent. He then calculated the average ratio for the top-quartile companies every year from 1920 to 1930. He did the same for the other quartiles. In every case, the quartile ratios converged over time. The companies in the top 2 quartiles in 1920 were more nearly average in 1930. The companies in the bottom 2 quartiles in 1920 were more nearly average in 1930. The most extreme quartiles showed the greatest movement.

Evidently, he had discovered a universal economic truth. Over time, the most successful and least successful firms tended to become more nearly average. American business was converging to mediocrity. His book documenting and describing his discovery was titled *The Triumph of Mediocrity in Business*. The book was a statistical tour de force, 468 pages long, with 140 tables and 103 charts, supporting his remarkable discovery.

Secrist summarized his conclusion:

Complete freedom to enter trade and the continuance of competition mean the perpetuation of mediocrity. New firms are recruited from the relatively "unfit"—at least from the inexperienced. If some succeed, they must meet the competitive practices of the class, the market, to which they belong. Superior judgment, merchandizing sense, and honesty, however, are always at the mercy of the unscrupulous, the unwise, the misinformed, and the injudicious. The results are that retail trade is overcrowded, shops are small and inefficient, volume of business inadequate, expenses relatively high, and profits small. So long as the field of activity is freely entered, and it is; and so long as competition is "free," and, within the limits suggested above, it is; neither superiority or inferiority will tend to persist. Rather mediocrity tends to become the rule.

The nation's economic problems were evidently due to the new economic principle he had discovered: competitive pressures inevitably dilute superior talent. The evident solution? Protect superior companies from competition from less-fit companies trying to enter the market.

Before publishing his work, Secrist asked thirty-eight prominent statisticians and economists for comments and criticism. They apparently found nothing amiss. After publication, the initial reviews from eminent colleagues were unanimous in their praise.

> This book furnishes an excellent illustration of the way in which statistical research can be used to transform economic theory into economic law, to convert a qualitative into a quantitative science. . . . [T]he book reflects in a most creditable manner the painstaking, long-continued, thoughtful, and highly successful endeavor of an able statistician and economist to strengthen our knowledge of the facts and theory of competition. (*Journal of Political Economy*)

> One cannot withhold a tribute of admiration for the author and his assistants for the enthusiasm and pertinacity with which they have carried to the end an extremely laborious task. (*Journal of the Royal Statistical Society*)

> [T]he author concludes that the interaction of competitive forces in an interdependent business structure guarantees "the triumph of mediocrity." The approach to the problem is thoroughly scientific. (*American Economic Review*)

> The economic future of the competitive business regime would seem to be a hopeless one from the social standpoint except in two respects: that some business planning might be introduced as the result of such studies, and that although the exceptional unit tends to become mediocre, the general level of mediocrity may be raised by some form of private or social control. . . . The results confront the business man and the economist with an insistent and to some degree tragic problem. (*Annals of the American Academy of Political and Social Science*)

Then a brilliant statistician named Harold Hotelling wrote a devastating review that politely but firmly demonstrated that Secrist had wasted ten years proving nothing at all. Instead of securing his reputation, Secrist became a classic example of being fooled by regression toward the mean.

■ REGRESSION TOWARD THE MEAN

I once did some research with a student on regression to the mean in baseball. Not 468 pages, but at least we recognized regression when we saw it. A reviewer for the journal that published our paper wrote that:

> There are few statistical facts more interesting than regression to the mean for two reasons. First, people encounter it almost every day of their lives. Second, almost nobody understands it.
>
> The coupling of these two reasons makes regression to the mean one of the most fundamental sources of error in human judgment, producing fallacious reasoning in medicine, education, government, and, yes, even sports.

Yes, we encounter regression to the mean almost every day and, yes, almost nobody understands it. This is a lethal combination—as Secrist discovered.

To understand regression, suppose that one hundred people are asked twenty questions about world history. Each person's "ability" is what his or her average score would be on a large number of these tests. Some people have an ability of ninety, some eighty, and some near zero.

Someone with an ability of, say, 80 will average 80 percent correct on tests, but is not going to get 80 percent correct on *every* test. Imagine a test bank with zillions of questions. By the luck of the draw, a person with an ability of 80 will know the answers to more than 80 percent of the questions on one test and to less than 80 percent on another test. A person's score on any single test is an imperfect measure of ability.

What, if anything, can we infer from a person's test score? A key insight is that someone whose test score is high relative to the other people who took the test probably also had a high score relative to his or her own ability. Someone who scores in the 90th percentile on a test could be someone of more modest ability—perhaps the 85th, 80th, or 75th percentile in ability—who did unusually well, or could be someone of higher ability—perhaps the 95th percentile in ability—

who did poorly. The former is more likely because there are more people with ability below the 90th percentile than above it.

If this person's ability is in fact below the 90th percentile, then when this person takes another test his or her score will probably also be below the 90th percentile. Similarly, a person who scores well below average is likely to have had an off day and should anticipate scoring somewhat higher on later tests. This tendency of people who score far from the mean to score closer to the mean on a second test is an example of regression toward the mean.

We encounter regression in many contexts—pretty much whenever we see an imperfect measure of what we are trying to measure. Standardized tests are obviously an imperfect measure of ability. It follows that school children who are given special tutoring because of their low test scores are generally not as weak as their low scores suggest. They can consequently be expected to do better on subsequent tests even if the tutor does nothing more than snap his or her fingers and say, "Improve!"

Medical tests are imperfect measures of a patient's condition, so the results regress. Suppose that a patient is given twenty tests during a routine medical checkup and one of the test's results are worrisome. The patient's condition is most likely not as bad as the test results suggest. After being given some treatment, the patient can be expected to improve even if the treatment is worthless.

Investment success is an imperfect measure of investor prowess. Therefore, we will see regression in that those investment advisors who make the best stock picks in any given year will, on average, be more mediocre the next year.

There was regression for the Internet company in Chapter 7 that tested different web page layouts; for example, one-click and two-click formats and different page colors and fonts. The company bases its recommendation on the following experiment. When a user goes to the web site, a random-event generator is used to take the user to one of several versions of the page. The company then records the user's reaction (how long the user stays at the page, whether the user clicks through for more information, and so on). After several days of tests, the company reports which version of the page was the most successful. One recurring problem they encounter is that when the client follows their advice and changes the layout, the actual benefits generally turn out to be smaller than observed in the experiment. How would you explain this?

Sure enough, regression to the mean. Each experimental score is an imperfect measure of "ability," the benefits from the layout. To the extent there is randomness in this experiment—and there surely is—the prospective benefits from the layout that has the highest score are probably closer to the mean than was the score. If the experiment showed a 30 percent increase in user clicks, the actual increase might be only 20 percent. There is nothing wrong with that. It is still the most successful layout. The company just needs to recognize that it is perfectly natural for the actual benefits to be more modest than predicted by the test.

Nobel Prize–winner Daniel Kahneman once told Israeli flight instructors that their trainees would progress faster if they were praised instead of punished. A senior instructor strongly objected:

> On many occasions I have praised flight cadets for clean execution of some aerobatic maneuver, and in general when they try it again, they do worse. On the other hand, I have often screamed at cadets for bad execution, and in general they do better the next time. So please don't tell us that reinforcement works and punishment does not, because the opposite is the case.

Kahneman immediately recognized that the instructor was being fooled by regression to the mean. The cadets who had the best flights are generally not as far above average in ability as their performance indicated. On average, they will not do as well on their next flight, whether the instructor praises them, screams at them, or says nothing at all. The senior instructor who chastised Kahneman mistakenly thought that his praise made the cadets do worse when the truth is that they were not as good as they seemed. Similarly, the cadets who had the weakest flights were, on average, not as incompetent as they seemed and will do better on their next flight if the instructor can control his screaming.

Kahneman later wrote:

> This was a joyous moment, in which I understood an important truth about the world: because we tend to reward others when they do well and punish them when they do badly, and because there is regression to the mean, it is part of the human condition that we are statistically punished for rewarding others and rewarded for punishing them.

Kahneman wasn't the first to recognize the importance of regression to the mean. In the 1800s, Sir Francis Galton observed regression toward the mean in his study of the heights of parents and their adult children. Unusually tall parents tend to have somewhat shorter children, while the reverse is true of unusually short parents. The erroneous conclusion is that heights are regressing to mediocrity; indeed, Galton titled his study "Regression Towards Mediocrity in Hereditary Stature."

Regression toward the mean does not imply that everyone will soon be the same height any more than it implies that everyone will soon get the same score on history tests. What regression toward the mean does say is that observed heights are an imperfect measure of the genetic influences that we inherit from our parents and pass on to our children. A person who is six-feet, six-inches tall might have six-foot genes and experienced positive environmental influences or might have seven-foot genes and had negative environmental factors. The former is more likely, simply because there are many more people with six-foot genes than with seven-foot genes. Thus, the observed heights of very tall parents usually overstate their genetic heights and, therefore, the average height of their children.

Regression works in both directions since it reflects nothing more than random fluctuations. Tall parents tend to have somewhat shorter children, and tall children tend to have somewhat shorter parents. I am six-foot four-inches tall and I am not only taller than my adult children, I am also taller than my parents.

It is not just heights. Regression occurs with any genetic trait that is imperfectly reflected in observed characteristics: height, weight, intelligence, foot size, hair density. Abnormal parents generally have less abnormal children, and abnormal children typically have less abnormal parents.

■ SECRIST'S FOLLY

In the same way, Secrist's study of successful and unsuccessful companies involved regression toward the mean. In any given year, the most successful companies are likely to have had more good luck than bad, and to have done well not only relative to other companies, but also relative to their own long-run profitability. The opposite is true of the least successful companies. This is why the subsequent performance of the top and bottom companies is usually closer to the average company. At the same time, their places at the extremes are taken by other companies experiencing fortune or misfortune. These up-and-down fluctuations are part of the natural ebb and flow of life and do not mean that all companies will soon be mediocre.

Let's work through a detailed example. Suppose that there are three kinds of firms in an industry: strong, weak, and average. Each strong firm has an average profit of 40 percent, calculated as a rate of return on assets. Each weak firm has an average profit of 20 percent. Each firm in the middle averages 30 percent. There are an equal number of companies in each group.

A firm's average profit is its "ability." Each company's profit in any year is equal to its ability plus 6, plus 3, minus 3, or minus 6. Thus, a firm with an ability of 40 is equally likely to have a profit of 46, 43, 37, or 34 percent in any given year. Their annual profit fluctuates randomly around their ability, which is constant. I'm not saying that, in practice, abilities never change. I'm making that assumption here in order to show that regression occurs even if abilities do not change.

These assumptions were used to generate data for 2 years, which I will call 1920 and 1930. There are 12 equally likely observed profit percentages in each year: 46, 43, 37, 36, 34, 33, 27, 26, 24, 23, 17, and 14.

Following Secrist, suppose that we group the firms into quartiles based on their observed profit. The top quartile consists of the firms with observed profits of 46, 43, and 37. The next quartile has firms with profits of 36, 34, and 33. The third quartile is 27, 26, and 24. The fourth quartile is 23, 17, and 14.

Regression to the mean occurs because firms with observed profits that are far from the mean tend to have abilities that are closer to the mean. Thus, their profits in any other year will be closer to the mean. In our example, the firms with observed profits in the top quartile had profits of 46, 43, or 37. Their average profit was 42. But all these firms have abilities of 40. They averaged 42 in their top-quartile year, but they can be expected to average 40 in any other year. Table 9.1 shows this convergence when the firms are grouped into quartiles based on their 1920 profits.

Table 9.1: Average Profits, Quartiles Formed Using 1920 Profits

	1920	1930
First quartile, 1920	42	40
Second quartile, 1920	34	33
Third quartile, 1920	26	27
Fourth quartile, 1920	18	20

The firms in the top two quartiles in 1920 tend to have more nearly average profits in 1930. The firms in the bottom two quartiles in 1920 also tend to be more nearly average in 1930.

This regression doesn't depend on which year we use to group the firms into quartiles. No matter which year is used to form quartiles, profits regress in the other year. Table 9.2 shows the convergence using quartiles based on 1930 profits.

Table 9.2: Average Profits, Quartiles Formed Using 1930 Profits

	1920	1930
First quartile, 1930	40	42
Second quartile, 1930	33	34
Third quartile, 1930	27	26
Fourth quartile, 1930	20	18

Figure 9.1: Quartiles Formed Using 1920 Profits Regress in 1930

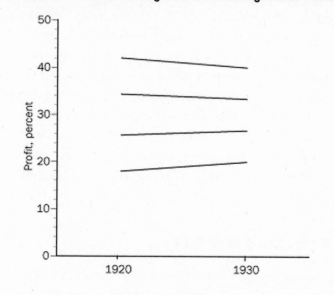

Figure 9.2: Quartiles Formed Using 1930 Profits Regress in 1920

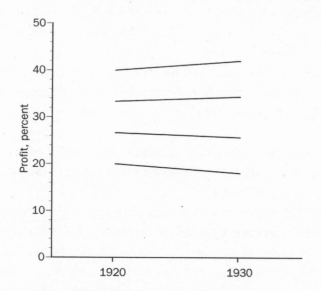

Figure 9.1 is a visual demonstration that if we use 1920 to form quartiles, as did Secrist, profits regress in 1930. Figure 9.2 shows that if we use 1930 profits to form quartiles, profits regress in 1920.

There is absolutely no convergence in abilities. We assumed that abilities are the same for each firm in each year. Regression occurs simply because profits fluctuate randomly about abilities.

Just as abnormal parents generally have less abnormal children, and vice versa, profits regress whether we go forward or backward in time. This observed regression simply confirms that when profits fluctuate about ability, the observed differences in profits are larger than the actual differences in ability. As Hotelling put it, "These diagrams really prove nothing more than that the ratios in question have a tendency to wander about." With that, ten years of work circled down the drain.

■ DO OLD FALLACIES EVER DIE?

Even though Secrist's error was clearly dissected by Hotelling, the error lives on. In 1970, an eminent political economist wrote:

> An early, completely forgotten empirical work with a related theme has the significant title *The Triumph of Mediocrity in Business*, by Horace Secrist, published in 1933 by the Bureau of Business Research, Northwestern University. The book contains an elaborate statistical demonstration that, over a period of time, initially high-performing firms will on the average show deterioration while the initial low performers will exhibit improvement.

Unfortunately, the author was blissfully unaware of the reason that Secrist's conclusions had no impact whatsoever. He remembered Secrist, but he forgot Hotelling.

A 1980s investments textbook written by a Nobel Prize winner argued that, "Ultimately, economic forces will force the convergence of the profitability and growth rates of different firms." To support this assertion, he looked at the firms with the highest and lowest profit rates in 1966. Fourteen years later, in 1980, the profit rates of both groups were closer to the mean. He concluded triumphantly: "Convergence toward an overall mean is apparent . . . the phenomenon is undoubtedly real." Déjà vu, déjà vu. Like Secrist fifty years earlier, he did not consider the possibility that this convergence is simply regression to the mean.

Several years later, two other distinguished finance professors—one was another Nobel Prize winner—made the very same error. They found earnings regression in the data and, like Secrist, attributed it entirely to competitive forces:

> In a competitive environment, profitability is mean reverting within as well as across industries. Other firms eventually mimic innovative products and technologies that produce above normal profitability for a firm. And the prospect of failure or takeover gives firms with low profitability incentives to allocate assets to more productive uses.

Competitive forces may exist. But they are surely not the whole story. Part of the story—perhaps the whole story—is the purely statistical observation that companies with relatively high earnings are more likely to have experienced good luck than bad.

Another variation on this recurring error cropped up in a book and book review, both written by prominent economists, arguing that the economic growth rates of entire nations converge over time. They completely ignored the role of regression to the mean in this convergence. Milton Friedman wrote an apt commentary titled, "Do Old Fallacies Ever Die?"

> I find it surprising that the reviewer and the authors, all of whom are distinguished economists, thoroughly conversant with modern statistical methods, should have failed to recognize that they were guilty of the regression fallacy. . . . However, surprise may not be justified in light of the ubiquity of the fallacy both in popular discussion and in academic studies.

If prominent statisticians, finance professors, and economists can ignore regression to the mean, so can anyone.

▪ DOW DELETIONS

The Dow Jones Industrial Average (the "Dow") is an average of the prices of thirty blue-chip stocks that represent the United States' most prominent companies. In the words of the Dow Jones company, these are "substantial companies—renowned for the quality and wide acceptance of their products or services—with strong histories of successful growth."

An averages committee periodically changes the stocks in the Dow. Sometimes, this is because a firm's stock is no longer traded after it merges with another company or is taken over by another company. Other times, a company has some tough years and is no longer considered to be a blue-chip stock. Such fallen companies are replaced by more successful companies.

For example, Home Depot replaced Sears on November 1, 1999. Sears is a legendary American success story, having evolved from a mail order catalog selling everything from watches and toys to automobiles and ready-to-assemble houses into the nation's largest retailer. Sears had been in the Dow for 75 years, but now was struggling to compete with discount retailers like Walmart, Target, and, yes, Home Depot. Revenue and profits were falling, and Sears' stock price had dropped nearly 50 percent in the previous 6 months. Home Depot, on the other hand, was booming along with home building and remodeling, and was opening a new store every 56 hours. Its tools competed directly with Sears' legendary Craftsman tools and it seemed to be winning this sales battle. Home Depot's stock price had risen 50 percent in the past 6 months.

When a faltering company is replaced by a flourishing company, which stock do you think does better subsequently—the stock going into the Dow or the stock going out? If you take into account regression to the mean, the stock booted out of the Dow probably will do better than the stock that replaces it.

This is counterintuitive because it is tempting to confuse a great company with a great stock. Suppose you find a great company (let's call it LeanMean) with a long history of strong, stable profits. Is LeanMean a good investment? The answer depends on the stock's price.

Is it an attractive investment at $10 a share? $100? $1,000? There are some prices at which the stock is too expensive. There are prices at which the stock is cheap. No matter how good the company, we need to know the stock's price before deciding whether it is an attractive investment.

The same is true of troubled companies. Suppose that a company with the unfortunate name Polyester Suits is on a downward death spiral. Polyester currently pays a dividend of $1 a share, but expects its dividend to decline steadily by 5 percent a year. Who would buy such a loser stock? If the price is right, who wouldn't? Would you pay $5 for a $1 dividend, then 95 cents, then 90 cents, and so on? If the $5 price doesn't persuade you, how about $1? How about 10 cents?

Let's go back to the Dow additions and deletions. The question for investors is not whether the companies going into the Dow are currently more successful than the companies they are replacing, but which stocks are better investments. The stocks going into and out of the Dow are all familiar companies that are closely watched by thousands of investors. In 1999, investors were well aware of the fact that Home Depot was doing great and Sears was doing poorly. Their stock prices surely reflected this knowledge. That's why Home Depot's stock was up 50 percent, while Sears was down 50 percent.

However, regression to the mean suggests that the companies taken out of the Dow are generally not in as dire straits as their recent performance suggests and that the companies replacing them are typically not as stellar as they appear. If so, stock prices will often be unreasonably low for the stocks going out and undeservedly high for the stocks going in. When a company that was doing poorly regresses to the mean, its stock price will rise; when a company that was doing well regresses to the mean, its price will fall. This argument suggests that stocks deleted from the Dow will generally outperform the stocks added to the Dow.

Sears was bought by Kmart in 2005, five and a half years after it was kicked out of the Dow. If you bought Sears stock just after it was deleted from the Dow, your total return until its acquisition by Kmart would have been 103 percent. Over the same five-and-a-half-year period, an investment in Home Depot, the stock that replaced Sears, would have *lost* 22 percent. The Standard & Poor's 500 Index of stock prices during this period had a return of -14 percent. Sears had an above-average return after it left the Dow, while Home Depot had a below-average return after it entered the Dow. (The Kmart-Sears combination has been ugly, but that's another story.)

Is this comparison of Sears and Home Depot an isolated incident or part of a systematic pattern of Dow deletions outperforming Dow additions? There were actually four substitutions made in 1999: Home Depot, Microsoft, Intel, and SBC replaced Sears, Goodyear Tire, Union Carbide, and Chevron. Home Depot, Microsoft, Intel, and SBC are all great companies, but all four stocks did poorly over the next decade.

Suppose that on the day the four substitutions were made, November 1, 1999, you had invested $2,500 in each of the four stocks added to the Dow, a total investment of $10,000. This is your Addition Portfolio. You also formed a Deletion Portfolio by investing $2,500 in each of the stocks deleted from the Dow.

Table 9.3 shows how these portfolios did compared to the S&P 500 during the decade following the substitutions. After 10 years, the S&P 500 was down 23 percent. The Addition Portfolio did even worse, down 34 percent. The Deletion Portfolio, in contrast, was up 64 percent.

Table 9.3: The Stocks Added and Deleted on November 1, 1999

	Initial Portfolio	Five Years Later	Ten Years Later
Addition Portfolio	$10,000	$6,633	$6,604
Deletion Portfolio	$10,000	$9,641	$16,367
S&P 500	$10,000	$8,295	$7,652

Still, these are just the four Dow substitutions made in 1999. Maybe 1999 was an unusual year and substitutions made in other years turned out differently? Nope. A 2006 study of all 50 changes in the Dow back to October 1, 1928, when the Dow 30-stock average began, found that deleted stocks did better than the stocks that replaced them in 32 cases and did worse in 18 cases. A portfolio of deleted stocks beat a portfolio of added stocks by about 4 percent a year, which is huge difference compounded over 78 years. A $100 portfolio of added stocks would have grown to $160,000 by 2006; a $100 portfolio of deleted stocks would have grown to $3.3 million.

The Dow Deletions, companies doing so poorly that they are booted out of the Dow, have been better investments than the darlings that replace them.

■ CHAMPIONS CHOKE

Many sports fans are convinced that champions choke—that athletes who achieve something exceptional usually have disappointing letdowns afterward. Evidently, people work extraordinarily hard to achieve extraordinary things, but once they are on top, their fear of failing causes the failure they fear. The same seems to be true in many professions.

After Roger Maris surpassed Babe Ruth by hitting 61 home runs in 1961, he hit only 33 homers in 1962 and 23 in 1963. After Martin Scorsese made *Taxi Driver* in 1976, he made the god-awful *New York, New York* in 1977.

The most famous example is the *Sports Illustrated* cover jinx. After Oklahoma won 47 straight college football games, *Sports Illustrated*'s cover story was, "Why Oklahoma is Unbeatable." Oklahoma lost its next game, 28–21, to Notre Dame. After this debacle, people started noticing that athletes who appear on the cover of *Sports Illustrated* are evidently jinxed in that they do not perform as well afterward. In 2002, *Sports Illustrated* ran a cover story on the jinx with a picture of a black cat and the cute caption "The Cover No One Would Pose For." More recently, we have the Madden Curse, which says that the football player whose picture appears on the cover of *Madden NFL*, a football video game, will not perform as well afterward.

Sorry to all you true believers out there, but it's just regression toward the mean again.

Athletic performances are an imperfect measure of skills and consequently regress toward the mean. Table 9.4 shows the 10 Major

League Baseball players with the highest batting averages in 2010. Josh Hamilton had the highest batting average, 0.359. Do you think that Josh is a 0.400 hitter who had a disappointing season in 2010, or a 0.300 hitter who had a great year? All 10 of the top-10 batters in 2010 did better than their career average that year. Overall, these top-10 batters have career averages of about 0.301, but averaged 0.327 in 2010.

In only three of twenty cases (highlighted in italics) did a player do better in 2009 or 2011 than he did in 2010. In seventeen of twenty cases (regression is a tendency, not a certainty), the batting averages of the top ten batters in 2010 regressed toward the mean in 2009 and 2011.

Regression does not describe changes in ability that happen as time passes—for example, companies undermined by competition or baseball players losing a step as they age. Regression is caused by performances fluctuating about ability, so that performances far from the mean reflect abilities that are closer to the mean. That's why we observe regression with baseball players whether we look forward to the next year or backward to the year before.

Table 9.4: How the Ten Players With the Highest BAs in 2010 Did in 2009 and 2011

	2009	2010	2011	Career
Josh Hamilton	0.268	**0.359**	0.298	0.308
Carlos Gonzalez	0.284	**0.336**	0.295	0.298
Miguel Cabrera	0.324	**0.328**	*0.344*	0.317
Joe Mauer	*0.365*	**0.327**	0.287	0.323
Joey Votto	0.322	**0.324**	0.309	0.313
Adrian Beltre	0.265	**0.321**	0.296	0.276
Omar Infante	0.305	**0.321**	0.276	0.275
Robinson Cano	*0.320*	**0.319**	0.302	0.308
Billy Butler	0.301	**0.318**	0.291	0.297
Troy Tulowitzki	0.297	**0.315**	0.302	0.293
AVERAGE	0.305	**0.327**	0.300	0.301

The triumph-of-mediocrity fallacy is to conclude that the skills of good players and teams deteriorate, but the correct conclusion is that the best performers in any particular season generally aren't as skillful as their lofty records suggest. Most had more good luck than bad, causing one season's performance to be better than the season before and better than the season after—when their place at the top is taken by others.

The *Sports Illustrated* Curse and the John Madden Curse are extreme examples of regression toward the mean. When a player or team does something exceptional enough to earn a place on the cover of *Sports Illustrated* or *Madden NFL*, there is essentially nowhere to go but down. To the extent luck plays a role in athletic success, and it surely does, the player or team who stands above all the rest almost certainly benefitted from good luck—good health, fortunate bounces, and questionable officiating. Good luck cannot be counted on to continue indefinitely, and neither can exceptional success.

■ SEARCHING FOR DEANS AND SOULMATES

Several years ago, a small private college had a nationwide search for a new college dean. None of the internal candidates were deemed good enough but, from hundreds of external applicants, the search committee identified several who, based on their résumés and references, were invited to interviews held at neutral airports to keep the process confidential. The three candidates who most impressed the search committee were invited to the college for two days of meetings with the faculty, administration, staff, and students.

The search committee was bursting with enthusiasm for these three godlike candidates. However, each candidate came and went, and each was disappointing relative to the pre-visit hoopla. Rumors circulated that the fix was in, that the search committee had deliberately invited two losers in order to make their favorite stand out as the best candidate. However, there was considerable disagreement about which candidate was the committee's favorite.

Do you suspect regression to the mean? No one knows how good any of the candidates really are based solely on résumés, references, and airport interviews. Do you think that the three candidates who look the best are, in reality, even more wonderful than they appear? Or not so spectacular? It would be an extraordinary person who is even better than he or she seems and still manages to rank among the top three candidates. Disappointment is almost inevitable, in that the three candidates who appear to be the best are almost surely not as good as they seem to be. Regression to the mean also explains why internal candidates are at an inherent disadvantage. Someone who has been at a college for twenty or thirty years does not have very many hidden virtues or warts. Unlike the largely unknown external candidates, with an internal candidate what you see is pretty much what you get.

I discussed this experience in my statistics class one year and a student came up to me after class with a remarkable coincidence. The previous night, he had been talking on the phone with his father, who was a sociology professor at another university, and his father was lamenting that when they invite the strongest applicants for faculty positions to come to campus, the candidates are generally not as exciting as they seemed on paper and in brief interviews beforehand. The student said he would call his father that afternoon and have a little talk about regression to the mean.

The same is true of our search for soul mates. Everyone looks for different things, so let's call it "pizzazz." Of the dozens, or hundreds, or thousands of people we meet, a few will stand out. When we see signs of pizzazz and summon the courage to get to know this person better, we are usually disappointed. The bad news is that this is just what we should expect. The good news is that we get to keep looking. The sobering news is that the other person probably feels the same way about us.

It is indeed true that we encounter regression to the mean almost every day of our lives. We should try to anticipate it, recognize it, and not be fooled by it. Remember Secrist.

■ **Don't be Fooled:** When a trait, such as academic or athletic ability, is measured imperfectly, the observed differences in performance exaggerate the actual differences in ability. Those who perform the best are probably not as far above average as they seem. Nor are those who perform the worst as far below average as they seem. Their subsequent performances will consequently regress to the mean.

This does not mean that the best performers are jinxed, only that their exceptional performances were assisted by good luck. Nor does regression to the mean imply that abilities are converging to the mean and everyone will soon be average, only that extreme performances rotate among people who experience good luck and bad luck. Nor does regression to the mean imply that successful and unsuccessful companies are converging to a depressing mediocrity.

10

EVEN STEVEN

N THE *SEINFELD* EPISODE "THE OPPOSITE," GEORGE ADMITS THAT the reason his life is the opposite of what he wants it to be is that every decision he has ever made has been wrong. Jerry tells George that the solution is to do the opposite of what he would normally do, so when George sees a beautiful woman eating alone, he walks over to her and says, "My name is George. I'm unemployed and I live with my parents." Incredibly, it works. When he interviews for a job with the New York Yankees, he chastises the owner George Steinbrenner for ruining the team. He is hired on the spot.

Meanwhile, Elaine's life is falling apart as she loses her boyfriend, her job, and her apartment. By the end of the episode, Elaine is bemoaning that she has become George. Jerry's life, in contrast, goes on as it ever has. Kramer nicknames Jerry "Even Steven" because anything bad that happens to Jerry is offset by something good. When a stand-up comedy gig is cancelled, Jerry gets a new job five minutes later on the same weekend for the same pay. When he plays poker, the winning and losing hands balance out and he breaks even. When his girlfriend dumps him, Jerry is unperturbed because he is confident a new one will soon appear.

Jerry isn't the only one who feels that things have a way of evening out. Many people believe that every time a coin lands heads, tails becomes more likely because heads and tails must come up equally often in the long run. Using the same reasoning, a baseball manager will bring in a pinch hitter for a player who had four hits in a row, reasoning that this hitter is due for an out.

One variation is to imagine that nature has a fixed supply of good and bad things. I once watched a kicker miss three field goals and an extra point in an early-season college football game. The television commentator said that the coach should be happy about those misses as he looked forward to some tough games in coming weeks. The commentator said that every kicker is going to miss some over the course of the season and it is good to get these misses "out of the way" early in the year.

A reader wrote to columnist Marilyn vos Savant saying that he had a lot of job interviews, but no offers. He hoped that the odds of an offer were increasing with every rejection. Another reader wrote Marilyn:

> At a lecture on fire safety that I attended, the speaker said: "I know that some of you can say you have lived in your homes for 25 years and never had any type of fire. To that I would respond that you have been lucky. But it only means that you are moving not farther away from a fire, but closer to one."

Explaining why he was driving to a judicial conference in South Dakota, the chief justice of the West Virginia State Supreme Court said that, "I've flown a lot in my life. I've used my statistical miles. I don't fly except when there is no viable alternative."

This commonplace reasoning is based on the fallacious *law of averages*. Some people think that in 1,000 coin flips there must be exactly 500 heads and 500 tails; therefore, if heads come up more often than tails in the first ten, fifty, or one hundred flips, tails must now come up more often than heads in order to balance things out. This belief is widespread, but wrong. A coin has no control over how it lands. If the coin is unbent and fairly tossed, heads and tails are equally likely to appear no matter what happened on the last flip or the last 999 flips.

Nonetheless, many gamblers believe in the fallacious law of averages because they are eager to find a profitable pattern in the chaos created by random chance. When a roulette wheel turns up a black number several times in a row, there are always people eager to bet on red, counting on the law of averages. Others rush to bet on black, trying to catch a hot streak. The casino cheerfully accepts wagers from both, confident that future spins do not depend on the past.

One of the most dramatic roulette runs occurred at Monte Carlo on August 18, 1913. At one table, black came up again and again. After ten blacks in a row, the table was surrounded by people betting on red and counting on the law of averages to reward them. But black kept coming. After fifteen straight blacks, there was near panic as people tried to reach the table so that they could place even heavier bets on red. Still black came up. By the twentieth black, desperate bettors were wagering every chip they had left on red, hoping to recover a fraction of their losses. When this extraordinary run ended, black had come up twenty-six times in a row and the casino had reaped millions of francs.

Surely some of the losers thought the game was rigged, and perhaps it was. But in honest games, at Monte Carlo and elsewhere, betting strategies based on the law of averages do not work. In fact, the few gambling systems that do work are based on the opposite principle—that physical defects in the apparatus cause some numbers to come up more often than others. In the late 1800s, an English engineer named William Jaggers hired six assistants to spend a month recording the winning numbers on Monte Carlo roulette wheels. Instead of betting *against* these numbers, counting on things to average out, he bet *on* these numbers, counting on wheel imperfections to cause these numbers to continue winning more often than others. He won nearly $125,000—more than $6 million in today's dollars—until the casino caught on and began switching wheels nightly.

Unlike coins and roulette wheels, humans have memories and do care about wins and losses. Still, the probability of a hit in baseball does not increase just because a player has not had one lately. Four outs in a row may have been bad luck, line drives hit straight into fielders' gloves. This bad luck does not ensure good luck the next time at bat. If it is not bad luck, then a physical problem may be causing the player to do poorly. Either way, a baseball player who had four outs in a row is not due for a hit, nor is a player who made four hits in a row due for an out. If anything, a player with four hits in a row is probably a better batter than the player who made four outs in a row.

Likewise, missed field goals need not be balanced by successes. A poor performance may simply suggest that the kicker is not very good. Being rejected for jobs does not make a job offer more likely. If anything, the evidence is mounting that this person is not qualified or interviews poorly. Not having a fire does not increase the chances of a fire—it may just be the mark of a careful homeowner who does not put paper or cloth near a stove, put metal in the microwave, leave home with the stove on, or fall asleep smoking cigarettes. Every safe airplane trip does not increase the chances that the next trip will be a crash.

Bad luck does not make good luck more likely, or vice versa. Every failure does not make success more likely, or vice versa. Chance is just that: chance.

■ **Don't be Fooled:** When we have a run of bad luck, we hope that we are due for a change of fortune. It is unlikely that our bad luck will continue forever, but the bad things that happen to us do not automatically make good things more likely. We often have to change our behavior to change our fortune. For example, if we are accumulating a collection of job rejections, we should think about how to present ourselves better, or perhaps apply for different jobs.

Even Steven is just a joke, not something to be counted on.

11

THE TEXAS SHARPSHOOTER

C HISWICK IS A PICTURESQUE, AFFLUENT WEST LONDON SUBURB located along a part of the Thames River that is popular for rowing competitions. The legendary annual boat race between Oxford and Cambridge finishes near the Chiswick Bridge. Chiswick was also home to novelist E. M. Forster, the Pissarro family of painters, rock musician Pete Townshend, actress Helen Mirren, and Fuller's Brewery, London's largest and oldest brewery, best known today as the brewer of London Pride.

This tranquil, idyllic town was hit by several German bombing raids during World War II, including one that came with no warning shortly before 7 p.m. on Friday, September 8, 1944. Robert Stubbs, the sixty-four-year-old caretaker of the Staveley Road School, was walking across the school's playing field, thinking about some chores and the approaching rain when he was suddenly tossed twenty feet across the grass. As he picked himself up, he saw that his body was not the only thing thrown about.

Debris and rubble were everywhere. Many trees along the road had been knocked flat or literally blown to bits. Despite their nine-inch-thick walls, eleven houses on Staveley Road had been destroyed and another twenty-seven had been damaged so badly that they were unlivable. A soldier walking along the road to visit his girlfriend lay dead. A three-year-old child died in her crib when the blast sucked the air out of her lungs. A woman was killed when her house caved in on top of her. Another seventeen people were seriously injured inside their collapsing homes. The toll would have been much larger had not so many people evacuated Chiswick that summer in fear of such an attack.

A witness said that it sounded like a gas main had exploded. A government official agreed that it well might have been a gas main, and that became the official explanation. Oddly enough another "gas main explosion" occurred fifteen seconds after the Chiswick explosion in another part of London. Citizens were skeptical and sarcastically referred to similar explosions as "flying gas pipes." They were right to be skeptical. The British government eventually acknowledged that Chiswick had been hit by a V-2 rocket launched from German-occupied Holland.

The V-2 rocket, weighing eight thousand pounds and traveling three thousand feet per second, hit the ground with an impact equal to that of fifty one-hundred-ton locomotives traveling at sixty miles per hour. After hitting the ground, the rocket's warhead exploded, creating a crater in Staveley Road thirty feet wide and ten feet deep. The blast waves pounded everything within a quarter mile radius.

During the final stages of World War II, the German army fired thousands of V-1s and V-2s at London. The V-1s were twenty-five feet long, pilot-less airplanes that used an internal gyroscope to control the flight path. The planes chugged along at three hundred miles an hour and took around thirty minutes to reach London from their launch sites in German-occupied France. A small windmill device mounted on the plane estimated the distance the V-1 had traveled based on the number of times the windmill revolved as the plane flew towards London. After a preset number of revolutions, the V-1 was sent into a steep dive toward earth.

The V-2s were the first long-range combat rockets and the first to reach outer space. Flying at more than three thousand miles per hour, they took only a few minutes to reach London. Because the V-2s traveled at four times the speed of sound and at an altitude of more than fifty miles, it was virtually impossible to stop them with fighter planes or anti-aircraft guns. Each rocket carried one-ton warheads capable of damaging everything within a quarter-mile radius.

Between June 1944 and March 1945, London was hit by 2,419 V-1s and 517 V-2s. The V-1s made a monotonous *duv-duv-duv* sound as they flew over London, warning people that a bomb was on its way. In addition, the initial V-1s had a design flaw that shut off the engine when they dove towards the ground. Londoners learned to scramble for shelter when the *duv-duv-duv* stopped. The V-2s were more ominous because they traveled faster than the speed of sound and gave no warning before they hit. Even more eerily, people heard the roar of the rocket descending *after* the rocket had already hit the ground and exploded, and this roar was followed by a sonic boom in the upper atmosphere. It was as if time was reversed. A massive explosion, followed by a deafening roar descending from the sky, followed by a sonic boom from where the deafening roar had begun.

One of the V-1s hit the Guards Chapel at Wellington Barracks during a Sunday service. The chapel was an imposing building with a reinforced roof, but the bomb blew off the roof and split the large building in half, killing 119 people and injuring another 141. Another V-2 hit a Woolworth's store in London. The entire building was demolished and collapsed into a pile of rubble in the store's basement. One hundred and sixty-eight shoppers were killed, some by the force of the explosion, others by the collapse of the building. When a bomb landed in a residential area, an entire block might be destroyed.

There were tens of thousands of casualties and millions of homes, offices, and factories were damaged. Perhaps even worse was the effect on civilian morale. It was not safe to go to church or to go shopping or to stay home and watch the telly. More than a million people evacuated London.

Despite the devastation they caused, the V-1s and V-2s had very limited accuracy. For example, the windmill system on the V-1s was easily thrown off by winds that sped up or slowed down the windmill. The Germans aimed the V-1s at London's Tower bridge but were satisfied if they landed anywhere in London. In practice, hundreds crashed harmlessly into the countryside or ocean.

Nonetheless, many Londoners believed that the Germans were targeting certain neighborhoods. There seemed to be clusters of bombs in some areas and an absence of bombs in others, suggesting that the Germans were aiming at some neighborhoods and avoiding others. Looking for an explanation for these data clusters, some suggested that German spies lived in the areas the Germans were not bombing. They were too quick to assume that if there is a pattern, there must be a reason. Not necessarily.

Clustering appears even in random data. I flipped a quarter ten times and here's what I got:

T   H   H   T   T   H   H   H   H   H

There is a cluster of 5 heads at the end of my little experiment. What happened? Did I face a different direction or sit in a different chair? No. Nothing happened that was special or unusual. When we see a data cluster, we naturally think that something special is going on—that there is a reason that these heads (or tails) are bunched together. But there isn't. Data clusters appear even in completely random coin flips. If you don't believe it, flip a coin 10 times. Even though every flip is completely random, there is a 47 percent chance that you will have a cluster of at least 4 heads in a row or 4 tails in a row.

The same is true of the geographic location of randomly dropped bombs. There will inevitably be bomb clusters in some areas and no bombs in other areas. A British statistician named R. D. Clarke analyzed data for an area of South London that had been hit by 537 bombs. He divided the area into 576 squares of 1 square kilometer each, and counted the number of bombs that landed in each square. This was compared to the distribution of bombs that would be expected if 537 bombs were randomly dropped on South London. Table 11.1 shows what he found.

Table 11.1: Randomly Dropped Bombs

Number of Bombs in the square	Expected Number of Squares	Actual Number of Squares
0	227	229
1	211	211
2	98	93
3	31	35
4	7	7
5 or more	2	1
TOTAL	576	576

If the bombs had been dropped randomly, we expect 227 squares to not have any bomb hits. In fact, 229 squares escaped damage. Similarly, we expect 211 squares to have 1 bomb, and 1 had one bomb. Overall, the observed distribution is very similar to the anticipated result of random bombing. Differences as large as or even larger than those observed could be anticipated 95 percent of the time with random bombing. The observed bomb clusters are absolutely meaningless. They are just what we expect if bombs are dropped randomly.

Because data clusters appear even in completely random data, they need not lead us on a wild goose chase for fanciful explanations. Unfortunately, it is very hard to resist the temptation to assume that every pattern must have a reason.

■ THE CANCER CLUSTER SCARE

In the 1970s, an unemployed epidemiologist named Nancy Wertheimer drove through Denver, looking at homes that had been lived in by people who had died of cancer before the age of 19. She looked for something—anything—these homes had in common.

What she found was that many cancer-victim homes were near large power lines. Her life partner, a physicist named Ed Leeper, drove through Denver with her and estimated the exposure to electromagnetic fields (EMFs) from power lines by measuring the distance of each home from different types of electrical wires and transformers and making assumptions about the strength of the fields. They did the same for a sample of Denver homes with no childhood cancer victims. Although they admitted that they had no idea why power lines might cause cancer, they nonetheless concluded that the risk of cancer increased by a factor of two or three for children living near large power lines.

Their published report set off a nationwide fear, fueled by frightening stories. A man who committed suicide had lived near a power line. Some chickens that stopped laying eggs lived near power lines. A journalist named Paul Brodeur wrote three *New Yorker* articles that reported an unusually large number of cancer cases among people living near a power station in Guilford, Connecticut, and fifteen cancer cases among people working at a school near power lines in Fresno, California. Brodeur put these articles (with minor changes) in a book titled *The Great Power-Line Cover-Up: How the Utilities and Government Are Trying to Hide the Cancer Hazard Posed by Electromagnetic Fields.* He ominously warned that, "Thousands of unsuspecting children and adults will be stricken with cancer, and many of them will die unnecessarily early deaths, as a result of their exposure to power-line magnetic fields."

The resulting national hysteria offered lucrative opportunities for consultants, researchers, lawyers, and gadgets, including Gauss meters that would allow people to measure EMFs in their own homes (rooms with high EMF readings were to be blocked off and used only for storage).

Once again, the problem is that clusters appear even in random data. Even if cancer is randomly distributed among the population, there will, more likely than not, be a geographic cluster of cancer victims. To demonstrate this, I created a fictitious city with ten thousand residents living in homes evenly spaced throughout the city, each having a one-in-a-hundred chance of cancer. (I ignored the fact that people live in families and that cancer is related to age.) I used computerized coin flips to determine the cancer victims in this imaginary town. The resulting cancer map is shown in Figure 11.1. Each black dot represents a home with a cancer victim. There are no cancer victims in the white spaces.

There is clearly a cancer cluster in the lower part of the map. If this were a real city, we could drive through the neighborhood where these people live and surely find something special. Perhaps the city's Little League fields are nearby. If we now compare the cancer rates for people who live near these Little League fields with the cancer rates for people who live far away, guess what? The cancer rates would be higher near the fields, suggesting that living near a Little League field causes cancer. Tear down the fields!

Figure 11.1 also shows a cancer fortress, a part of town where nobody has cancer. If we drive through this cancer-free neighborhood, we are sure to find something unusual. Perhaps, the town's water tower is nearby. If we now compare the cancer rates for people who live near the water tower with cancer rates for people who live far away, cancer rates would of course be lower near the water tower. That's why we looked at that neighborhood in the first place. Because nobody there has cancer.

Figure 11.1: A Cancer Map

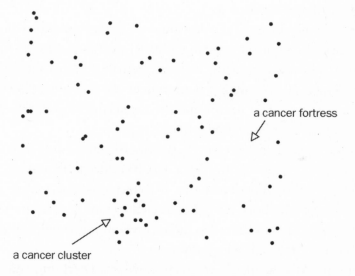

a cancer fortress

a cancer cluster

In each case, near the Little League fields and near the water tower, we have the same problem. If we use the data to concoct the theory (Little League fields cause cancer, water towers protect against cancer), then of course the data support the theory! How could it be otherwise? Would we make up a theory that did not fit the data? Of course not. A theory cannot be fairly tested by looking at the data that were used to create the theory. We need fresh data. The theory also needs to make sense.

Sometimes, data clusters do turn out to be important. In the summer of 1976, a mysterious lung disease hit 182 people (with 29 deaths) at the annual convention of the Pennsylvania American Legion, a group of military veterans. After considerable detective work, scientists identified the airborne bacteria that caused the pneumonia these people suffered—now called Legionnaires' disease—and these scientists identified antibiotics that work much better than the ones used when the outbreak hit.

With Legionnaires' disease, a data cluster led to a theory that was tested with new data. Without the theory or the fresh data, all we have is a cluster. The Wertheimer-Leeper cluster of cancer victims is one version of the "Texas sharpshooter" fallacy. In this first variation, a man with a gun but no skill fires a large number of bullets at the side of a barn and then paints a bullseye around the spot with the most bullet holes. Even if the geographic incidence of cancer is completely random, there will be coincidental clusterings—just as in one hundred random gunshots there will be clusterings of bullet holes.

For a valid statistical test, the researcher should paint the target before firing bullets—making an argument for why power lines might cause cancer and *then* comparing the cancer incidence in neighborhoods with and without power lines.

Another problem with the Wertheimer-Leeper study is that their estimates of the exposure to EMFs may have been influenced by how they expected the study to turn out. Biased estimates can easily double or triple a very small risk ratio. For a scientific study, neutral observers should estimate the exposure to EMFs without knowing which homes had cancer victims and which did not.

After the Wertheimer-Leeper report, Maria Feychting and Anders Ahlbom embarked on a more rigorous study of power line EMFs by identifying Swedish families that lived within three hundred meters of high voltage power lines. Instead of guestimating EMF exposure, Sweden's meticulous utility records were used to calculate the EMFs that these people had been exposed to each year for twenty-five years. After a meticulous analysis of their data, Feychting and Ahlbom concluded that those children who were most exposed were four times more likely to suffer from childhood leukemia than were unexposed children.

The Feychting-Ahlbom study is an example of another version of the Texas sharpshooter fallacy. Instead of firing shots and then painting a bullseye around the largest cluster, our deceptive sharpshooter fires lots of bullets at lots of targets. Afterward, he finds a target that he hit, covers the other bullet holes with putty, and repaints everything but the one target he hit.

The Feychting-Ahlbom study created hundreds of targets by considering several cancers, several age groups, several EMF measures, and several cutoffs for separating "unexposed," "somewhat exposed," "more exposed," and "most exposed." They calculated nearly eight hundred risk ratios before choosing childhood leukemia. If power lines are completely benign, some observed risk ratios will, by bad luck alone, be higher than others. Other risk ratios will turn out to be far below average. Feychting and Ahlbom naturally chose to report the highest risk ratio and not mention the others. They covered up the missed targets.

This version of the sharpshooter fallacy is also called the Feynman Trap, a reference to the Nobel Laureate Richard Feynman, who we will meet again later in Chapter 13. Feynman asked his Cal Tech students to calculate the probability that, if he walked outside the classroom, the first car in the parking lot would have a specific license plate, say 8NSR261. Cal Tech students are very smart and they quickly calculated the probability of 8NSR261 by assuming each number and letter in the plate were independently determined. Their answer was 1 in 176 million. When they finished, Feynman revealed that the correct probability was 1 because he had seen this license plate on his way to class. Something extremely unlikely is not unlikely at all if it has already happened.

And yet researchers do it all the time. Predicting what the data look like after looking at the data is easy, and meaningless. In our power line example, predicting childhood leukemia after observing childhood leukemia is not compelling. When data are used to invent a theory, the evidence is unconvincing unless the theory has a logical basis and has been tested with fresh data. The sharpshooter should draw a single target and he should draw it before, not after, firing his gun.

Is there any basis for the power-line theory? Scientists know a lot about EMFs and there is no plausible theory for how power line EMFs could cause cancer. The electromagnetic energy is far weaker than that from moonlight and the magnetic field is weaker than the earth's magnetic field.

Also, Feychting and Ahlbom found a correlation between cancer and a child's EMF exposure during the year the cancer was diagnosed, but no correlation between cancer and a child's EMF exposure one, five, or ten years before the diagnosis even though it generally takes several years for cancer symptoms to appear. Finally, if there were a link between power line EMFs and cancer, people exposed to higher doses should have had higher risk ratios, but they did not. Their own data contradict their theory.

Has the Swedish study been confirmed with fresh data? No. For example, the UK Childhood Cancer Study, covering children in England, Scotland, and Wales, found that children with more EMF exposure generally had *less* chance of leukemia and other forms of cancer, though the observed differences were not statistically persuasive. In addition, the publicity following the Swedish study motivated several experimental studies of rodents which found that EMFs far larger than those generated by power lines had no effect on mortality, cancer incidence, immune systems, fertility, or birth abnormalities.

Weighing the theoretical arguments and empirical evidence, the National Academy of Sciences concluded that power lines are not a public health danger and there is no need to fund further research, let alone tear down the power lines. One of the nation's top medical journals weighed in, agreeing that we should stop wasting research resources on this issue. Even one of the coauthors of the Swedish study conceded that there is no point in doing further research until there is a theory that explains how EMFs cause cancer.

In 1999, *The New Yorker* published an article titled "The Cancer-Cluster Myth," which implicitly repudiated the earlier articles written by Paul Brodeur.

■ **Don't be Fooled:** Data clusters are everywhere, even in random data. Someone who looks for an explanation will inevitably find one, but a theory that fits a data cluster is not persuasive evidence. The found explanation needs to make sense and it needs to be tested with uncontaminated data.

Similarly, someone who fires enough bullets at enough targets is bound to hit one. A researcher who tests hundreds of theories is bound to find evidence supporting at least one. Such evidence is unconvincing unless the theory is sensible and confirmed with fresh data.

When you hear that the data support a theory, don't be persuaded until you've answered two questions. First, does the theory make sense? If it doesn't, don't be easily persuaded that nonsense is sensible. Second, is there a Texas sharpshooter in the house? Did the person promoting the theory look at the data before coming up with the theory? Were hundreds of theories tested before settling on the theory being promoted? If there is a smoking gun, withhold judgment on the theory until it has been tested with different data.

12

THE ULTIMATE PROCRASTINATION

I N THE EARLY 1970S, THE AMERICAN STATISTICAL ASSOCIATION sponsored a collection of essays illustrating the widespread application of statistical tools. One essay, written by David P. Phillips, a professor of sociology at the University of California at San Diego, began with this provocative question:

> In the movies and in certain kinds of romantic literature, we sometimes come across a deathbed scene in which a dying person holds onto life until some special event has occurred. For example, a mother might stave off death until her long-absent son returns from the wars. Do such feats of will occur in real life as well as in fiction?

An interesting question, to be sure. Many of us put off doing today what we can do tomorrow. But can death, like dieting and house cleaning, be put off? What evidence could be used to see whether death can be postponed? Nobody collects data on children visiting dying parents. And even if they did, we have no way of knowing whether the impending visit had any effect on the timing of the parent's death.

Phillips is a clever man with a bachelor's degree, *magna cum laude*, from Harvard and a PhD from Princeton, and he had the clever idea of investigating whether famous people can postpone death until after the celebration of their birthdays. Birthdays are not always joyous for the elderly, since they are an insistent reminder that the clock is ticking, but Phillips argued that the birthdays of famous people are publicly celebrated occasions that are worth staying alive for. There are many anecdotes of famous people dying on their birthdays or other memorable dates. Perhaps this is because they postponed death until they could celebrate?

Sir Thomas Browne, a seventeenth century English doctor, scientist, and writer died on his birthday, October 19, and seemed to have foretold this: "The first day should be the last, that the Tail of the Snake should return into its Mouth precisely at that time, and they should wind up on the day of their Nativity, is indeed a remarkable coincidence." Not only that, but Browne's friend and admirer, Sir Kenelm Digby, died on his birthday, June 11, which was also the date of his naval victory over the Dutch and Venetians at Scanderoon, inspiring this epitaph by Richard Farrar:

> Born on the day he died, the eleventh of June
> And that day bravely fought at Scanderoon;
> 'Tis rare that one and the same day should be
> His day of birth, of death, of victory!

Were these two birthday deaths unusual or do they happen quite often, more often than expected by coincidence? Gilbert Geis, a professor at the University of California at Irvine, selected a random sample of 2,250 persons from *Who Was Who in America* and found only three people who died on their birthdays, fewer than one would expect by chance alone. Geis concludes wryly, "Perhaps Sir Thomas Browne, dedicated to science, wanted to provide some data to support his own theory."

Geis's data do not show that people postpone death until their birthday. However, some famous people have died on other noteworthy days. John Adams and Thomas Jefferson, the second and third US presidents, both died on July 4, 1826, the fiftieth anniversary of the signing of the Declaration of Independence. James Monroe, the fifth president, also died on July 4, five years later. Did they postpone death until July 4, or are these just coincidences?

Probably just coincidences. George Washington, the first president, died on December 14, and nobody remembers this because it is not memorable. It is not Independence Day, Christmas, New Year's, Washington's birthday, his wife's birthday, the anniversary of his marriage, the anniversary of any battles, or anything else special. Because we are hardwired to look for patterns, we find it striking that three presidents died on July 4, and do not remember all the presidents, generals, and other American leaders who did not die on July 4. And what about James Madison, the fourth president, who died on June 28? If three other presidents could die on Independence Day, why couldn't Madison? Wasn't he patriotic enough to postpone his death six days until July 4?

There are thousands of famous Americans and only 365 days in the year—which means that many people will die on special days or on the same day as someone else. We remember these "special" death days and pay no attention to the rest. The fact that somebody happened to die on a noteworthy day is not noteworthy. It is inevitable.

Cherry-picking people and days will never prove anything except that we spent a lot of time picking cherries. For a valid statistical test, we need to say *beforehand* that we are going to look at a well-defined group of people and a well-defined list of days and see if there are an unexpectedly large number of deaths on these special days. Phillips's postponement theory could be tested by looking at a group of famous people and seeing whether more of these people died on their birthdays (or shortly after) than died shortly before their birthdays.

■ DEATH DIPS AND BLIPS

Phillips sort of did this. He looked at the deceased people with known death dates in *Four Hundred Notable Americans* which was part of the *Encyclopedia of American History*, an ambitious compilation of the most important facts of American history. He concluded that famous people were often able to postpone their deaths, in that there were fewer than expected deaths (a "death dip") in the months before the birth month and more than expected deaths (a "death blip") during the birth month and the next few months. This famous study of famous birthdays and deathdays was cited in many statistics textbooks, including my own.

Phillips followed this study with other widely publicized studies with various coauthors that supported his theory: Jews postpone death until after Yom Kippur; Jews postpone death until after Passover; elderly Chinese women postpone death until after the Harvest Moon Festival. Maybe there really is something to this idea of the ultimate procrastination.

But then the doubts started. Three students taking my statistics classes wrote term papers attempting to replicate Phillips's birthday/deathday findings with different data sets. None found a statistically significant death dip and blip. Figure 12.1 shows their combined data. The values on the horizontal axis, death month minus birth month, are negative for those who died before their birth month, zero for those who died in their birth month, and positive for those who died after their birth month.

While there were slightly fewer deaths than expected one month before the birth month, there were far more than expected two and three months before the birth month and there was no death blip on or after the birth month. Random data would show differences between the actual and expected number of deaths each month at least as large as those in Figure 12.1 about half the time.

Figure 12.1: Three Studies Comparing the Death Month with the Birth Month

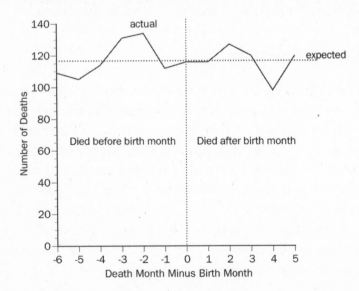

Puzzled by the fact that three independent attempts to confirm Phillips's theory failed, another student (Heather Royer, now a professor herself) and I reexamined the birthday/deathday data that launched Phillips's postponement ship. One perplexing aspect of his analysis, given his description of the dramatic deathbed scene, is that Phillips lumped together all deaths that occurred during the birth month, not distinguishing those that occurred before the birthday from those that occurred afterward. Instead, Phillips counted all deaths that occurred during the birth month as having been postponed until after the birthday celebration. If you were born on November 22 and died on November 11, he counted this as a successful postponement. There is no logical explanation for this bizarre accounting other than it gave Phillips the results he wanted.

Heather and I found that of the twenty-six famous people who died during their birth month, thirteen died before their birthdays, one died on his birthday, and twelve died after their birthdays! The twenty-six people who died close to their birthdays were completely unsuccessful in postponing death. We also separated deaths into thirty days before the birthday, thirty days after, and so on, and found no evidence that people are able to postpone death.

■ UPON FURTHER INVESTIGATION

These discoveries made me wonder about Phillips's other studies that showed death postponement until after Yom Kippur, Passover, and the Harvest Moon Festival. Did these studies have problems, too?

Turns out they did. Another student (Peter Lee, now a doctor) and I looked at the Jewish data. For Yom Kippur, Phillips didn't compare mortality before and after Yom Kippur. Instead he compared September mortality for ten years (1922, 1925, 1930, 1933, 1941, 1949, 1952, 1960, 1963, and 1968) in which Yom Kippur occurred between September 28 and October 3 with the average September mortality in two adjacent years. This is an extraordinarily awkward way of looking for a death dip before Yom Kippur and completely ignores the predicted death blip after the holiday. Remember, the theory is that death postponement creates a death dip before and a death blip afterward. We need both the dip and the blip to support the theory. It would have been far more natural to compare the number of deaths in the days before and after Yom Kippur in every year, but Phillips did not report this obvious comparison. Even more oddly, his Passover study *did* compare the number of deaths during the week preceding Passover with the number of deaths during the week afterward.

It is certainly suspicious that the birthday, Yom Kippur, and Passover studies all used different methodologies: adjacent months (not centered on the ceremonial occasion), the month preceding the ceremonial occasion in different years, and adjacent weeks (centered on the ceremonial occasion). Why would someone use a different calculation in each study, unless this had to be done to get the desired results? It is also suspicious that the reported results used one set of data for Yom Kippur and a different set of data for Passover. Why weren't results for both holidays reported for both sets of data, unless this had to be done to get the desired results?

These weren't the only problems. Amazingly enough, the deceased were not necessarily Jewish! In the Yom Kippur study, the data consisted of all New York City residents during a time (1921–69) when the population was 28 percent Jewish and all Budapest residents during a time (1875–1915) when its population was 22 percent Jewish. The Passover study used data for California decedents whose last names suggested that they were "probably Jewish."

Living in New York or Budapest is an astonishingly weak indicator of whether a person is Jewish. Having a name that is probably Jewish is not only a weak indicator but ripe for convenient placements. The researchers included people named Asher or Brody, but excluded people named Ash or Bach. Was this because the former are more clearly Jewish than the latter, or because the timing of their deaths supported the researchers' theory? (Pop quiz: Is Green a Jewish or non-Jewish name?)

Peter Lee collected data from a Jewish Memorial Chapel for more than five thousand deceased people who were not only definitely Jewish, but felt strongly enough about their faith to be given services in a Jewish mortuary. Peter and I compared their death dates to four major Jewish holidays: Channukah, Passover, Rosh Hashanah, and Yom Kippur.

Overall, there were *more* deaths before these celebrations than after, although none of the results for any holiday were close to statistically significant. In every case, the observed differences could be expected to occur by chance more than half the time.

■ MOON CAKES AT MIDNIGHT

Next, I turned to Phillips's data for one of the most important Chinese holidays—the Harvest Moon Festival, which occurs on the fifteenth day of the eighth moon of the lunar calendar. The family customarily gathers for bonding, celebration, and a festival meal including traditional moon cakes eaten outdoors at midnight.

Phillips and yet another coauthor analyzed California mortality data and concluded that some elderly Chinese American women postponed their deaths until after the celebration of the Harvest Moon Festival. Their strongest evidence was an observed death dip in the week preceding the Harvest Moon Festival and a rise in the week afterward for Chinese women at least seventy-five years old.

An oddity in their data is that there happened to be a large number of deaths on the Harvest Moon Festival day. Should these deaths be counted as occurring before or after the celebration? Phillips counted them as after so that these deaths would be recorded as evidence of death postponement. However, the main ceremonial ritual occurs at midnight. If a person can postpone death until after a celebration, shouldn't she be able to postpone death until after the main ceremonial activity? In his study of Jewish deaths near Passover, Phillips counted deaths as successfully postponed if they occurred *after* midnight on the night of the traditional Passover meal. The only apparent reason for counting deaths that occur on the day of the Harvest Moon Festival as being after the celebration is that this bolsters the evidence for the death-postponement theory.

Similarly, Phillips justified his focus on seventy-five year old women by arguing that older women are in charge of preparing an elaborate meal. However, age sixty-five was used by Phillips to identify elderly Jewish males in his Passover study. Perhaps seventy-five was used in the Harvest Moon Festival study and sixty-five in the

Passover study so that the results would support his otherwise insupportable theories.

It is completely unsurprising that the Harvest Moon results are not statistically significant unless we artificially restrict our sample to women over seventy-five and implausibly assume that deaths on the festival day occurred after the midnight ceremony.

These oddities cry out for an independent test, using fresh data that have not been massaged as needed. Death postponement for the Harvest Moon Festival was retested using new Chinese American, Korean American, and Vietnamese American mortality data. No matter how deaths on the festival day were recorded, elderly Chinese women had *more* deaths during the week before the festival than during the week after. The same is true of elderly Vietnamese women. Elderly Korean women had either more deaths before the festival day or the same number before and after. None of these differences are statistically significant.

What is the real lesson here? Not that people can postpone death, but that if your goal is to get published and a straightforward analysis of the data doesn't work, try less obvious analyses. Be a Texas sharpshooter! Sooner or later, something will work. Do lots of tests and report only the results that support your theory.

■ THE LONG GOODBYE

Shortly after I did this detective work, Donn Young, a statistician and research scientist at Ohio State University's Comprehensive Cancer Center, sent me a copy of his study that had just been published in the *Journal of the American Medical Association*. He recounted that,

> Healthcare workers involved in caring for patients dying of cancer commonly recall those who apparently held on to life and defied the odds by surviving a major holiday or significant event only to die immediately thereafter. By "willing" themselves to survive the holiday, these patients have been able to spend an important event with their families and have seemingly saved their family and friends from having to associate a joyous holiday with a tragic event.

To see whether these anecdotes reflected a systematic phenomenon or the selective recall of heartwarming incidents, Young and an associate looked at the timing of more than three hundred thousand cancer deaths in Ohio. They had three reasons for focusing on cancer patients. First, death postponement is presumably most relevant for people with a chronic disease, as opposed to a sudden death from, say, a heart attack. Second, cancer patients are seldom on life support, where the timing of death can be determined by family members. Third, unlike many other diseases, cancer deaths do not have seasonal patterns—for example, rising in winter months and falling in the summer.

They compared the number of death during the weeks before and after Christmas, Thanksgiving, and the patients' birthdays. For all three ceremonial occasions, there were slightly *more* deaths before the event than after, though the differences were not statistically significant for any of the three events. Their data do not indicate that cancer patients are able to postpone death for significant events.

Young attributed the anecdotal folklore to wishful thinking and selective memory (we remember memorable coincidences and forget the rest). One unfortunate consequence of this folklore is that families may feel guilt or shame when a patient dies before a holiday: John didn't love us enough to stay around to celebrate with us. Young's advice is quite different. If a loved one has a terminal disease and an important event is coming up, don't take a chance. Celebrate it now:

My father died of chronic renal failure last summer, a week after his 88th birthday. We celebrated his birthday early, because we just didn't know if he'd make it or not. Fortunately he did make it, so we simply celebrated it again. I don't think anyone's going to say that celebrating an event like that twice is a bad idea.

■ **Don't be Fooled:** Be skeptical—very skeptical—of theories that seem fanciful. Watch out for unnatural groupings of data. Watch out for studies where it seems that the researchers are reporting only a carefully selected portion of their statistical tests.

13

SERIOUS OMISSIONS

ONDAY, OCTOBER 12, 1987, WAS THE START OF A NERVOUS
week on Wall Street, though it initially seemed no more nervous than usual and that there was no good reason to be especially nervous. Then the market started shaking. The Dow
dropped 4 percent on Wednesday, 1 percent on Thursday, and another
5 percent on Friday, with a record 339 million shares traded on the
New York Stock Exchange (NYSE) and losers outnumbering winners
17 to 1—though it was hard to think of a reason why prices fell.

Monday's "Abreast of the Market" column in *The Wall Street
Journal* suggested that Friday's bloodletting might have been the selling climax that many technical analysts believe signals the beginning
of a bull market. One said that "the peak of intensity of selling pressure has exhausted itself" and another said "if we haven't seen the
bottom, we're probably very close."

If it were so easy to predict the stock market, the gurus would
get rich trading stocks instead of making a living by making predictions. The very day this article appeared was Black Monday, a frightening market convulsion. When the market opened, the excess of sell
orders was so large that trading on the New York Stock Exchange
was suspended for an hour for 8 of the 30 stocks in the Dow. For
the day, an astounding 604 million shares were traded and the
Dow dropped 508 points (23 percent). Losers outnumbered gainers
by 40 to 1 and the total market value of stocks fell by roughly
$500 billion.

The next day, Terrible Tuesday, the stock market came close to a total collapse. The Dow opened with a two hundred point gain, but by noon had fallen back below Monday's close. During the day, trading was temporarily suspended in many of the most well-known stocks, including IBM for two hours, and Merck for four hours. Several major financial institutions were rumored to be bankrupt and some banks cut off lending to securities firms who, in turn, demanded that traders who had borrowed money sell their stocks and repay their loans. Some of the largest securities firms urged the NYSE to shut down completely in order to stop this downward spiral.

The day was saved when the Federal Reserve reduced interest rates, promised to supply much needed cash, and pressured banks to lend money. With vigorous encouragement from investment bankers, several major corporations announced plans to repurchase their stock, and the system held together—if just barely. One market participant said that, "Tuesday was the most dangerous day we had in fifty years. I think we came within an hour [of the disintegration of the stock market]." The Dow closed on Tuesday up 6 percent with 608 million shares traded and rose another 10 percent the next day—ending the short-run crisis.

When a few data are very different from the rest, these are called *outliers*. For example, the daily changes, up or down, in the Dow Jones Industrial Average of stock prices are seldom larger than 4 percent. The 23 percent drop that occurred on October 19, 1987, was an outlier. Sometimes, an outlier is just a clerical error, like the misplacement of a decimal point, and can be corrected. Sometimes, an outlier reflects a unique situation—for example, the day a natural disaster occurred—and the outlier can be discarded if we are not interested in such unusual events. In other cases, the outlier may be worth looking at. It could be very interesting to see how the stock market reacted to a natural disaster, a presidential assassination, or the end of a war.

The stock market meltdown on October 19, 1987, was a Black Monday worth studying. One lesson learned was that the Federal Reserve was willing and able to do whatever is needed to prevent a stock market meltdown. In addition, the Brady Commission, a presidential task force, concluded that so-called portfolio insurance—a wildly mis-named investment strategy of buying stocks after prices have risen and selling after prices have fallen—was the trigger that precipitated the crash on October 19 and threatened further panic on October 20. The Brady Commission also concluded that the markets for stocks, options, and futures became disconnected during the panic and went into virtual free fall. To avoid a repeat, the commission recommended that markets be supervised by a single regulatory authority (such as the Federal Reserve), that markets be subject to consistent borrowing rules, and that trading be halted simultaneously in all three markets during crises to allow time to match buyers and sellers. This outlier was a painful and expensive lesson—but it was a lesson.

In other situations, outliers might be discarded because they are potentially misleading. For example, a national magazine once re-ported that a group of Colorado teachers had failed a history test, with an average score of 67. It turned out that only four teachers had taken the test and one had a score of 20. The other three averaged 83. The one very low score pulled the mean down to 67 and misled a magazine that interpreted the average score as the typical score. Here, the outlier was atypical and misleading.

On the other hand, discarding outliers is sometimes misleading. A dramatic example occurred in the 1980s when scientists discovered that the software analyzing satellite ozone readings over the South Pole had been automatically omitting a large number of very low readings because these were outliers in comparison to readings made in the 1970s. The computer program assumed that readings so far from what had been normal in the 1970s must be mistakes.

When scientists reanalyzed the data, including the previously ig-nored outliers, they found that an ominous hole in the ozone layer had been developing for several years, with Antarctic ozone declining by 40 percent between 1979 and 1985. Susan Solomon of the National Oceanic and Atmospheric Administration's Aeronomy Laboratory said, "This is a change in the ozone that's of absolutely unprecedented proportions. We've just never seen anything like what we're experi-encing in the Antarctic." Outliers are sometimes clerical errors, meas-urement errors, or flukes that, if not corrected or omitted, will distort the data. At other times, as with the ozone readings, they are the most interesting observations.

While it is sometimes misleading to exclude outliers, it is almost always misleading to exclude data that are *not* outliers.

■ ROCKET SCIENCE

The evening before the scheduled 1986 launch of the space shuttle *Challenger*, engineers discussed postponing the launch. For nearly a decade, the engineers had been concerned about the rubber O-rings that sealed the joints used to contain the high-pressure gases produced by the burning propellant. A 1978 NASA memo warned that a design change was "mandatory to prevent hot gas leaks and resulting catastrophic failure."

Some O-rings had failed on previous flights and the engineers were worried that this was because O-rings become less resilient at low temperatures. Now, the temperature was predicted to be below freezing at takeoff and some engineers opposed the launch.

Figure 13.1 shows the number of O-ring failures on the seven flights where there had been O-ring failures. There were no data for temperatures below 53°. However, for the data they had, Figure 13.1 showed no apparent relationship between temperature and the number of O-ring failures (unless we have a theory why there should be more failure at high *and* low temperatures). The absence of a clear relationship between temperature and O-ring performance and a strong desire to avoid disrupting the launch schedule trumped the concerns of some engineers.

The failure of Figure 13.1 is that it excludes the 17 flights where there had been no O-ring failures. When these are included in Figure 13.2, a very different picture emerges. On the 20 flights when the temperature was above 65°, only 3 flights had O-ring failures. On the 4 flights where the temperature was below 65°, there were always failures. Even more ominously, the largest number of failures had been at the lowest previous temperature (53°) and the forecast was now below freezing.

Figure 13.1: Seven Flights and No Relationship

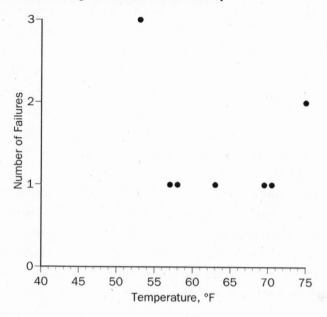

Figure 13.2: A Different Picture With All 24 Flights

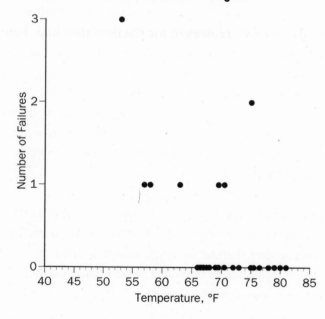

Tragically, the engineers' fears were well-founded. An O-ring failed during liftoff and the *Challenger* broke apart seventy-three seconds later, killing all seven crew members. A presidential commission investigating this disaster included Richard Feynman, the flamboyant Cal Tech professor who prepared his lectures in topless bars. When he worked at Los Alamos on the Manhattan Project to develop the atomic bomb, he demonstrated the insecurity of this high-security facility by breaking into locked cabinets and sneaking out of the compound through a hole in the fence. An autobiography was titled *Surely You're Joking, Mr. Feynman!*

Here, Feynman was deadly serious. During nationally televised hearings, this Nobel Prize–winning theoretical physicist demonstrated that O-rings lost their resiliency at low temperatures simply by dunking one in a glass of ice water. Odd that the rocket scientists hadn't thought of that. Sort of like the parable told by Francis Bacon in the seventeenth century:

> In the year of our Lord 1432, there arose a grievous quarrel among the brethren over the number of teeth in the mouth of a horse. For thirteen days the disputation raged without ceasing. All the ancient books and chronicles were fetched out, and wonderful and ponderous erudition, such as was never before heard of in this region, was made manifest. At the beginning of the fourteenth day, a youthful friar of goodly bearing asked his learned superiors for permission to add a word, and straightway, to the wonderment of the disputants, whose wisdom he sore vexed, he beseeched them to unbend in a manner coarse and unheard-of, and to look in the open mouth of a horse and find answer to their questionings.

In the *Challenger* example, the omission of important data was an innocent, but fatal, mistake. In other cases, data are deliberately omitted because they do not support preconceived notions. Wanting to believe that something is true, data that challenge these beliefs are discarded.

■ THE HOUND OF THE BASKERVILLES

In Japanese, Mandarin, and Cantonese, the pronunciation of *four* and *death* are very similar. Not surprisingly, many Japanese and Chinese consider four to be an unlucky number. Surprisingly, it has been argued that this aversion to four is so strong that Japanese and Chinese Americans are susceptible to heart attacks on the fourth day of every month. The idea is clearly preposterous, but a study making this silly claim was published in one of the world's top medical journals.

The study was called "The Hound of the Baskervilles Effect," referring to Sir Arthur Conan Doyle's story in which Charles Baskerville is pursued by a vicious dog and dies of a heart attack:

> The dog, incited by its master, sprang over the wicket-gate and pursued the unfortunate baronet, who fled screaming down the yew alley. In that gloomy tunnel it must indeed have been a dreadful sight to see that huge black creature, with its flaming jaws and blazing eyes, bounding after its victim. He fell dead at the end of the alley from heart disease and terror.

We see the number four every day—in times, addresses, phone numbers, page numbers, prices, and car odometers. Are Asian Americans really so superstitious and fearful that the fourth day of the month—which, after all, happens every month—is as terrifying as being chased down a dark alley by a ferocious dog?

The Baskervilles study (isn't the BS acronym tempting?) examined data for Japanese and Chinese Americans who died of coronary disease. A natural test would be a comparison of the number of coronary deaths on the third, fourth, and fifth days of the month. In their data, 33.9 percent of the coronary deaths on these 3 days occurred on the fourth day of the month, which does not differ substantially or statistically from the expected 33.3 percent. If days 3, 4, and 5 are equally likely days for coronary deaths, we can expect a difference this large more often than not.

So, how did the Baskervilles study come to the opposite conclusion? The authors didn't report the 33.9 percent figure. Instead, they reported deaths from some kinds of heart disease, but not others. In the International Classification of Diseases, coronary deaths are divided into several categories. In some categories, more than one-third of the deaths occurred on day four. In other categories, fewer deaths occurred. The Baskervilles study reported results only for the former. They discarded data that did not support their theory.

The lead author of the Baskervilles study coauthored two different studies that used all of the heart disease categories and a third study that used completely different categories. The only reason for using different categories in different studies is to manufacture support for otherwise unsupported theories.

When we suspect that a researcher made choices after looking at the data, this suspicion can be tested by trying to replicate the results with fresh data. The Baskervilles study used data for the years 1989–98. When 1969–88 and 1999–2001 data were used to retest the heart disease categories reported in the Baskervilles study, the results were neither substantial or statistically significant. In the 1969–88 data, there were more deaths on day five than on day four; in the 1999–2001 data, there were more deaths on day three. It is also revealing that the authors could have used the 1969–88 data (and did so in other studies), but chose not to do so in the Baskervilles study. We can guess why.

The only evidence supporting this disparaging theory was obtained by omitting diseases and years that did not support the theory. Without this helpful pruning, there is no evidence that the fourth day of the month is fatal for Asian Americans. What this study really demonstrates is that support can be found for any theory—no matter how silly—by discarding data that don't support the silly theory.

■ BORN UNDER A BAD SIGN

Each year in the Chinese lunar calendar is associated with one of five elements (fire, earth, metal, water, or wood). In traditional Chinese medicine, each of these elements is associated with a zang organ, which stores energy, and a fu organ, which produces energy and removes waste (Table 13.1).

Table 13.1: The Five Elements and Human Organs

Element	Zang Organ (Yin)	Fu Organ (Yang)
fire	heart	small intestine
earth	spleen	stomach
metal	lungs	large intestine
water	kidney	urinary bladder
wood	liver	gall bladder

The lead author of the Baskervilles study coauthored another provocative study, this time arguing that Chinese people may be "ill-fated" for diseases that affect the organs associated with their birth year. For example, because 1937 is a fire year and the zang fire organ is the heart, Chinese people born in 1937 may be more likely to die of heart disease.

Perhaps a person who feels doomed to die of heart disease does not try to prevent it. Or is so anxious that his chronic anxiety produces the anticipated outcome. Or perhaps there is no relationship at all.

The authors reported that mortality data for Chinese Americans support their theory. However, they only reported results for a few narrow subgroups of diseases related to the ten organs in Table 13.1. For example, they reported results for nephritis and nephrosis, but not for other kidney diseases and they reported results for bronchitis, emphysema, and asthma, but not for other respiratory system diseases. They discarded data that did not support their theory.

The authors also divided heart diseases into unusual subgroups and again discarded inconvenient data. Their purported theory is that Chinese people born in a fire year are more susceptible to heart disease, not that they are more susceptible to some kinds of heart disease and less susceptible to other kinds. Even more suspiciously, the lead author did not use these subgroups in the Baskervilles study. They evidently chose the subgroups for each study after looking at the data, which renders the statistical tests meaningless.

Suppose that I claim that I can flip heads consistently because I spent my childhood practicing coin flips while other kids were shooting basketballs or hitting baseballs. (There is, in fact, an extraordinary magician and mathematician, Persi Diaconis, who can consistently flip heads. I cannot.) But I can nonetheless manufacture evidence of my coin-flipping prowess. Suppose I just flipped a coin twenty times and got nine heads and eleven tails. Nothing remarkable yet. But if I can think up a flimsy excuse for discarding ten of the tails, then, voilà, I flipped heads nine out of ten times. Is that convincing evidence? Of course not.

When real empirical research (not my coin flips) is reported, we often don't know whether data were discarded. A researcher may say, "We used data for these years, these people, and these diseases," so that it appears the categories were chosen ahead of time. The researcher does not say, "After looking at the data, we discarded data for these years, these people, and these diseases because they didn't support our theory." Why do researchers do this? First, they want publishable results and feel they need statistical significance to get published. Second, they sincerely believe that their theory is true and, therefore, see no harm in ignoring evidence to the contrary.

For the ill-fated study, every year corresponds to one of the five elements (fire, earth, metal, water, or wood). The most natural test of the theory that disease is related to birth year is to see whether more than one-fifth of the Chinese people dying of a certain disease had ill-fated birth years. For example, since the zang fire organ is the heart, were more than one-fifth of the Chinese people who died of heart disease born in fire years?

The authors did not report this test, but I will. For the fifteen diseases that they reported, 20.08 percent had ill-fated birth years. This is neither substantial or statistically significant evidence of a relationship between disease and birth year. For the broader disease categories in Table 13.1, 19 percent had ill-fated birth years. This is almost statistically significant, but in the wrong direction.

Another plausible test would be to see whether, among Chinese persons dying of a particular disease, those with ill-fated birth years died younger than those with other birth years. For the fifteen reported diseases, only two are statistically significant. With broader disease categories, the statistical significance vanishes. For example, the authors reported that the ill-fated with bronchitis, emphysema, or asthma have relatively short lives—however, the ill-fated have relatively long lives if we look at all respiratory system diseases.

What do we find with independent data that haven't been contaminated by data grubbing? Data for 1960–68 and 1991–2002 do not replicate the results the authors reported using plundered data for 1969 through 1990. For the diseases they claimed to be statistically significant, almost exactly 20 percent of the deceased had ill-fated birth years and there were no substantial or statistically significant differences in the average age at death of ill-fated and other Chinese Americans.

As with the Baskervilles study, what the bad-sign study really demonstrates is that support for a theory—any theory—can inevitably be amassed by looking at lots of data and discarding data that don't support the theory.

■ MONOGRAMMIC DETERMINISM

"Our cup of joy is now overflowing! We have a daughter of as fine proportions and of as angelic mien as ever gracious nature favor a man with, and her name is Ima!" This angelic baby's name was chosen because the heroine in an epic Civil War poem written by the baby's uncle was named Ima. We do not know if Ima's exuberant father, James Stephen ("Big Jim") Hogg, the man who wrote this announcement of his daughter's birth, was aware of the unfortunate consequence: Ima Hogg.

Ima later said that, "My grandfather Stinson lived fifteen miles from Mineola and news traveled slowly. When he learned of his granddaughter's name he came trotting to town as fast as he could to protest but it was too late. The christening had taken place, and Ima I was to remain."

At some point, Big Jim recognized the humor in his daughter's name and an enduring Texas legend is that he used it to political advantage, telling crowds during his re-election campaign for governor that he had two daughters, Ima and Ura. The *Kansas City Star* newspaper embellished the story even more, reporting that there was a third daughter, named Hoosa. In truth, Ima had no sisters, only three brothers with ordinary names: Michael, Thomas, and William.

Ima Hogg survived her comical name quite well. Big Jim bought land near West Columbia, Texas, and his will stipulated that the land could not be sold until fifteen years after his death. Twelve years after Jim's death, oil was discovered and Ima and her brothers escalated from merely prosperous to *very* rich. Ima became known as the "First Lady of Texas" because of her love of Texas and her wide-ranging philanthropic activities.

Should parents consider not only their babies' names, but also their initials? My initials are GNS (Gary Nance Smith); my brother's initials are RAS (Robert Alan Smith). What if my parents had named me Gary Alan Smith? Would the shame of the initials GAS have ruined my life, or could I somehow have overcome the stigma?

A group of researchers from the psychology and sociology departments at the University of California at San Diego (UCSD) argued that three-letter initials *are* important, in that people with positive initials (such as ACE or VIP) live longer than people with negative initials (such as PIG or DIE). The idea that longevity is affected by initials has been dubbed "monogrammic determinism." Oddly enough, the UC San Diego researchers also found that negative initials are more common than positive initials and that their popularity has increased over time. Are parents sadistic, and increasingly so?

It seems unlikely that negative initials would be so popular if they had such damaging effects on health. Surely, caring parents do not choose baby names that cut years off their children's life expectancy. Surely, this study had a few problems.

The UCSD researchers used these twelve positive initials: ACE, GOD, HUG, JOY, LIF, LIV, LOV, LUV, VIP, WEL, WIN, and WOW; and these nineteen negative initials: APE, ASS, BAD, BUG, BUM, DED, DIE, DTH, DUD, HOG, ILL, MAD, PIG, RAT, ROT, SAD, SIC, SIK, and UGH. They confirmed their choices by asking college students to label these initials and nine neutral initials as positive, negative, or neutral.

We do not know whether the UCSD researchers chose their initials before or after looking at the data. The fact that students could distinguish between the good and bad initials does not tell us how the list was compiled. An attempt to replicate this study started with an independent list of one hundred positive or negative initials, including the thirty-one used by the UCSD researchers. A group of students and faculty were given the list and asked to select the best and worst.

Table 13.2 shows the top twelve positive initials and top nineteen negative initials. Only five of the UCSD researchers' twelve positive initials (shown in bold) were among the top twelve vote-getters; only six of their nineteen negative initials were among the top nineteen vote-getters. It is hard to explain some omissions, particularly among the negative initials. Perhaps they chose the initials after looking at the data?

Why did they use twelve positive initials and nineteen negative initials when they could have used the same number of each? Why did they use BUG instead of FAG, DUD instead of DUM, HOG instead of FAT? They apparently discarded initials that did not support their theory.

Table 13.2: Top Vote-Getters for Positive and Negative Initials, in Order

Positive	Negative	
ACE	**ASS**	GAS
ICE	KKK	FAT
JOY	FAG	**BAD**
VIP	**DIE**	POX
CEO	GAY	HOR
WOW	ZIT	**BUM**
GEM	FUK	SIN
FLY	**PIG**	
FOX	DUM	
HIP	**RAT**	
WIT	SOB	
WIN	TIT	

Using mortality data for 1969 through 1995, the UCSD researchers grouped the deceased by the year they died and compared the average age at death for those with positive or negative initials to those with neutral initials (which may also have been chosen after looking at the data) who died in the same year. They reported that, on average, males with positive initials lived 4.5 more years, males with negative initials lived 2.8 fewer years, females with positive initials lived 3.4 more years, and that there was no difference for females with negative initials. A 4.5-year difference in life expectancy is larger than the difference between the United States and Venezuela and almost as large as the difference between the United States and Algeria. There are plausible explanations for the differences between the United States and Venezuela or Algeria. There is no comparable scientific explanation for why initials might have such large effects on life expectancy.

One problem with grouping people by the year they died is that the popularity of various initials change over time. Suppose, for example, that mortality rates are identical for people with positive and negative initials, but that negative initials are more common today than in the past (which is true). If so, recently deceased people with negative initials will be younger than people with other initials.

To take an extreme example, suppose that the initials ACE stopped being used fifty years ago and the initials GAS only started being used at the same time. This is obviously unrealistic, but it is an easy-to-understand dramatization of the fact that negative initials are becoming increasingly popular. In our stylized example, everyone who died last year with the initials ACE was at least fifty years old and everyone who died with the initials GAS was not yet fifty when they died. This difference has nothing to do with the effects of initials on life expectancy. It has everything to do with changes in the popularity of different initials.

How do we circumvent this problem? By grouping people by the year they were born in. People who was born, say, sixty years ago with the initials ACE would be compared to people born sixty years ago with other initials. People who was born, say, forty years ago with the initials GAS would be compared to people born forty years ago with other initials. Any observed differences in the ages at death would be due to differences in life expectancy, not to changes in the popularity of different initials.

It turns out that when we compare people who were born in the same year, there is no relationship between initials and mortality. On average, males and females with negative initials lived slightly longer than those with positive initials (the opposite of the results reported by the UCSD researchers), but the differences are small and not statistically significant.

An attempt was also made to replicate the UCSD study using data for a longer time period, 1905 through 2003. This, too, did not support the results they reported. Using either the UCSD list of initials or the survey initials, males with negative initials lived slightly *longer*, on average, and the reverse was true of females, but the observed differences are neither substantial or statistically significant.

■ **Don't be Fooled:** A study that leaves out data is waving a big red flag. A decision to include or exclude data sometimes makes all the difference in the world. This decision should be based on the relevance and quality of the data, not on whether the data support or undermine a conclusion that is expected or desired.

It is okay to correct data that were recorded incorrectly. It is sometimes okay to omit outliers. However, the best rule for researchers is, when in doubt, don't leave it out. The best rule for readers is to be wary of studies that discard data. Ask yourself if anything is really clearly wrong with the omitted data. If not, be suspicious. Data may have been discarded simply because they contradicted the desired findings.

14

FLIMSY THEORIES AND ROTTEN DATA

MAJOR LEAGUE BASEBALL (MLB) IS A MAGNET FOR STATISTICIANS because meticulous records have been kept for more than one hundred years. Even better, a baseball fanatic named Sean Lahman allows everyone to download the massive collection of statistics he has maintained on every player and team in MLB history. Let the ransacking begin!

Many statisticians, including the legendary Bill James, have revolutionized our understanding of baseball by developing sabermetrics, which are objective, data-based measurements of player and team performance. Many of the statistics that sabermetricians developed and championed have now become commonplace.

For example, a player's hitting prowess has traditionally been measured by his batting average: the number of base hits divided by the number of times at bat, not including walks, being hit by a pitch, and sacrifice flies. Sabermetricians consider batting average a poor measure of how much a batter helps his team score runs, which is what really counts. Batting average does not give a player credit for getting on base by walking or being hit by a pitch and does not distinguish among singles, doubles, triples, and home runs.

An alternative that sabermetricians have developed is on-base plus slugging (OPS), where the on-base average includes hits, walks, and being hit by a pitch, and the slugging average counts the total bases (1 for a single, 2 for a double, 3 for a triple, and 4 for a home run). OPS is not a perfect measure, but it is easily understood and is a big improvement over the traditional batting average. It is now commonly reported in the news and on baseball cards, and is even calculated for Little League players.

The sabermetrics movement was given publicity and credibility by Michael Lewis's 2003 book *Moneyball* which describes how the Oakland Athletics compete against teams with much higher payrolls by using sabermetrics to identify players that are undervalued (i.e., cheap). If another team thinks Bob is better than Juan because Bob has a higher batting average, and Oakland thinks Juan is better than Bob because Juan has a higher OPS, Oakland will try to trade Bob for Juan. Ironically, sabermetrics is now used by so many major league teams that Oakland's advantage has dissipated and perhaps disappeared.

For academics, the treasure trove of baseball statistics offers a very different opportunity—the chance to uncover patterns in the data that are statistically significant and therefore publishable, especially if the data are tweaked. Many of these discovered patterns make little or no sense, but they get published anyway simply because they are statistically significant.

■ BASEBALL SUPERSTITIONS

Using a rounded wooden stick to hit a round baseball traveling ninety miles an hour and perhaps veering left, right, up, or down may be the most difficult challenge in any sport. If the ball is hit, it might go right to a fielder for an out or it might land safely for a base hit. On average, professional baseball players only get a base hit on one out of four times at bat. Increase that fraction to one out of three and you're headed for the Hall of Fame. From the pitcher's viewpoint, small differences are just as critical in separating all-star pitchers, journeymen, and failures.

Perhaps this is why baseball players are notoriously superstitious, looking for something—no matter how ridiculous—that might tilt the odds in their favor. Heck, researchers often do the same thing, looking for something—no matter how ridiculous—that resembles a pattern.

Wade Boggs had an illustrious career playing third base, mostly with the Boston Red Sox. He had a career batting average of 0.328 (one out of three), played in twelve straight All-Star Games, and was elected to the Baseball Hall of Fame in 2005. If there was a Superstition Hall of Fame, he would be in that too. Boggs woke up at exactly the same time every day and ate chicken at 2:00 p.m. using a 13 recipe rotation over every 14 days (he ate lemon chicken twice). For a night game at Fenway Park, the Chicken Man got to his locker at exactly 3:30, put on his uniform, and went to the dugout to warm-up at 4:00. He then went through a precise warm-up routine, including fielding exactly 150 ground balls. At the end of his fielding warm-up, he stepped on third base, second base, first base, and the baseline (during the game he entered the field by jumping over the baseline) and taking 2 steps to the coach's box and 4 steps to the dugout. By the end of the season, Bogg's footsteps had left permanent footprints in the grass. Boggs always took batting practice at 5:17 and ran wind sprints at 7:17 (an opposing manager once tried to disorient Boggs by having the stadium clock skip from 7:16 to 7:18).

During the game, when Boggs took his position at third base, he smoothed the dirt in front of him with his left foot, tapped his glove three times, and straightened his hat. Every time he batted, he drew the Hebrew word *Chai* ("life") in the batter's box. (He isn't Jewish.)

As obsessive as Boggs was, he seems almost sane compared to Turk Wendell, who pitched in the major leagues for 11 years, from 1993 to 2004. He wore uniform 99 because this was Charlie Sheen's uniform number when he played pitcher Ricky Vaughn ("Wild Thing") in the movie *Major League*. When Wendell signed a contract with the New York Mets in 2000, he asked for a contract of $9,999,999.99. He wore a necklace made from the teeth of wild animals he had killed. Before walking to the mound to pitch, Wendell put 4 pieces of black licorice in his mouth to chew on while he was pitching. Instead of stepping on the baseline (as some players do) or stepping over the baseline (as other players do), Wendell would leap over the baseline. When he reached the mound, Wendell waved to the center fielder until the player waved back. When he needed a new ball, he asked the umpire to roll it to him so he wouldn't have to catch it; if the umpire threw the ball to him, Wendell would either let it bounce off his chest or let it go by him. After every inning, he brushed his teeth in the dugout, something so unusual that it is shown on his Upper Deck rookie baseball card.

Baseball superstitions also apply to teams, the most famous being the Curse of the Bambino. The Boston Red Sox won their fifth world series in 1918, making them the most successful baseball franchise of the time. Before the start of the 1920 season, the Red Sox owner sold the team's best player, Babe Ruth ("the Bambino") to the New York Yankees (who had never won a World Series) for $125,000 cash and a $300,000 loan to finance a Broadway musical starring the owner's girlfriend.

In his first season with the Yankees, Ruth hit fifty-nine home runs, more than any other *team*. The Yankees went on to win more World Series championships than any other team, and the Red Sox went year after disappointing year without a championship. On the four occasions that they played in the World Series, they lost every time—always in dramatic fashion in the seventh and deciding game. Finally, in 2004, after eighty-six years of frustration, the Red Sox won the World Series.

The Chicago Cubs have not yet broken their curse. The Chicago Cubs won the World Series in 1907 and 1908, but have not won since—a drought of more than one hundred years. The legend is that the curse has to do with a goat fell that off a truck and walked inside a Chicago tavern owned by Billy Sianis. Looking for a gimmick, Sianis kept the goat, grew a goatee, started calling himself Billie Goat, and changed the name of his bar to the Billy Goat Tavern.

Billy had two box seat tickets to the fourth game of the 1945 World Series against the Detroit Tigers, with the Cubs ahead two games to one. Billy took his goat with him to the game wearing a blanket with the sign "We got Detroit's goat."

Cubs owner Phil Wrigley told his staff that "the goat stinks," and Sianis was asked to leave and take his goat with him. As he was leaving, Sianis yelled, "The Cubs ain't gonna win no more!" The Cubs lost Game 4 and the next two games, too, thereby losing the World Series. Sianis sent Wrigley a curt telegram, "Who stinks now?"

Attempts by Cubs fans to reverse the curse by bringing goats—alive or butchered—to Wrigley Field and donating goats to people in developing countries have been unsuccessful.

Baseball superstitions are generally amusing and harmless. Ernest Abel and Michael Kruger, two prolific researchers at Wayne State University, have argued that some superstitions can be deadly.

■ IF YOU GIVE ME A D, I'LL DIE

Several studies have found that people with unpopular first names are considered by themselves and others to be inferior to people with popular names. If health is related to self esteem, then life expectancy might be lower for people with unpopular first names. However, a careful study of this very question found no relationship between name popularity and life expectancy.

There is even less reason to think that life expectancy might be affected by the first letter of your name. A small study of MBA students did find that students whose first or last names begin with C or D tended to have lower grade-point averages. However, the difference in average grades for C and D students compared to other students was only 0.02 on a 4-point scale. We also don't know whether this result was the tip of an iceberg of unreported tests.

Nonetheless, inspired by this flimsy finding, Abel and Kruger reported that Major League Baseball players whose first names began with the letter D died, on average, 1.7 years younger than did players whose first names began with the letters E through Z. Their explanation? "Professional athletes are notoriously superstitious." True enough, but this stereotype refers to superstitious *behavior* like wearing the same (unwashed) socks to every game or touching first base when entering the field. Wearing unwashed socks is different from being upset about the first letter of your name. Does anyone seriously believe that a person will die young because he is named Donald instead of Ronald?

There is no persuasive reason for focusing on the letter D. Abel and Kruger argued that, "D is not one of the ABCs and is considered almost a failure." Well, almost failing is not as bad as actually failing, which is generally denoted by an F, and there are twenty-three letters in the alphabet that are not A, B, or C, many of which might seem undesirable.

Pepsi-Cola once had a blind taste test in which people tasted Pepsi from a glass marked M and Coca-Cola from a glass marked Q. More than half preferred Pepsi. Coca-Cola then ran its own test, letting people drink Coke from a glass marked M and Coke from a glass marked Q, They found that most people preferred Coke from the glass labeled M. This prompted their advertising headline: "The Day Coca-Cola Beat Coca-Cola." Evidently, Q is an unattractive letter.

Among twenty-six letters, we can inevitably turn up statistical patterns, particularly if we analyze several subsets and permutations of the data, and then (after the fact) think of explanations for these coincidental relationships. If F turns out badly, F stands for failure. If X turns out badly, X is an unusual letter. If Z turns out badly, Z is the last letter of the alphabet. A valid statistical test identifies the "bad" letter before the test, not afterward.

The GPA study used the five categories A, B, C, D, and E–Z and considered each person's first and last initials, excluding people with conflicting initials. David Jones and James David were put into the D category, while Allen David and David Allen were excluded from the analysis. The only persons in the E–Z category were people like Ethan Fleming whose first and last initials were both E–Z.

Although they cited the MBA study as motivating their own study, Abel and Kruger only reported results for first names. Allen David is A, David Allen is D, and James David is E–Z. Furthermore, Abel and Kruger only reported results for people who were born between 1875 and 1930. They offered no justification for restricting their analysis to the letter D, first names, and this time period, other than . . . well, they worked.

These were not innocent assumptions. Abel and Kruger's conclusion that baseball players whose names began with the letter D die young depends on these artificial restrictions: using first names rather than first and last names and only considering players who were born between 1875 and 1930. Otherwise, there is no statistically significant difference in the average age at death of Major League Baseball players whose names begin with the letter D.

■ A BAD MONTH TO BE BORN

A 1958 Academy Award–winning Disney documentary showed thousands of lemmings marching in tight procession to the edge of a cliff and then falling into the ocean and dying. The narrator solemnly observed that, "A kind of compulsion seizes each tiny rodent and, carried along by an unreasoning hysteria, each falls into step for a march that will take them to a strange destiny." This dramatic scene made "behaving like lemmings" part of our national vocabulary—describing people who imitate each other, mindless of the consequences.

Lemmings are rodents and, ironically for a company with a mouse at the center of its identity, this Disney documentary is completely false. Lemmings prefer to be alone, avoid water if possible, and can swim if they must. So how did Disney film the lemmings' suicidal march? A few dozen lemmings were put on a snow-covered turntable and filmed from different angles as they ran on the spinning table and were launched into the air. With editing, it looked like thousands of lemmings had hysterically followed each other to their deaths. And this staged scene was labeled a documentary! Fiction is stranger than truth.

Lemmings are not suicidal, let alone prone to mass suicides. All living things have an innate will to live. Yet, people do commit suicide. What desperate circumstances could overpower their natural will to survive?

Suicidal people evidently think their lives are so hopelessly depressing that they make the irreversible decision to stop living. Suicide tends to be more common in the spring and early summer—perhaps because some people are crushed by the contrast between their depression and the happiness others feel as the air warms, flowers sprout, and love blooms. This makes sense. However, Abel and Kruger—the two researchers who concluded that D's die young—

made the nonsensical claim that suicidal tendencies depend on the month a person is born in—not the month they choose to die in. This would be a remarkable finding if it were true. But it isn't. Their data and statistical tests were both incorrect.

Abel and Kruger looked at the birth months of Major League Baseball players who committed suicide. Their data are in the column labeled "Observed Number" in Table 14.1. There is a striking dip in July and a spike in August, followed by a decline in September, which led Abel and Kruger to conclude that people born in August tend to be suicidal.

Table 14.1: Baseball Suicides by Birth Month

	Observed Number	Adjusted Number	Expected Value
January	6	9	10.5
February	7	13	10.5
March	5	8	10.5
April	5	10	10.5
May	5	9	10.5
June	6	11	10.5
July	2	3	10.5
August	19	29	10.5
September	5	8	10.5
October	7	11	10.5
November	3	5	10.5
December	6	10	10.5
TOTAL	76	126	126

Some birth months will inevitably have more suicides than other months. Before condemning August, we need to consider whether the observed pattern makes sense and whether it is statistically persuasive. For the first question, there is no credible reason why people born in August should be more inclined to commit suicide than are people born in July or September.

For a statistical analysis, we can compare the observed number of monthly suicides with the expected number, taking into account the number of births in each month. For example, if 10 percent of all players have January birth months, we expect 10 percent of the suicides to have January birth months.

Abel and Kruger did something completely different—and completely wrong. They calculated something they called the "adjusted number" of suicides by dividing the observed number of suicides in each birth month by the total number of players born in that month, multiplying this ratio by 1,000, and rounding off to the nearest whole number. This puzzling calculation (shown in the "Adjusted Number" column in Table 14.1) increased the total number of suicides by 66 percent, from 76 to 126. They then divided 126 by 12 to obtain a 10.5 expected value for each month. When these manipulations were finished, they concluded that there was a statistically significant relationship between birth month and suicide.

Not so fast! We can't invent 66 percent more suicides. The only valid way to get more data is to collect more data, for example, by including other professional athletes. Another problem is that their data are wrong! At the time they wrote their paper, 86 players with known birth months had committed suicide—not the 76 players they reported. In addition, there were 5 suicides with July birth months (3 more than Abel and Kruger reported) and 16 with August birth months (3 fewer than they reported). They counted 3 July birth months as August birth months.

When the errors in their analysis are corrected, the observed monthly variations in suicides are not statistically significant. In fact, we can anticipate variations among the birth months as large as those actually observed more than half the time.

The proverbial bottom line is that there is no theoretical basis for a July dip, August surge, and September crash in suicide birth months; the data were misreported; and the statistical procedure was incorrect. When the correct data are correctly analyzed, there is no relationship between birth month and suicide.

■ THE HALL OF FAME KISS OF DEATH

In another paper, Abel and Kruger argued that "baseball fame may carry a heavy price" in that Major League Baseball players who are elected to the Hall of Fame die, on average, five years younger than other players. This surprising assertion contradicts the widespread belief that positive self-esteem enhances physical health. Indeed, remember that it was Abel and Kruger who argued that baseball players whose first names begin with the letter D live shorter lives because of low self-esteem. If something as trivial as having D for a first initial causes an early death, then surely something as real and tangible as being the best at one's chosen profession should lengthen life expectancy.

Something must be wrong with their research. And indeed there is.

Abel and Kruger took their data from the Lahman database. For each Hall of Famer who was alive when elected, Abel and Kruger identified peers who were still living on the election date and had the same birth year as the Hall of Fame player. They recorded each player's year of death or, if no death date was listed, assumed the player was still alive. They then applied a statistical procedure specifically designed to handle situations like this where some members of the sample are not yet deceased. So far, so good.

The problem is that in many cases, the reason no death date is listed in the Lahman data base is not because the player is still alive, but because the death date is unknown. *Every* Hall of Fame player is either known to be alive or has a known death date. In contrast, many obscure players, particularly from the early years of baseball, have unknown death dates. Abel and Kruger's treatment of deceased players with unknown death dates as still alive artificially increased the calculated longevity of players who are not in the Hall of Fame.

For example, Cy Young, who was elected to the Hall of Fame in 1937, was born in 1867 and died in 1955 at age 88. For comparison, Abel and Kruger used 22 players who were born in 1867 and were apparently still alive in 1937, when Cy Young was elected to the Hall of Fame. Nineteen of these 22 peers have known death dates and their average age at death is 83 years, 5 years younger than Cy Young. Three peers do not have death dates, so Abel and Kruger assumed these 3 players were still alive in 2005 when they did their study—even though they would have been 138 years old! If these 3 players had died in 2005, the average age at death of the 22 peers would increase to 90 years. Because these 3 players were presumed alive in 2005, their implied longevity is even longer.

So, the peers with known death dates died, on average, 5 years younger than Cy Young, but incorrectly adding in 3 players with unknown death dates as if they were still going strong at 138 makes it seem that Cy Young's peers lived, on average, more than 2 years longer than he did.

Another mistake Abel and Kruger made is that, instead of calculating the age at death for each player, they calculated the number of years they lived after being elected to the Hall of Fame. This is problematic, most obviously because life expectancy depends on a person's age. Abel and Kruger's procedure does not distinguish between Elmer Flick, who was eighty-seven years old when he was elected to the Hall of Fame, and Cal Ripken, Jr., who was forty-seven years old when he was elected. Abel and Kruger's calculation of the average number of years that players lived past their induction to the Hall of Fame is a useless statistic. Age at death is a better number.

Their analysis was redone using the age at death for players with known death dates. As of 2010, there were 292 persons in the Baseball Hall of Fame, of whom 164 were alive in the year they were elected. Of these 164 Hall of Famers, 62 were still alive and 102 were deceased in 2010. Each deceased Hall of Famer was matched with all deceased players who were born in the same year and, like the Hall of Famer, were alive when he was elected to the Hall of Fame.

Contrary to the conclusion reached by Abel and Kruger, Hall of Fame players, on average, lived about one year longer than their peers. However, this difference is not close to being statistically significant. There is no statistically persuasive difference in the life expectancy of players elected to the Hall of Fame and their peers.

■ **Don't be Fooled:** In a fervent quest for publishable theories—no matter how implausible—it is tempting to tweak the data to provide more support for the theory and it is natural to not look too closely if a statistical test gives the hoped-for answer. Be wary of studies where the researcher ransacked the data for a pattern and then bolstered the statistical significance by massaging or pruning data that did not fit the pattern. If a statistical conclusion seems unbelievable, check the data and the tests. Even professionals make mistakes.

15

DON'T CONFUSE ME
WITH FACTS

N JUNE 1972 FIVE MEN BROKE INTO THE HEADQUARTERS OF THE
Democratic National Committee at the Watergate Hotel complex
in Washington, DC. They were evidently trying to steal copies of
the Democrats' campaign plans and install listening devices on the
telephones and elsewhere in the offices.

A Watergate security guard noticed that some of the doors' latches
had been taped to keep the doors from locking. He called the police and
they caught and arrested the five burglars. The nation wondered, who
but Republicans would break into Democratic committee headquarters? There was nothing of value there except perhaps to Republicans.
Who authorized this break-in? How high up the Republican chain of
command did this go? Did President Richard Nixon know?

Nixon's press secretary dismissed the incident as "a third-rate
burglary attempt." Nixon told the nation, "I can say categorically
that . . . no one in the White House staff, no one in this administration, presently employed, was involved in this very bizarre incident."
Nixon had long been called "Tricky Dick" because of his dirty and
sometimes bizarre campaign tactics, and many wondered if this was
yet another one of his dirty tricks.

The Watergate burglary turned into the Watergate scandal as evidence mounted that the White House had been involved in the planning and, even worse, that Nixon had misled the nation about his
involvement. Americans tend to forgive politicians and celebrities who
admit their mistakes and to punish those who lie. One of the burglars

turned out to be a Republican Party security aide. Tens of thousands of dollars in donations to Nixon's re-election campaign had been deposited in the burglars' bank accounts. This was not a third-rate burglary.

A special US Senate committee held Watergate hearings which were televised live to the nation with day after day of incriminating testimony. The most dramatic was something completely unexpected. Nixon had installed microphones that secretly recorded conversations in the Oval Office, the Cabinet Room, and his private office. These recordings would settle once and for all the question of Nixon's involvement in the initial planning and subsequent cover-up of the burglary. The Supreme Court forced Nixon to turn over the tapes and, even with eighteen and a half minutes suspiciously erased, there was still plenty of evidence that Nixon had been involved in efforts to hinder the FBI investigation and pay hush money to the burglars.

The House Judiciary Committee voted to recommend impeachment of the president for obstruction of justice, abuse of power, and contempt of Congress. Nixon's support within his own party melted away and it became clear that he was on his way out. Clear to everyone but an otherwise obscure congressman who could not see what he did not want to see.

Representative Earl Landgrebe from Indiana achieved notoriety mostly for his unwavering support of Nixon throughout the Watergate hearings. At one point, he told reporters, "Don't confuse me with facts; I've got a closed mind." On another occasion, he said, "I'm going to stick with my president even if he and I have to be taken out of this building and shot." Nixon resigned the next day. Langrebe earned a place on the *The New Times Magazine*'s 1974 list of the "ten dumbest" congressmen.

Landgrebe is certainly not the only politician with a closed mind. Nor are politicians alone. Even supposedly dispassionate scientists are said to be like artists, in that they fall in love with their models. We all have theories. Why the stock market went down. Why a company is successful. Why someone got promoted. And we are all tempted to emphasize data that confirm our theories and either ignore contradictory data or else misinterpret conflicting data as actually confirming our theory. It is, however, more disappointing and disillusioning when supposedly objective scientists turn out to be as human as the rest of us, failing to see what is clear to everyone else.

ESP

Extrasensory perception (ESP) is the ability to receive information without using the five physical senses: sight, hearing, taste, smell, and touch. ESP includes both telepathy (reading another person's mind) and clairvoyance (identifying an unseen object). These psychic abilities are generally immediate, but could involve precognition—receiving information about something that has not yet happened.

We can illustrate these psychic abilities with tricks a mentalist might perform in a magic show:

- Telepathy: A volunteer selects a card from a shuffled deck, looks at it, and places it back in the deck. The mentalist says that he can read the volunteer's mind and proves it by identifying the selected card.
- Clairvoyance: Audience members write personal notes (perhaps the name of a deceased relative) on slips of paper, which are then put into a hat. The mentalist says that he can see the unseen and proves it by removing papers from the hat one by one, holding each paper tightly clinched in his hand, and then identifying what is written on the slip of paper.
- Precognition: The mentalist says that he can predict which of four colors will be selected by a volunteer. After the volunteer chooses a color (either by looking at face up cards or turning over a face down card), the mentalist opens an envelope that was sealed beforehand and has been lying in plain sight. The color written on a slip of paper removed from the envelope matches the volunteer's choice.

These are all standard magic tricks performed by magicians who have no special powers except the ability to put on a convincing and entertaining performance.

Do such psychic powers really exist, or are they just clever tricks? No one but a magician has ever demonstrated 100 percent accuracy, but some serious researchers believe that ordinary people can consistently outperform random guessing.

The most famous ESP researcher was J.B. Rhine. While working on his PhD in botany at the University of Chicago, Rhine abruptly changed careers after he attended a talk on spiritualism given by Sir Arthur Conan Doyle. Doyle was famous because of the stories he had written about Sherlock Holmes, a fictional detective who was known for his meticulous examination of crime scenes and his extraordinary logical reasoning.

Doyle was the antithesis of the Holmes character he created. He was fascinated by paranormal phenomena, which by definition, have no logical explanation, and his desire to believe was so strong that he ignored all evidence that might threaten his beliefs.

Perhaps the most embarrassing example involved five fairy photographs taken in 1917 and 1920 by two young girls who lived in Cottingley, England. The first of these photographs is shown in Figure 15.1.

Figure 15.1: Fairies are Real (and Santa Claus, too)

Despite the two-dimensional appearance of the fairies, the odd lighting, the absence of movement in the fairy wings, and the overall implausibility, Doyle was so certain of the authenticity of the fairy photos that he wrote a book about them, *The Coming of the Fairies*. Many years later, long after Doyle had died, one of the girls admitted the obvious. The fairies were photographs cut out of magazines and stuck on hat pins.

Doyle also firmly believed that the living could communicate with the dead. Modern spiritualism started with the Fox sisters, three teenagers in rural New York, who conducted séances in which they sat with gullible customers at a table in a dark room, while the deceased used rapping sounds to communicate with the living. When one of the sisters finally confessed that it was trickery (the mysterious rapping sounds were made by cracking her toe joints!), Doyle refused to believe her: "Nothing that she could say in that regard would in the least change my opinion."

The magician Harry Houdini tried to convince Doyle that he was being taken advantage of by frauds, but Doyle did not believe him. When Houdini showed Doyle the tricks that fake spiritualists used, Doyle concluded that Houdini was covering up his own supernatural powers. Doyle even believed that Houdini accomplished his famous escape tricks by dematerializing himself. We are all resistant to evidence that threatens our beliefs, but Doyle's gullibility and self-deception were astonishing.

We might suppose that Doyle's embarrassing acceptance of the fairy photos and his stubborn denial of the Fox sister's confession would undermine his credibility, especially among scientists. We would be wrong. J.B. Rhine's reaction to Doyle's Chicago talk on spiritualism was euphoric. He recalled later that, "This mere possibility [of communication with the deceased] was the most exhilarating thought I had had in years."

Soon after completing his PhD in botany, Rhine enrolled in the psychology program at Harvard to study with Professor William McDougall, who had recently been president of two organizations devoted to supporting research on psychic phenomena. While they were in Boston, Rhine and his wife attended a séance given by a then famous, now infamous, medium named Mina ("Margery") Crandon.

The Rhines were suspicious (after all, why are séances always done in the dark?). Afterward, they published a detailed exposé, explaining why they were convinced that "the whole game was a base and brazen trickery."

Arthur Conan Doyle was incensed. He sent a letter to the *Boston Herald* condemning the Rhines's "colossal impertinence" and paid for display ads in Boston newspapers that said simply, "J.B. RHINE IS A MONUMENTAL ASS." As in other cases, Doyle was completely unwilling to consider evidence that might undermine his beliefs. This incident is also interesting because it shows that, early in his career, Rhine had an open mind about psychic phenomena. He genuinely wanted to investigate whether they were real. However, his judgment soon became clouded by a desire to believe.

After a year at Harvard, Rhine followed McDougall to Duke University in 1927, where McDougall became chair of the psychology department and supported Rhine's establishment of the Parapsychology Laboratory where Rhine conducted decades of research on extrasensory perception.

His most famous experiments involved the Zener cards, which we saw earlier in chapter two. A Zener pack consists of twenty-five cards, five cards of each of five designs: circle, cross, wavy lines, square, and star. In a typical experiment, one person (the sender) shuffles the deck and then turns the twenty-five cards over, one by one, staring at each card for a few moments and then recording the symbol. Another person (the receiver) tries to identify each card. Sometimes, the receiver is told during the test whether a guess is correct or incorrect; other times, the sender does not reveal the correct answers until after the deck is finished. Either way, the answers are recorded and a statistical analysis is done after the test is over.

Rhine's 1934 book *Extra-Sensory Perception* described the promising results of his Duke experiments. *The New York Times* science editor gushed that, "[T]here can be no doubt of the value of his work . . . Dr. Rhine has made a name for himself . . . because of his originality, his scrupulous objectivity, his strict adherence to the scientific method." Articles about ESP popped up in newspapers and magazines worldwide. Rhine became famous. Ordinary citizens bought packs of Zener cards for ten cents and did ESP tests in their own homes. ESP fever was contagious.

Irving Langmuir was a distinguished chemist and physicist who won the Nobel Prize in Chemistry in 1932. He had a deep respect for science and a deep skepticism of implausible claims that had not been tested rigorously. Around the time Rhine's ESP book was published, Langmuir arranged for a visit to Rhine's Duke laboratory so that he could see for himself what was going on. Several years later, in 1953, Langmuir gave a talk titled "Pathological Science," a term he invented to describe "the science of things that aren't so." Part of this talk involved Langmuir's recollection of his visit to Rhine's laboratory. Langmuir had been amazed to discover that Rhine was discarding some of his data, putting hundreds of thousands of Zener cards in sealed envelopes in a file cabinet because Rhine felt that some participants were deliberately giving wrong answers! If you believe something strongly enough, excuses can always be found.

A neutral researcher would analyze all the data, the correct and incorrect predictions, the positive and negative results. For example, if the receivers are simply guessing randomly in a test involving twenty-five Zener cards, we expect the receivers to average five correct guesses. (It is a little more complicated than this because the receiver knows that there are only five circles, five pluses, and so on in the pack, but five correct is approximately correct.)

Suppose one person gets seven right and another person gets three right. An impartial observer would say nothing unusual happened, since they averaged five correct. Someone looking for evidence of ESP might say that the first person demonstrated ESP by getting more than five correct, and the second person also demonstrated ESP, since she was successful in her efforts to embarrass Rhine by making incorrect predictions.

This is what Rhine did. Because he strongly believed in ESP, he felt that it was perfectly legitimate to separate the positive and negative results and count each as evidence of ESP. The positive results showed that people had ESP. The negative results also showed that people had ESP, but were using their ESP to humiliate him.

Langmuir came away convinced that Rhine was an honest victim of self-deception. Rhine's experiments were not evidence of ESP but, instead, evidence of how well-intentioned researchers are blind to the statistical mischief they are committing.

Langmuir also said that when he told Rhine that he thought his ESP research was pathological science, Rhine replied, "I wish you'd publish that. I'd love to have you publish it. That would stir up an awful lot of interest . . . I'd have more graduate students. We ought to have more graduate students. This thing is so important that we should have more people realize its importance. This should be one of the biggest departments in the university." Rhine unintentionally revealed that he was no longer an impartial researcher, trying to determine whether ESP is real, but a partisan advocate striving for fame and funding.

ESP experiments are also a classic example of selective reporting. Even if ESP does not exist, we expect one out of every twenty people tested to make enough correct guesses to be considered statistically significant. With thousands of people tested multiple times, some incredible results are inevitable—and these remarkable results are the ones that get reported. A test result with a one-in-a-thousand chance of occurring is not so remarkable if we know that a thousand tests were conducted.

In his 1953 talk, Langmuir gave a personal example that involved his nephew, David Langmuir:

> [David] and a group of other young men thought they would like to check up Rhine's work so they got some cards and they spent many evenings together finding how these cards turned up and they got well above 5. They began to get quite excited about it and they kept on, and they kept on, and they were right on the point of writing Rhine about the thing. And they kept on a little longer and things began to fall off, and fall off a little more, and they fell off a little more. And after many, many, many days, they fell down to an average of five—grand average—so they <u>didn't</u> write to Rhine. Now if Rhine had received that information, that this reputable body of men had gone ahead and gotten a value of 8 or 9 or 10 after so many trials, why he would have put it in his book. How much of that sort of thing, when you are fed information of that sort by people who are

interested—how are you going to weigh the things that are published in the book?

This kind of selective reporting is also called the "publication effect," in that statistically significant results find their way into journals and books, while insignificant results are not reported.

The first antidote to data grubbing and selective reporting is common sense. Many people believe in ESP, but others do not. Perhaps the safest thing to say is that if ESP does exist, it does not seem to be of much practical importance. There is no evidence, for example, that people can use ESP to bankrupt casinos in Las Vegas, Atlantic City, or Monte Carlo.

The second antidote is fresh data. People who score well should be retested. Rhine reported that when he retested his high scorers, their scores almost always declined. This happened so often that he called it the "decline effect." His explanation: "They were no doubt fatigued and bored." An alternative explanation is that the initial high scores were just the selective reporting of lucky guesses.

The large number of persons tested isn't the only difficulty in assessing the statistical significance of Rhine's results. He also looked for parts of a test where a subject did well, which is also data grubbing. A remarkable performance by 5 percent of the people tested or by 1 person on 5 percent of a test isn't really surprising.

Rhine also looked for "forward displacement" or "backward displacement," where a person's choices didn't match the contemporaneous cards, but did match the next card, the previous card, two cards hence, or two cards previous. This multiplicity of potential matches increases the chances of finding coincidental patterns. Rhine also considered it remarkable when a person got a high score on parts of a test and a low score ("negative ESP") on other parts. Rhine explained how a subject

may begin his run one one side of the mean and swing to the other side just as far by the time he ends a run; or he may go below in the middle of the run and above it at both ends. The two trends of deviations may cancel each other out and the series as a whole average close to "chance."

He described the results of one test as follows:

> [T]he displacement was both forward and backward when one of
> the senders was looking at the card, and only in the forward direc-
> tion with another individual as sender; and whether the displace-
> ment shifted to the first or second card away from the target
> depended on the speed of the test.

With so many subjects and so many possibilities, it should be easy
to find patterns, even in random guesses.

The main lesson learned from Rhine's research is to watch out for
research based on ransacking the data. People who examine the data
from every angle are sure to find something. All this proves is that
they examined the data from every angle.

Rhine's ESP research was provocative, but his understandable enthusiasm fueled the data grubbing and selective reporting that undermined the credibility of his results. ESP tests would be less controversial
and more convincing—one way or the other—if there were more uses
and fewer abuses of statistical tests. Since 1996, James Randi, a magician
and self-proclaimed skeptic, has offered a $1 million prize to anyone
who can demonstrate "under proper observing conditions, evidence of
any paranormal, supernatural, or occult power or event." The prize is
still unclaimed.

■ THE HOUDINI CHALLENGE

Early in his career, Harry Houdini posed as a medium who could
carry messages from the spirit world. For part of his act, Houdini allowed himself to be tied to a chair in a "spirit cabinet" with bells and
tambourines at his feet. After pretending to go into a trance, a curtain
was closed. The instruments then made loud noises before flying over
the heads of the audience. When the curtain was opened, Houdini was
found still tied firmly to his chair. The trick is that, tied in the right way,
it is very easy to slip one's hands in and out of ropes as needed to shake
bells and tambourines and throw them out of the cabinet. (I know this
because a medium once chose me from the audience to come up on

stage and go into a spirit cabinet with her. Once we were inside the cabinet, she asked me to play along with her act. I did.) The trick is comical in its simplicity and audacity. However, with proper presentation before an audience that wants to believe in spirits, it can be very impressive.

For another part of his act, Houdini went into a trance and transmitted messages from the deceased. Here, the trick was that Houdini compiled the messages beforehand by talking to local residents, reading old newspaper articles, and writing down names and dates from a local cemetery. One performance was reportedly so convincing that when Houdini spelled the name of a man whose throat had been cut, people fled in panic.

Later in his career, his beloved mother died and Houdini was desperate to contact her. He met with several spiritualists and was repeatedly disappointed. Houdini easily identified the tricks they used to fool the gullible and none of the spiritualists could guess the last word his mother said before she died ("forgive"). He became obsessed with exposing mediums as "vultures who preyed on the bereaved." Houdini went to séances wearing a disguise and accompanied by a reporter and police officer. When he figured out the trickery, he would take off his disguise and announce, "I am Houdini and you are a fraud!"

He also made spiritualism part of his stage show, revealing the tricks of the most famous mediums. He offered a $10,000 prize to anyone who could perform a supernatural feat that he could not replicate. No one could claim the prize.

As a final challenge, Houdini and his wife Bess agreed on a secret message that would be sent by whoever died first. The first part of the message was "Rosabelle." This was his wife's nickname and was inscribed on the inside of her wedding band. The second part of the message was based on a code they used when they performed together, using ten words to represent numbers:

1. Pray
2. Answer
3. Say
4. Now
5. Tell

6. Please
7. Speak
8. Quickly
9. Look
10. Be Quick (could also represent 0)

For example, Bess might enter the audience, take a coin from a volunteer, and ask Harry, "Please tell me the last two digits of the date." The words Please and Tell signaled Harry that 65 was the correct answer. For other stunts, each number corresponded to a letter—for example, Answer represents the second letter of the alphabet (B) and Now is the fourth letter (D). For later letters in the alphabet, words can be combined with a pause signifying the end of the letter. Thus a phrase using Answer (2) and Pray (1) would represent U, the twenty-first letter in the alphabet.

The secret coded message that Harry (or Bess) would try to send from the afterlife was Answer (B), Tell (E), Pray Answer (L), Look (I), Tell (E), Answer Answer (V), Tell (E). The complete decoded message was "Rosabelle, believe."

After Houdini's death in 1926, Bess held hundreds of unsuccessful séances, including annual Halloween séances, with a $10,000 reward for anyone who could receive the ten words from Houdini (Rosabelle plus the nine code words). In 1929, Bess announced that a spiritualist named Arthur Ford had broken the Houdini code, but both later admitted that this had been faked. Bess said that it had been deliberately faked (perhaps because of her romantic involvement with Ford or because she wanted publicity); Ford said that he had tricked Bess into revealing the secret. In any case, Ford did not claim the prize.

In 1936, after yet another unsuccessful Halloween séance performed on top the legendary Knickerbocker Hotel in Hollywood and broadcast by radio around the world, Bess put out a candle she had kept burning next to Houdini's photograph. She later said that "ten years is long enough to wait for any man."

■ A FAMILY'S INFATUATION WITH THE PARANORMAL

In 1872 Sir Francis Galton reported that, "An eminent authority has recently published a challenge to test the efficacy of prayer by actual experiment." Galton responded to this challenge by proposing a comparison of the recoveries of two groups of people hospitalized for fractures and amputations: "The one consisting of markedly religious, piously-befriended individuals, the other of those who were remarkably cold-hearted and neglected."

Galton did not carry out this study, but he did report the longevity of eminent British clergymen and the British Royal Family, who received public prayers from churches all over England every Sunday: "Grant him/her in health long to live." Galton calculated that the life expectancy of clergymen (66.4 years) was slightly *lower* than that of lawyers (66.5 years) and doctors (67.0 years). For the Royal Family, the most prayed-for people in England, life expectancy was only 64.0 years, substantially *less* than for other aristocrats (67.3 years). If anything, it seemed that prayer did more harm than good.

Galton concluded that, "The civilised world has already yielded an enormous amount of honest conviction to the inexorable requirements of solid fact; and it seems to me clear that all belief in the efficacy of prayer, in the sense which I have been considering it, must be yielded also." In ordinary English, prayer does not prolong life.

However, Galton's comparisons are not really scientific comparisons. In his proposed observation of hospitalized persons who were prayed for and those who were neglected, there may be systematic differences between the two groups. Perhaps the "cold-hearted and neglected" tend to be poorer, older, or less concerned with hygiene. In addition, the proposed comparison was not double-blind, with neither patient or doctor aware of who was being prayed for. If the doctors know who is being prayed for, this might influence their subjective assessments of the recoveries.

Galton's comparison of the clergy and the British Royal Family with lawyers, doctors, and aristocrats is undermined by the fact that people are not randomly assigned to these groups, but are in these groups by ancestry or choice. Maybe there is something special (good or bad) about royal genes. Maybe people who choose to become lawyers or doctors are systematically different (perhaps more energetic or wealthier) than clergymen. Perhaps doctors are more proactive about their health and more informed about proper treatment. Galton's proposed and actual studies both had serious flaws.

Now, fast forward a hundred years to a serious study of the power of prayer. This story begins with a remarkable family, the Targs, and their prominent involvement in the investigation of many paranormal phenomena, including space aliens, the spirit world, remote viewing, distant healing, and the power of prayer. The most important lesson is that even very intelligent people latch onto flimsy beliefs and won't let go.

WILLIAM TARG

William Targ was the son of Russian parents who immigrated to the United States. He had a lifelong love of books and a fascination with the paranormal. When he was only twenty-two years old, he borrowed $800 from his mother and opened a Chicago bookstore with a large section of books about ESP, UFOs, ghosts, teleportation, and other paranormal phenomena.

Targ later became editor-in-chief at Putnam and published many paranormal books, including Erich Von Däniken's *Chariots of the Gods*, which claims that the Egyptian pyramids, Stonehenge, and other ancient marvels were created by space aliens ("ancient astronauts") or by humans who had been taught by aliens. Von Däniken's primary "evidence" for this absurd theory are his beliefs that prehistoric people could not do such incredible things on their own and that many ancient religious gods were, in fact, aliens. He even found ancient pottery depicting humans interacting with these alien "gods."

Targ described *Chariots of the Gods* as "quasi-scientific." Scientists and historians have been less charitable, generally viewing it as uninformed, illogical, deceptive, fabricated, and even plagiarized from other books derived from short stories written by H. P. Lovecraft. The

Public Broadcasting System science show *NOVA* found the person who made the pots that Von Däniken claimed came from a prehistoric archeological site and depicted human encounters with aliens. When confronted with this deception, Von Däniken explained that "some people would only believe if they saw proof." Some skeptics have suggested that *Chariots of the Gods* may itself be a hoax, an intentionally deceptive book written for the gullible.

Perhaps even more incredible is a Putnam book called *The Book of James (William James, That Is)*. The author, Susy Smith, wrote thirty books on parapsychology and the survival of consciousness after physical death, including *Life is Forever: Evidence for Survival after Death*, *Prominent American Ghosts*, and *Today's Witches*. Smith says that *The Book of James* came to her via automatic writing controlled by William James, a deceased Harvard professor.

The messages sent by James through Smith are very comforting, both for those who have lost loved ones and for those anxious about their own eventual deaths. After death, the spirit leaves the body and enters the Etheric, where there are many amusements including poker games, theatre, and ballet lessons. Smith/James gushes that, "No one, you see, has to hunt for a baby-sitter, drive through traffic halfway across town, or remain home because of illness. And no one refrains from going out at night for fear of being mugged." Despite these conveniences, some spirits choose to watch soap operas on television. When a spirit tires of these diversions, it can move on to Ultimate Perfection and eternal bliss. Laggards will regret the time they wasted in the Etheric.

Before her death in 2001, Smith designed an afterlife experiment with a $10,000 prize to anyone who could receive an encrypted message that Smith had stored on a computer at the University of Arizona's Human Energy Systems Laboratory and that she would send from the spirit world after her death. No one has collected the prize.

Smith's experiment is similar to Houdini's famous challenge— except that Smith hoped to demonstrate that the deceased can communicate with the living, while Houdini anticipated that he would demonstrate the opposite.

RUSSELL TARG

William Targ's son, Russell, was a physicist who published more than one hundred papers and received two NASA awards for his pioneering work on lasers and laser communications. He also strongly believed that humans have paranormal abilities to read each other's minds and to move objects just by willing them to move.

Russell cofounded a $25 million project at the Stanford Research Institute as part of the STARGATE program funded by the CIA and the Defense Intelligence Agency to investigate psychic abilities. Russell concluded that virtually everyone is capable of "remote viewing," the ability to perceive unseen objects. Russell also believed that an Israeli magician named Uri Geller had demonstrated a psychic ability to control dice, but he was less certain of Geller's ability to use mental powers to bend keys and spoons.

Outside scientists criticized the SRI experiments for inadequate controls and record keeping. They attributed the reported successes to inadvertent cues from the researchers or deception by the participants. Several professional magicians, including James Randi, have shown how Geller's feats could be performed using magic tricks that are familiar to magicians, but mystifying to others.

In the 1990s, the government concluded that nothing useful had come from remote-viewing research and stopped supporting it.

One of Geller's managers has admitted that he saw Geller cheating during his stage performances and even helped him on occasion—for example, taking notes on people entering the theatre and their seat numbers so that Geller could pretend to divine objects in the pockets and purses of audience members.

Geller has taken to calling himself an entertainer and mystifier rather than a psychic. In a 2007 interview published in a magician's magazine, Geller said, "I'll no longer say that I have supernatural powers. I am an entertainer. I want to do a good show. My entire character has changed." In 2008, Geller received a Services to Magic Award at the International Magic Convention and said, "I had the idea and cheekiness to call it psychic, in fact all I wanted was to be rich and famous, I wanted to buy my mother a TV."

ELISABETH TARG

Elisabeth Targ was Russell's daughter and William's grand-daughter—an apple that didn't fall far from the family tree. As a child, she tried to remote-view wrapped presents, predict presidential elections, and guess random colors on her father's ESP machine. Her father recalled that he "expected her to be intelligent, bright, and psychic." Elisabeth graduated from high school at fifteen, already fluent in French, German, and Russian, and enrolled at Pomona College. During her first semester, she conducted a variation on her father's remote-viewing experiment by having student volunteers guess the contents of a box when neither the student or Elisabeth knew the contents. Her professor didn't like the experiment. Elisabeth left Pomona and earned a bachelor's degree and medical degree from Stanford University.

In the 1990s Elisabeth investigated whether patients with advanced AIDS could be healed by distant prayer. Unlike Galton's speculative study a century earlier, Elisabeth wanted to do a scientific study. Twenty patients with advanced AIDS at the University of California San Francisco Medical Center were randomly divided into two groups, with 10 patients sent prayers and positive energy from self-proclaimed healers living an average of 1,500 miles away. The 6-month study was double-blind in that neither the patients or the doctors knew which patients were being prayed for. (The healers of course knew who they were praying for.) Four of the 20 patients died (the expected mortality rate), but none were in the prayer group.

Encouraged by these results, Elisabeth did a second six-month study involving forty AIDS patients divided into two double-blind groups. Photos of those in the prayer group were sent to forty experienced distance healers (including Buddhists, Christians, Jews, and shamans) who took turns trying to work their magic. This study found that those in the prayer group spent fewer days in the hospital and suffered from fewer AIDS-related illnesses. The results were statistically significant and published in a prestigious medical journal.

Elisabeth became a celebrity because of her provocative findings and scientific rigor. People with agendas cited her work as proof of the existence of God or the inadequacy of conventional views of mind, body, time, and space. Elisabeth did not speculate about why it worked. She just knew that it worked.

She was awarded a $1.5 million grant from the National Institute of Health (NIH) for an even larger study of AIDS patients and for investigating whether distant healers could shrink malignant tumors in patients with brain cancer. Shortly after being awarded this grant, Elisabeth was discovered to have brain cancer herself and, despite prayers and healing energy from all over the world, she died four months later.

After her death, problems were discovered with her research. By the luck of the draw, the four oldest patients in her original study had been put in the non-prayer group. The fact that all four died may have been because of their age, not the absence of prayer.

The second study had planned to compare the mortality of the prayer and non-prayer groups. However, one month after the six-month study began, triple-cocktail therapy became commonplace and only one of the forty patients died—which demonstrated the effectiveness of the triple cocktail but eliminated the possibility of a statistical comparison of the prayer and non-prayer groups.

Elisabeth and her colleague, Fred Sicher, turned instead to physical symptoms, quality of life, mood scores, and CP4+ counts. There were no differences between the prayer and non-prayer groups. Her father told Elisabeth to keep looking. If you believe something, evidence to the contrary is not important. If you believe something, what harm is there in finding evidence that supports your belief? Finally she found something—hospital stays and doctor visits, although medical insurance was surely a confounding influence.

Then Elisabeth and Fred learned about a paper listing twenty-three AIDS-related illnesses. Maybe they could find a difference between the prayer and non-prayer groups for some of these twenty-three illnesses. Unfortunately, data on these illnesses had not been recorded while her double-blind test was being conducted. Undeterred, Elisabeth and Fred pored over the medical records even though they now knew which patients were in the control group and which were in the prayer group. When they were done, they reported that the prayer group fared better than the non-prayer group for some illnesses. Their published paper suggested that the study had been designed to investigate these illnesses and did not reveal that the illness data were assembled after the study was over and the double-blind controls had been lifted. Perhaps they found what they were looking for simply because they kept looking. Perhaps they found what they was looking for because the data were no longer double-blind.

Elisabeth's NIH study continued after her tragic death. It found no meaningful differences in mortality, illnesses, or symptoms between the prayer and non-prayer groups. An even larger study, conducted by the Harvard Medical School, looked at 1,800 patients who were recovering from coronary artery bypass graft surgery. The patients were randomly assigned to 3 groups: some patients were told they would receive distant prayer and did; other patients were told they *might* receive prayer and did; the final group were told they might receive prayer but did not. There was no difference between the prayer- and non-prayer patients but, oddly enough, those who were told they definitely would receive prayer were more likely to develop complications than were those who were only told that they might receive prayer.

Once again, wishful thinking doused by facts. Wanting something to be so does not make it so. The Houdini Challenge, the Susy Smith Challenge, the James Randi Challenge—the prizes are all unclaimed, yet some people still believe the unbelievable.

■ **Don't be Fooled:** Extraordinary claims require extraordinary evidence. True believers settle for less.

If Arthur Conan Doyle could refuse to believe a con woman's confession that she pretended to communicate with the deceased, so can anyone. If J. B. Rhine could conclude that a volunteer's failure to guess cards correctly was evidence that the volunteer was guessing cards correctly, so can anyone. If Elisabeth Targ could believe that there is no harm in ransacking data for evidence that people can be healed by distant prayer, so can anyone. It is very hard to be open to the possibility of being wrong. But we should try.

16

DATA WITHOUT THEORY

ATA ARE JUST DATA. EVEN IF WE SEE A CLEAR AND OBVIOUS PATTERN, we still need a logical reason for believing that the pattern is something more mere coincidence. Sometimes, an explanation is easily found and provides a good reason for predicting that the pattern will persist. Because of the Thanksgiving holiday, the consumption of turkey in the United States has shown a bulge in November for decades and will probably continue to do so for years to come. Because of the cold weather, construction activity declines in winter in the northern part of the United States and will most likely continue doing so.

Other times, all we have is data without theory—and that is treacherous. A well-meaning monitoring of cell-phone calls in Rwanda found that a decline in the movement of people outside their villages was usually followed a few weeks later by an outbreak of cholera. Perhaps people stayed home when the first symptoms hit? Who knows? Who cares that we don't have a logical explanation? All that matters is that the project had stumbled on an unexpected way to predict cholera outbreaks. Right?

Not really. It turns out that the reason people stopped venturing outside their villages was that flash floods had washed the roads away, and this flooding also increased the risk of cholera. The Rwandan government could observe flash floods easily without big-brother surveillance of its citizens' every movement, and cell-phone data couldn't predict cholera outbreaks that were not caused by floods that washed out roads.

Similarly, if we extrapolate a past trend into a future prediction without thinking about whether the trend makes sense, we may miss by a proverbial mile. If we ransack stock prices and winning lottery numbers for a nonsensical system for beating the stock market and winning the lottery, we will almost surely be poorer for it.

Data without theory can fuel a speculative stock market bubble or create the illusion of a bubble where there is none. How do we tell the difference between a real bubble and a false alarm? You know the answer: we need a theory. Data are not enough.

■ AS FAR AS THE EYE CAN SEE

For his second State of the Union Address, Abraham Lincoln calculated the percentage increase in the US population between each 10-year census from 1790 through 1860. The average 10-year increase was 34.60 percent. He noted that the percentage increase during each of these 7 decades was always within 2 percent of 34.60 percent, "thus showing how inflexible, and consequently how reliable, the law of increase in our case is." Using this 34.60 percent per decade figure, he predicted that the US population 70 years later, in 1930, would be 251,680,914. In addition to his incautious extrapolation, notice the unjustified precision in his prediction. If we can't count the exact population today, why are we predicting the exact population 70 years from now?

The actual US population in 1930 turned out to be 123 million, less than half what Lincoln had predicted. A 1938 presidential commission erred in the other direction, predicting that the population would never exceed 140 million. Just 12 years later, in 1950, the population was 152 million.

If we have no logical explanation for a historical trend and nonetheless assume it will continue, we are making an *incautious extrapolation* that may well turn out to be embarrassingly incorrect. Sometimes, incautious extrapolations are made just for the fun of it. A study of British public speakers over the past 350 years found that the average sentence length had fallen from 72.2 words per sentence for Francis Bacon to 24.2 for Winston Churchill. At this rate, the number of words per sentence will hit 0 and then go negative 100 years from now.

Mark Twain came up with this one:

> In the space of one hundred and seventy-six years the Lower Mississippi has shortened itself two hundred and forty-two miles. This is an average of a trifle over one mile and a third per year. Therefore, any calm person, who is not blind or idiotic, can see that in the Old Oolitic Silurian Period, just a million years ago next November, the Lower Mississippi River was upward of one million three hundred thousand miles long, and stuck out over the Gulf of Mexico like a fishing rod. And by the same token, any person can see that seven hundred and forty-two years from now the Lower Mississippi will be only a mile and three-quarters long. . . . There is something fascinating about science. One gets such wholesale returns out of a trifling investment of fact.

Unfortunately, incautious extrapolations are not always humorous—at least not intentionally so.

■ WE WILL ALL WORK FOR IBM

In 1924 the Computing-Tabulating-Recording Company changed its awkward name to something more ambitious—International Business Machines (IBM)—and went on to become the premier growth stock of all time. By 1978, its revenues had been growing (adjusted for inflation) by about 16 percent a year for more than 50 years. Some financial analysts, looking backward instead of forward, concluded that you could never go wrong buying IBM stock. A popular saying at the time was, "No purchasing manager ever got fired for buying IBM computers, and no portfolio manager ever got fired for buying IBM stock."

Figure 16.1 shows a 1978 prediction of IBM's earnings per share over the next ten years, based on an extrapolation of data for the preceding ten years. A smooth line fits these data closely and suggests that IBM's earnings per share would be $18.50 a share in 1988, triple its 1978 earnings. Based on such extrapolations, many stock analysts recommended buying IBM stock, predicting that its price would triple over the next ten years.

Figure 16.1, like all historical graphs, is merely descriptive. Before we extrapolate a past trend into a confident prediction, we should look behind the numbers and think about whether the underlying reasons for the past trend will continue or dissipate.

If these analysts had thought about it, they might have realized that there were persuasive reasons why IBM's phenomenal growth could not continue forever. IBM started small and grew rapidly as the use of computers spread throughout the economy. By 1978, IBM was a very large company, with limited room for continued growth. It is a lot harder for a giant company to grow by 16 percent a year than it is for a small company.

If IBM kept growing at 16 percent annually and the overall US economy continued to grow at its long-run 3 percent rate, by 2003 half of US output would be IBM products and in 2008 everything would have been made by IBM! At some point in this fanciful exercise, something has to give—either IBM's growth rate has to drop to 3 percent or the economy's growth rate has to rise to 16 percent. A sustained 16 percent growth for the entire economy is highly implausible because economic growth is constrained by the labor force and productivity and it is hard to see how these could increase fast enough to yield a 16 percent growth rate.

Figure 16.2 shows that IBM's 16 percent growth rate did not persist. A simple extrapolation of the 1968–78 earnings trend proved to be an incautious extrapolation that was recklessly optimistic. Instead of earning $18.50 a share in 1988, IBM earned half that. Subsequent years turned out to be more of the same. IBM could not grow by 16 percent forever. Investors who bought IBM stock in the 1970s, confident that IBM's remarkable growth rate would never end, were disappointed to learn that you seldom see the future by looking in a rearview mirror.

Figure 16.1: A Sure Thing?

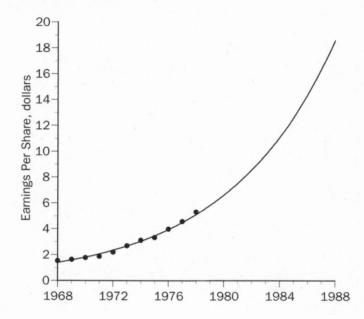

Figure 16.2: Oops!

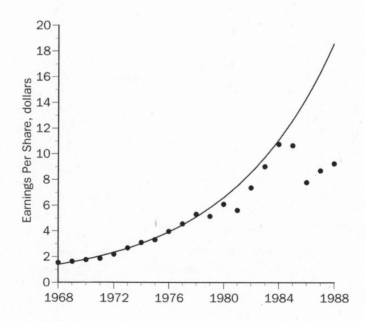

Figure 16.3: Stocks Are a Great Investment

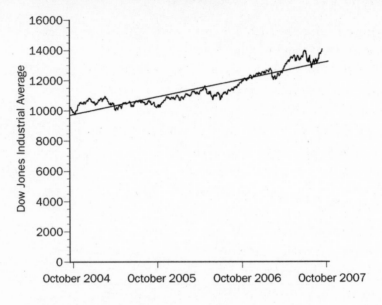

Figure 16.4: Stocks Are a Terrible Investment

■ STOCKS ARE A GREAT INVESTMENT

Figure 16.3, constructed in December 2008, shows that stocks are a wonderful investment. Stock prices increased by 38 percent between October 2004 and October 2007. Not only that, but the increase was smooth and steady—not at all like those scary newspaper stories about stock market volatility.

Why does Figure 16.3 stop in October 2007 when data for 2008 were available? Because these additional data (shown in Figure 16.4) tell a story that wasn't meant to be told—a 46 percent decline in stock prices between October 2007 and December 2008. Figure 16.4 suggests that stocks are a terrible investment.

A careful selection of when to start and stop a graph can create the illusion of a trend that would be absent in a more complete graph. Which data are more honest, October 2004 through October 2007, or October 2007 through December 2008? Both time periods are too brief to give an honest summary of volatile stock prices. As a truthful forecaster once said, "Stock prices will go up. Stock prices will go down. Not necessarily in that order."

A long perspective is needed for a balanced view. Over the past 100 years, stock prices have increased, on average, by about 4 percent a year.

Would anyone be so naive as to extrapolate stock prices based on only a few years of data? Investors do it all the time, over even shorter periods, hoping that the latest zig is the prelude to many happy profits or fearing that the recent zag is the beginning of a crash. In October 2007, some clients of a financial planner I know borrowed money so that they could earn double-digit returns in the stock market. Fifteen months later, they sold everything because they did not want to lose another 50 percent in the stock market.

We should be suspicious whenever someone presents data that begin or end at peculiar points in time. If someone prepares a graph in 2009 using data for October 2004 through January 2007, we should be puzzled why they didn't use data before October 2004 or after January 2007, and why their data begin in October and end in January. If the beginning and ending points seem to be peculiar choices that would be made only after scrutinizing the data, these choices probably were made to distort the historical record. There may be a perfectly logical explanation, but we should insist on hearing it.

■ BEATING THE STOCK MARKET (OR, WHY I LOVE THE PACKERS)

Our innate desire to find patterns and orderliness meshes well with our wishful thinking that we can get rich by buying the right stock or the right lottery ticket. The problem—the persistent problem—is that even though the stock market is mostly random and lotteries are completely random, patterns can always be found in random numbers. If we look for them, we will find them.

On Super Bowl Sunday in January 1983, both the business and sports sections of the *Los Angeles Times* carried articles on the "Super Bowl Stock Market Predictor." The theory is that the stock market goes up if the National Football Conference (NFC) or a former National Football League (NFL) team now in the American Football Conference (AFC) wins the Super Bowl and the market goes down otherwise. A Green Bay Packer win is good for the stock market; a New York Jets win is bad for stocks.

This theory had been correct for fifteen of the first sixteen Super Bowls and the *Times* quoted a stockbroker: "Market observers will be glued to their TV screens . . . it will be hard to ignore an S&P indicator with an accuracy quotient that's greater than 94 percent." The Washington Redskins (an NFC team) won, the stock market went up, and the Super Bowl Indicator was back in the news the next year, stronger than ever. The Super Bowl system worked an impressive twenty-eight out of thirty-one times through 1997, but then failed eight of the next fourteen years.

The stock market has nothing to do with the outcome of a football game. The accuracy of the Super Bowl Indicator is nothing more than an amusing coincidence fueled by the fact that the stock market usually goes up and the NFC usually wins the Super Bowl. The correlation is made more impressive by the gimmick of counting the Pittsburgh Steelers, an AFC team, as an NFC team. The excuse is that Pittsburgh once was in the NFL; the real reason is that Pittsburgh won the Super Bowl several times when the stock market went up. Counting Pittsburgh as an NFC team twists the data to support this cockamamie theory.

In 1989, inspired by the success of the Super Bowl Indicator, a *Los Angeles Times* staff writer tortured the data some more and discovered several comparable coincidences. His "Yo, Adrian Theory" states that if a Rocky or Rambo movie is released, the stock market will go up.

That same year, *The New York Times* reversed the direction of the prediction. Instead of using the Super Bowl to predict the stock market, why not use the stock market to predict the Super Bowl? Why not? It's no more ridiculous than the original Super Bowl Indicator. The *Times* reported that, if the Dow Jones Industrial Average increases between the end of November and the time of the Super Bowl, the football team whose city comes second alphabetically usually wins the Super Bowl. (Hint: Why do you suppose they chose the end of November for their starting date, as opposed to January 1, a month before the game, a year before the game, or any other logical date?)

More recently, the Bespoke Investment Group discovered the SI Swimsuit Indicator, which says that the stock market does well if the model on the cover of the annual *Sports Illustrated* swimsuit issue is American and does poorly if she is a foreign model.

The performance of the Super Bowl Indicator has been mediocre since its discovery—which is unsurprising since there was nothing behind it but coincidence. What is genuinely surprising is that some people do not get the joke. The man who created the Super Bowl Indicator intended it to be a humorous way of demonstrating that correlation does not imply causation. He was flabbergasted when people started taking it seriously!

■ THE FOOLISH FOUR

In 1996 the Gardner brothers wrote a wildly popular book with the beguiling name, *The Motley Fool Investment Guide: How the Fools Beat Wall Street's Wise Men and How You Can Too*. Hey, if fools can beat the market, so can we all.

The Gardners recommended what they called the Foolish Four Strategy. They claimed that during the years 1973–93, the Foolish Four Strategy had an annual average return of 25 percent and concluded that this strategy "should grant its fans the same 25 percent annualized returns going forward that it has served up in the past."

Here's their recipe for investment riches:

1. At the beginning of the year, calculate the dividend yield for each of the 30 stocks in the Dow Jones Industrial Average. For example, on January 2, 2014, Coca-Cola stock had a price of $40.66 per share and paid an annual dividend of $1.22 per share. Coke's dividend yield was $1.22/$40.66 = 0.0300, or 3.00 percent.
2. Of the thirty Dow stocks, identify the ten stocks with the highest dividend yields.
3. Of these ten stocks, choose the five stocks with the lowest price per share.
4. Of these five stocks, cross out the stock with the lowest price.
5. Invest 40 percent of your wealth in the stock with the next lowest price.
6. Invest 20 percent of your wealth in each of the other three stocks.

As Dave Barry would say, I'm not making this up.

Any guesses why this strategy is so complicated, verging on baffling? Data mining perhaps?

Steps 1 and 2 are plausible. Stocks with high dividend yields are appealing. There is even a long-established investment strategy, called the Dogs of the Dow, that favors buying the Dow stocks with the highest dividend yields and this sensible strategy has been reasonably successful. The basic idea is that contrarian investors should buck the trend by buying out-of-favor stocks that have low prices and high dividend yields. As super-investor Warren Buffett said so memorably, "Be fearful when others are greedy and greedy when others are fearful."

But beyond this kernel of a borrowed idea, the Foolish Four Strategy is pure data mining. Step 3 has no logical foundation since the price of one share of stock depends on how many shares the company has outstanding. If a company were to double the number of shares, each share would be worth half as much. There is no reason why a Dow stock with more shares outstanding (and a lower price per share) should be a better investment than a Dow stock with fewer shares outstanding (and a higher price per share). Later in this chapter, we will see that Warren Buffett's Berkshire Hathaway stock (which is not in the Dow) has *very* few shares outstanding and consequently sells for a mind boggling price of nearly $200,000 per share. Yet it has been a great investment.

What about Step 4? Why, after selecting the five stocks with the lowest price, as if it is good to have a low price, would we cross out the stock with the lowest price? Why indeed.

And Steps 5 and 6? Why invest twice as much money in the next lowest priced stock as in the other three stocks? We all know the answer. Because it worked historically. Period.

Shortly after the Gardners launched the Foolish Four Strategy, two skeptical finance professors tested it using data from the years 1949–72, just prior to the period data mined by the Gardners. It didn't work. The professors also retested the Foolish Four Strategy during the years that were data mined by the Gardners, but with a clever twist. Instead of choosing the portfolio on the first trading day in January, they implemented the strategy on the first trading day of July. If the strategy has any merit, it shouldn't be sensitive to the starting month. But, of course, it was.

In 1997, only one year after the introduction of the Foolish Four, the Gardners tweaked their system and renamed it the UV4. Their explanation confirms their data mining: "Why the switch? History shows that the UV4 has actually done better than the old Foolish Four." It is hardly surprising that a data-mined strategy doesn't do as well outside the years used to concoct the theory. The Gardners admitted as much when the Motley Fool stopped recommending both the Foolish Four and UV4 strategies in 2000.

The Foolish Four strategy was aptly named.

■ AN INVERTED HEAD AND SHOULDERS

The Super Bowl Indicator is a simple rule for predicting whether the stock market is going up or down. There is an entire profession, called technical analysis, dedicated to predicting stock prices by gauging investor sentiment. Fundamental analysis uses profits, interest rates, and other economic factors to measure what a stock is worth.

Technical analysis, in contrast, assumes that economic factors are already well known and taken into account by market prices. There is no point in looking at fundamentals. It is more useful to gauge investor moods, what Keynes called their "animal spirits."

The core of technical analysis is identifying patterns in stock prices that can be used to predict future prices. The analysis is made more legitimate by affixing labels to these patterns, such as a channel, support level, resistance level, double top, double bottom, head and shoulders, cup and handle. Despite the alluring labels, study after study has found that technical analysis is pretty much worthless—except for employing technical analysts and generating commissions for stockbrokers.

Figure 16.5: An Upward Channel

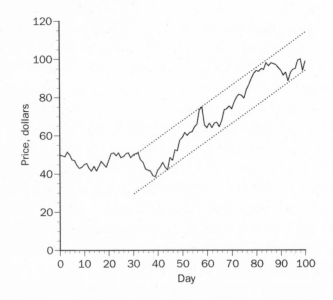

An academic economist once sent several stock-price charts, including Figure 16.5, to a technical analyst (let's call him Ed) and asked Ed's help in deciding whether any of these stocks looked like promising investments. The economist did not identify the companies because the purest technical analysts try to focus on the price patterns and not be swayed by information or feelings they may have about a company. Some technicians avoid all news and work in windowless rooms because they don't want to be influenced by good or bad news or by sunny or stormy days.

The analyst drew the two parallel lines in Figure 16.5 and saw a clear pattern. Since about Day 30, this stock had traded in a narrow upward-sloping channel. On Day 100, the price was near the lower boundary of this channel and clearly poised for an upward surge.

Figure 16.6: A Death Spiral

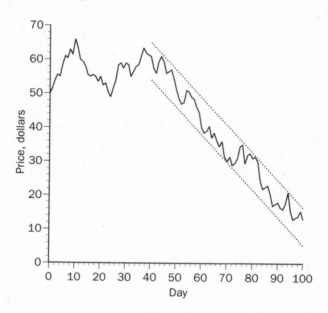

Figure 16.6 shows another chart with a clear pattern. The channel is downward sloping and the stock is clearly in a death spiral. Only a fool would buy a stock with this price history.

Figure 16.7 shows a stock with a support level that was established on Day 24 and confirmed twice. Every time the price fell to $28, it found support and rebounded upward. Even more powerfully, this chart shows a head-and-shoulders pattern, with the price rising off the support level at $28, falling back to $28, rising even more strongly, falling back to $28, and then rising modestly. The technical analyst believed that support levels that are established and confirmed by a head-and-shoulders pattern are extremely strong. When the price pierced the $28 support level on Day 99, this was an unmistakable signal that something had gone terribly wrong. It takes an avalanche of bad news to overcome such a strongly established support level. Once the $28 barrier had been breached, the price could only go down.

Figure 16.7: Piercing a Head-and-Shoulders Support Level

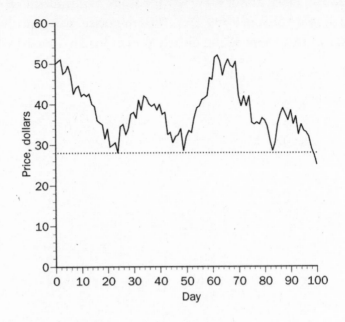

Figure 16.8: Breaking Through a Resistance Level

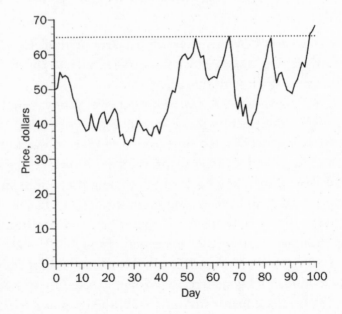

Figure 16.8 shows the opposite pattern. A resistance level was established and confirmed at $65. Every time the price approached $65, it bounced back. The more often this occurred, the stronger was the psychological resistance to the price going above $65. Even more powerfully, in the eyes of this technical analyst, this chart shows an inverted head-and-shoulders pattern, as the second bounce back from $65 was much stronger than the first and third bounce-backs. When the price surged through the resistance level on Day 98, eliminating the psychological barrier to the price going higher, this was an unmistakable buy signal.

The analyst was so excited when he saw these patterns that he overlooked the odd coincidence that all four price charts start at a price of $50 a share. This was not a coincidence.

These are not real stocks. The mischievous professor (I confess, it was me) who sent Ed these charts created these fictitious data from student coin flips. In each case, the "price" started at $50 and then each day's price change was determined by twenty-five coin flips, with the price going up fifty cents if the coin landed heads and down fifty cents if the coin landed tails. For example, fourteen heads and eleven tails would be a $1.50 increase that day. After generating dozens of charts, ten were sent to the analyst with the expectation that he would find seductive patterns. Sure enough, he did.

When this ruse was revealed, Ed was quite disappointed that these were not real stocks, with real opportunities for profitable buying and selling. However, the lesson he drew from this hoax was quite different from the intended lesson: Ed concluded that it is possible to use technical analysis to predict coin flips!

What this example really demonstrates is that it is very difficult, even for professional investors, to understanding that data grubbing will inevitably uncover statistical patterns that are nothing more than coincidence. Data without theory is alluring, but misleading.

■ HOW (NOT) TO WIN THE LOTTERY

In the New York State Lotto game, a player chooses 6 of 59 numbers, 1 through 59, and wins the grand prize if these 6 numbers match (not necessarily in order) the 6 numbers drawn live on television. The chances of winning are 1 in 45 million, but a ticket costs only fifty cents and the grand prize (spread over 25 years) is equal to 30 percent of the total ticket sales. Another 15 percent of ticket revenue is allocated to lesser prizes. The New York Lotto payout is the lowest of any pick-six game in the United States and the odds of winning are also the lowest. For example, players pick 6 of only 44 numbers in nearby Connecticut and 6 of 49 in New Jersey. Nonetheless, New York Lotto is the most popular US pick-six game.

State lotteries are essentially a stupidity tax, but the popularity of lotto games shows that many people lust for a chance—no matter how remote—to change their lives completely. In 2012, a Mega Millions lottery spanning most of the United States offered a record $656 million jackpot. Thousands of people waited in lines for hours or drove up to 100 miles to join the crowds that purchased a total of $1.5 billion in tickets. The only catch in this lottery frenzy is that the chances of winning were minuscule, 1 in 176 million for the record jackpot.

The chasm between dreams and reality gives enterprising people an opportunity to sell gimmicks that purportedly increase the chances of winning. One company sold a Millionaire Maker for $19.95, using this pitch: "Studies have shown that most lotto winners don't use a special system to select numbers. Instead, they tap the power of random selection." Their $19.95 product is a battery-powered sphere filled with numbered balls that "mixes the balls thoroughly" and chooses a "perfectly random set of numbers." Did I mention that lotteries are a stupidity tax?

Others have developed a very different approach. They argue that by collecting and analyzing winning lottery numbers, we can handicap the lottery just like handicapping horses. It is hard to imagine a more tedious waste of time. Maybe, calculating the average telephone number?

Gail Howard's web site claims that she has been "America's Most Credible Lottery Authority for 30 Years." The site also claims that she has been on hundreds of radio and television shows, including *The Today Show* and *Good Morning America*, and that her thirty-minute infomercial "Lottery Busters" was shown on cable television every day for more than a year. (Oddly, I counted that boast as a negative, not a positive. Ditto for her warning that, "You'd better hurry, while distribution of this controversial information is still permitted.") One of Howard's many books begins with the following statement, which is unremarkable, except for the fact that it completely contradicts everything else in her book: "You don't have to worry about the state lottery games being crooked or rigged . . . the winning numbers are selected through a completely random process." Undeterred, Howard offers several tips for "greatly improving your chances of winning."

Here are some top-six secrets offered by Howard and other experts for winning a pick-six lotto game:

1. Go with the hot numbers. The New York Lottery web site shows the winning numbers over the past several years. Enter these in a spreadsheet and identify the numbers that have come up most often.
2. Don't ignore overdue numbers. Numbers that haven't occurred recently are due for a hit.
3. Don't bet on consecutive numbers, like 11, 12, 13, 14, 15, 16. The winning numbers are hardly ever consecutive numbers.
4. Don't use the Quick Pick option where a computer chooses the numbers for you. What does a computer know?
5. Men win two out of three jackpots. If you are female, ask your husband, boyfriend, brother, or father to buy tickets for you.
6. The most common names among winners are Mary and Joseph, including variations such as Maria or Joe. If you have a different name, ask a friend named Mary or Joseph to buy tickets for you.

And here is a skeptic's response to those tips:

1. Unless the game is rigged (and no one seriously claims it is), every number is equally likely to be chosen. The apparatus that selects the winning numbers does not remember numbers drawn in the past and does not care about numbers drawn in the future.
2. This is not helpful. First, you tell me to bet on hot numbers; now you tell me to bet on cold numbers.
3. Yes, consecutive numbers are unlikely to win. So are any six numbers. Every six-number combination is equally unlikely.

4. Yes, computers can't predict the winning numbers. Neither can you. That's why it's called *random*.
5. Maybe men buy two out of three tickets. Or maybe female winners ask their husband, boyfriend, brother, or father to claim their prize.
6. Maybe, just maybe, the most common names among players are Mary and Joseph, including variations such as Maria or Joe.

Just as a careful study can identify worthless patterns in coin flips and dice rolls, so tedious scrutiny can discern worthless patterns in lottery numbers. The most persuasive reason for skepticism about lottery-beating systems is that if anyone had a system that really worked, they would get rich buying lottery tickets instead of peddling books and battery-powered gadgets.

There is no evidence that Gail Howard ever won a lottery. Howard was, in fact, a creation of Ben Buxton, who operated a variety of dodgy mail-order businesses peddling lottery advice, astrological predictions, and good-luck pieces using dozens of names, including Gail Howard, Astrology Society of America, Brother Rudy, Madame Daudet, Rothchild Depository, and Lourdes Water Cross.

The US attorney in Newark asked a federal district court to enjoin Buxton from "continuing to defraud hundreds of thousands of consumers through false and misleading promotions of horoscopes, lottery-winning systems, religious trinkets, and other products, all guaranteed to bring unwitting consumers wealth, good luck and prosperity." The US Postal Service also got involved and, working with the US attorney, secured a court order permanently stopping Buxton's various businesses, allowing the postal service to intercept tens of thousands of checks mailed to Buxton, and ordering Buxton to pay $300,000 in restitution to former customers.

■ BUBBLES THAT DO NOT POP

It's not only scam artists who separate us from our money. We sometimes do it to ourselves in collective, self-inflicted con games. It is hard to imagine life without the Internet—without e-mail, Amazon, and Wikipedia at our fingertips. When the electricity goes out or we go on vacation, Internet withdrawal pains can be overwhelming. Cell phones only heighten our addiction. Do we really need to be online and on call 24/7? Must we respond immediately to every e-mail, text, and tweet? Do we really need to know what all our friends are eating for lunch?

Back in the 1990s, when computers and cell phones were just starting to take over our lives, the spread of the Internet sparked the creation of hundreds of Internet-based companies, popularly known as dot-coms. Some dot-coms had good ideas and have matured into strong, successful companies. But many did not. In too many cases, the idea was simply to start a company with a dot-com in its name, sell it to someone else, and walk away with pockets full of cash. It was so Old Economy to have a great idea, start a company, make it a successful business, and turn it over to your children and grandchildren.

A dot-com company proved it was a player not by making a profit, but by spending money, preferably other people's money. (I'm not joking!) One rationale was to be the first-mover by getting big fast (a popular saying was "Get large or get lost"). The idea was that once people believe that your web site is the place to go to buy something, sell something, or learn something, you have a monopoly that can crush competition and reap profits.

It is not a completely idiotic idea. It sometimes even works. (Think Amazon and eBay.) The problem is that, even if it is possible to monopolize something, there were thousands of dot-com companies and there isn't room for thousands of monopolies. Of the thousands of companies trying to get big fast, very few can ever be monopolies.

Most dot-com companies had no profits. So, wishful investors thought up new metrics for the so-called New Economy to justify ever higher stock prices. They argued that, instead of being obsessed with something as old fashioned as profits, we should look at a company's sales, spending, web site visitors. Companies responded by finding creative ways to give investors what they wanted. Investors want more sales? I'll sell something to your company and you sell it back to me. No profits for either of us, but higher sales for both of us. Investors want more spending? Order another thousand Aeron chairs. Investors want more web-site visitors? Give gadgets away to people who visit your web site. Buy Super Bowl ads that advertise your web site. Remember, investors want web-site visitors, not profits. Two dozen dot-com companies ran ads during the January 2000 Super Bowl game, at a cost of $2.2 million for thirty seconds of ad time, plus the cost of producing the ad. Companies didn't need profits. They needed traffic.

Stock prices tripled between 1995 and 2000, an annual rate of increase of 25 percent. Dot-com stocks rose even more. The tech-heavy NASDAQ index more than quintupled during this 5-year period, an annual rate of increase of 40 percent. A fortunate person who bought $10,000 of AOL stock in January 1995 or Yahoo when it went public in April 1996 would have had nearly $1 million in January 2000. Stock market investors and dot-com entrepreneurs were getting rich and they believed that it would never end. But, of course, it did.

On March 11, 2000, I participated in a panel discussion on the booming stock market and the widely publicized "36K" prediction that the Dow Jones Industrial Average would more than triple, from below 12,000 to 36,000. The first speaker talked about Moore's Law (transistor density on integrated circuits doubles every two years). I listened intently and I had to agree that technology was wonderful. But I didn't hear a single word about whether stock prices were too high, too low, or just right.

The next speaker talked about how smart dot-com whizzes were. When you bought a dot-com stock, you were giving your money to very smart people who would soon figure out something profitable to do with it. I again listened intently and I had to agree that many dot-com companies were started by smart, likable people. Heck, one of my sons had joined with four other recent college graduates to form a company. The five of them rented a five-bedroom house in New Hampshire (low taxes, but close to Taxachusetts), slept upstairs, and commuted to work by walking downstairs. What kind of work were they doing downstairs? They didn't have a business plan. The key phrase was "nimble." They were bright, creative, and flexible. When a profitable opportunity appeared, these five nimble lads would recognize it and seize it with all ten hands. I agreed that these were terrific kids and there were undoubtedly hundreds of other terrific kids looking for ways to make a profit from the Internet. But I still hadn't heard a single word about whether stock prices were too high, too low, or just right.

The next speaker talked about how Alan Greenspan was a wonderful chair of the Federal Reserve (the "Fed"), the government agency in charge of monetary policy in the United States. The Fed decides when to increase the money supply to boost the economy and when to restrain the money supply to reduce inflationary pressures. As a cynic (me) once wrote, the Fed jacks up interest rates to cause a recession whenever they feel it is in our best interests to be unemployed. It is very important to have a Fed chair who knows what he's doing. I listened intently and I had to agree that Alan Greenspan was an impressive Fed chair. But, once again, I didn't hear anything about whether stock prices were too high, too low, or just right.

I was the last speaker and the grump at this happy party. I looked at stock prices from a variety of perspectives and concluded that not only was it farfetched to think that the Dow would hit 36,000 anytime soon, but that the current level of stock prices was much too high. My final words were, "This is a bubble, and it will end badly."

I was right—eerily so. The conference was on Saturday, March 11, 2000. The NASDAQ dropped the following Monday and fell by 75 percent over the next 3 years from its March 10, 2000, peak. AOL fell 85 percent, Yahoo 95 percent. The interesting question is not the coincidental timing of my remarks, but why was I convinced that this was a bubble?

During the dot-com bubble, most people did not use a persuasive theory to gauge whether stock prices were too high, too low, or just right. Instead, as they watched stock prices go up, they invented explanations to rationalize what was happening. They talked about Moore's Law, smart kids, and Alan Greenspan. Data without theory.

Here is a theory that makes sense. Think of a stock as a money machine that gives out, say, $2 in dividends every year. The *economic value* of this marvelous machine is the amount you would pay to get a $2 dividend every year.

In contrast to *investors* who buy a money machine with the expectation of receiving dividends every year, *speculators* buy a stock so they can sell it to someone else for a profit. To speculators, a stock is worth what someone else will pay for it, and the challenge is to guess what others will pay tomorrow for what you buy today. This guessing game is the Greater Fool Theory: buy something at an inflated price, hoping to sell it to an even bigger fool at a still higher price.

In a speculative bubble, the price of the money machine rises far above its economic value because people are buying the machine not for the annual $2, but so that they can sell the machine to someone else for a higher price. They think the price will go up in the future simply because it went up in the past. (Need I say data without theory?) The bubble pops when speculators stop thinking that the machine's price will keep going up and up and up. They start selling and the price goes down and down and down, because speculators won't pay a speculative price unless they believe they can sell it for an even higher price. When they stop believing, the party is over.

If a stock has an economic value of $100 and the market price is $500, this is a bubble in that the price is much, much higher than the economic value. You don't think a price could ever be so far above economic value? In the 1600s, tulip bulbs in Holland sold for tens of thousands of dollars (in today's dollars). More recently, worthless stuffed dolls sold for hundreds of dollars.

Beanie Babies, made by Ty Warner with a heart-shaped hang tag, are stuffed animal toys are filled with plastic pellets ("beans"). Around 1995, the same time the dot-com bubble was inflating, Beanie Babies came to be viewed as "collectibles" because buyers expected to profit from rising Beanie Baby prices by selling these silly bears to an endless supply of greater fools. Delusional individuals stockpiled Beanie Babies, thinking that these would pay for their retirement or their kids' college education.

What exactly is the economic value of a Beanie Baby? It doesn't pay dividends. It doesn't pay anything! You can't even play with a Beanie Baby. To preserve their value as a collectible, Beanie Babies must be stored in air-tight containers in a cool, dark, smoke-free environment. Yet, the hopeful and greedy paid hundreds of dollars for Beanie Babies that were originally sold in toy stores for a few dollars. They saw how much prices had increased in the past and assumed the same would be true in the future. They had no reason for believing, but they wanted to believe. Data without theory, once again.

In 1999, the Princess Beanie Baby honoring Diana, the Princess of Wales, was released. By 2000, the Princess was selling for as much as $500. Then the bubble popped. I bought a Princess bear on Amazon in 2008, and the shipping cost more than the bear itself.

■ THE SOUTH SEA BUBBLE

The dot-com bubble and the Beanie Baby bubble are nothing new. In 1720, the British government gave the South Sea Company exclusive trading privileges with Spain's American colonies. None of the company's directors had ever been to America, nor had they any concrete trading plans, but, stimulated by the company's inventive bookkeeping, people rushed to invest in this exotic venture. The price of the South Sea Company's stock soared from £120 on January 28 to £400 on May 19, £800 on June 4, and £1,000 on June 22. Some became rich and thousands rushed to join their ranks. It was said that you could buy stock as you entered Garraway's coffeehouse and sell it for a profit on the way out. People saw the pattern—buy it for some price, sell it for a higher price—and didn't think about whether it made any sense.

Soon other entrepreneurs with more brains than scruples were offering stock in ever more grandiose schemes and were deluged by frantic investors not wanting to be left out. It hardly mattered what the scheme was. One promised to build a wheel for perpetual motion. Another was formed "for carrying on an undertaking of great advantage, but nobody is to know what it is" (just like some dot-com companies!). The shares for this mysterious offering were priced at £100 each, with a promised annual return of £100. After selling all the stock within five hours, the promoter immediately left England and never returned. Yet another stock offer was for the *nitvender*— the selling of nothing. When the South Sea bubble popped, fortunes and dreams disappeared.

As with all speculative bubbles, there were many believers in the Greater Fool Theory. While some suspected that prices were unreasonable, the market was dominated by people believing that prices would continue to rise, at least until they could sell to the next fool in line. In the spring of 1720, Sir Isaac Newton said, "I can calculate the motions of the heavenly bodies, but not the madness of people" and sold his South Sea shares for a £7,000 profit. But later that year, he bought shares again, just before the bubble burst, and lost £20,000. When a banker invested £500 in the third offering of South Sea stock, he explained that, "When the rest of the world are mad, we must imitate them in some measure." After James Milner, a member of the British Parliament, was bankrupted by the South Sea Bubble, he lamented that, "I said, indeed, that ruin must soon come upon us but . . . it came two months sooner than I expected."

■ THE BERKSHIRE BUBBLE

Some investors think they can identify a bubble just by looking at how fast the price has increased relative to the Consumer Price Index (CPI). Looking at such data without any particular theory in mind, they reason that if an asset's price has soared, it must be a bubble. Not necessarily. Data without theory is always treacherous.

Most quality stocks sell for $20 to $200 a share. In 2005, Wells Fargo sold for around $30, Coca-Cola for $40, and Johnson & Johnson for $60. Astonishingly, Berkshire Hathaway sold for $90,000 a share. True, Berskshire was run by the legendary investor Warren Buffett, but how could one share of stock be worth more than a Porsche 911?

Figure 16.9 compares the percentage increase in Berskhire's price with the percentage increase in the CPI between 1995 and 2005. The CPI increased by 27 percent while Berkshire increased by an astonishing 269 percent. Was Berkshire a bubble waiting to pop?

Berkshire kept right on increasing, to a peak of $141,600 in 2007, fell with the rest of the stock market in 2009, and then surged upward to above $170,000 in 2013. Figure 16.10 shows that the gap between Berkshire and the CPI actually *increased* after 2005.

How could a single share of stock be worth more than a Porsche? How could a stock's price increase faster than consumer prices—the prices of food, clothing, and shelter?

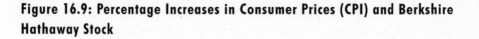

Figure 16.9: Percentage Increases in Consumer Prices (CPI) and Berkshire Hathaway Stock

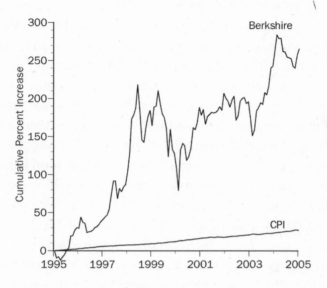

Figure 16.10: More Percentage Increases in the CPI and Berkshire Hathaway

Since a corporation is owned by its stockholders, the value of the stock depends on the value of the company. The value of a single share of stock, in turn, depends on the overall value of the company *and* the number of shares outstanding. If a company's total value is $100 million and the company has one million shares outstanding, each share is worth $100; if the company has one hundred million shares outstanding, each share is only worth $1.

Many companies use stock splits to keep their stock "affordable." Suppose that Things.com is worth $100 million and has one million shares outstanding, each worth $100. After several profitable years, the value of the company increases to $200 million, with each share worth $200. Things.com might have a two-for-one stock split so that the number of shares doubles to two million and the value of each share falls by half to $100. The stock split is a nonevent in that each stockholder has twice as many shares, but each share is worth half as much.

The reason Berkshire stock is so expensive is that it has *never* split, despite the remarkable increase in Berkshire's value under Buffett's guidance. Buffett has always recognized a stock split as a nonevent and he famously signed birthday cards, "May you live until Berkshire shares split." Berkshire has fewer than two million shares outstanding. IBM has more than one billion, Exxon has six billion. That's why a single share of Berkshire is worth more than a Porsche.

The answer to the second puzzle—how a stock's price could increase faster than consumer prices—is also simple. The value of a company is fundamentally different from the price of soup—even for a company that sells soup. A company's value depends on its profits, which depend not only on the price of soup but on how much soup it sells.

Berkshire Hathaway owns dozens of companies, including Benjamin-Moore, Burlington Northern, Dairy Queen, Fruit of the Loom, GEICO, and See's Candy, and owns substantial amounts of stock in many other companies, including American Express, Anheuser-Busch, Coca-Cola, Kraft, Procter & Gamble, Washington Post, and Wells Fargo. Berkshire's profitable investments generate tremendous income, which it invests in even more companies. The total value of its assets have grown by more than 20 percent a year for nearly 50 years.

The price of Berkshire stock can be more than \$100,000 and rise faster than the CPI, and still not be a bubble, because this extraordinary company is extraordinarily profitable.

■ REAL STOCK PRICES

Data that are adjusted for inflation are called *real* data. If our income increases by 10 percent while consumer prices also increase by 10 percent, our real income is constant in that we cannot buy any more or less than we could before.

In 1987 two business school professors used the S&P 500 index of stock prices and the consumer price index (CPI) to calculate real stock prices from 1857 through 1985. They found that real stock prices were higher in 1985 than in 1857: stock prices increased more than consumer prices.

That is not a new insight and the professors wanted something original, something that would be publishable. So, they compared actual stock prices with real stock prices, as in Figure 16.11, although there is no obvious reason why anyone would want to compare them.

Figure 16.11: Uh-oh, Another Bubble

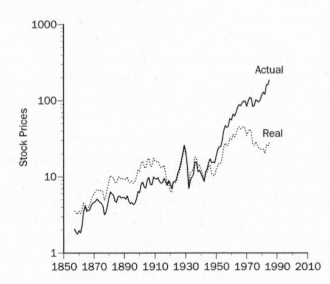

The professors set the consumer price index equal to 1 in 1864 so that real stock prices equaled actual stock prices that year. Actual stock prices fell below real prices after 1864, then the two series converged in 1918. Actual and real prices moved together between 1918 and 1946, then diverged again, suggesting that stock prices should fall in order for the two series to converge again. The post-World War II surge in stock prices was apparently a bubble that would not last.

This comparison was original enough to be published, just as the professors hoped. The problem is that a comparison of actual and real stock prices is data without theory and means nothing at all. Before comparing two things, we should think about why they might be related. A comparison of actual and real stock prices is superficially similar to the bogus argument that Berkshire stock was a bubble because its price increased faster than the CPI. But the prediction based on Figure 16.11 is quite different and even more bogus. The difference between actual and real stock prices has nothing to do with stock prices!

Remember that real stock prices are equal to actual stock prices adjusted for inflation. These were equal in 1864 because the CPI was set equal to 1 in 1864. Between 1865 and 1918, real stock prices were higher than actual stock prices because consumer prices fell. Real and actual stock prices were equal between 1918 and 1946 because consumer prices were (approximately) the same as in 1864. After 1946, real stock prices were lower than actual stock prices because consumer prices were higher than in 1864. That is all Figure 16.11 says. Compared to 1864, consumer prices were lower between 1865 and 1918 and higher after 1946.

A prediction that real stock prices will again equal actual stock prices is *not* a prediction about the stock market. It is a prediction that the CPI will fall back to its 1864 level.

Figure 16.12 shows that this implied prediction was completely wrong. The stock market has had exhilarating ups and terrifying downs, but the gap between actual and real stock prices has continued to grow year after year because consumer prices have continued to increase year after year. This gap will never disappear because consumer prices will never again be what they were in 1864.

The core problem is that these professors compared actual and inflation-adjusted stock prices without ever thinking about why anyone would want to make this comparison. All this comparison tells us is whether consumer prices are higher today than they were in 1864—and we already know the answer to that question.

In carpentry, they say, "Measure twice, cut once." With data, "Think twice, calculate once."

Figure 16.12: The Gap Keeps Widening Because the CPI Keeps Increasing

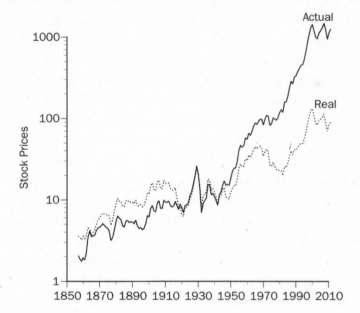

■ **Don't be Fooled:** Data without theory can lead to bogus inferences. For example, many comforting or alarming projections can be concocted by extrapolating a few years of data far into the future. Before being comforted or alarmed, consider whether it makes sense to extrapolate. Is there a persuasive reason why the future can be predicted simply by looking at the past? Or is that wishful thinking? Or no thinking at all?

The same is true of patterns in the data. Remember that even random coin flips can yield striking, even stunning, patterns that mean nothing at all. When someone shows you a pattern, no matter how impressive the person's credentials, consider the possibility that the pattern is just a coincidence. Ask why, not what. No matter what the pattern, the question is: Why should we expect to find this pattern?

A statistical comparison of two things is similarly unpersuasive unless there is a logical reason why they should be related. Why should stock prices go up at the same rate as consumer prices? Why should inflation-adjusted stock prices equal unadjusted stock prices? There may be nothing there but a spurious correlation. Ask yourself whether the people who did the study thought before calculating. Was a coherent theory specified before looking at the data? Was the theory tested with uncontaminated data? Or were the data plundered and pillaged?

17

BETTING THE BANK

N THE 1980s, AN INVESTMENT ADVISORY FIRM WITH THE SOPHISTI-
cated name Hume & Associates produced *The Superinvestor Files*,
which were advertised nationally as sophisticated strategies that
ordinary investors could use to reap extraordinary profits. Sub-
scribers were mailed monthly pamphlets, each about fifty pages long
and stylishly printed on thick paper, for $25 each plus $2.50 for shipping and handling.

In retrospect, it should have been obvious that if these strategies
were really as profitable as advertised, the company could have made
more money by using the strategies than by selling pamphlets. But,
being gullible and greedy, investors hoped that the secret to becoming
a millionaire could be purchased for $25, plus $2.50 for shipping and
handling.

One Superinvestor strategy was based on the gold-silver ratio
[GSR], which is the ratio of the price of an ounce of gold to the price
of an ounce of silver. In 1985, the average price of gold was $317.26
and the average price of silver was $5.88, so that the GSR was
$317.26/$5.88 = 54, which meant that an ounce of gold cost the same
as 54 ounces of silver.

In 1986 Hume wrote:

The [GSR] has fluctuated widely just in the past seven or eight years,
dipping as low as 19-to-1 in 1980 and soaring as high as 52-to-1 in
1982 and 55-to-1 in 1985. But, as you can also clearly see, it has always
—ALWAYS—returned to the range between 34-to-1 and 38-to-1.

Figure 17.1: The GSR 1970–85

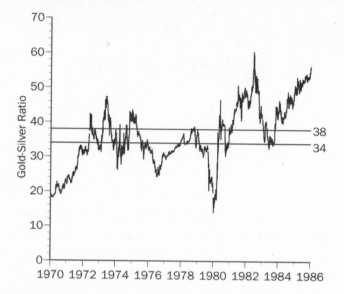

Figure 17.1 confirms that the GSR fluctuated around the range 34 to 38 during the years 1970 through 1985.

The Superinvestor strategy is to invest whenever the GSR goes above 45 or below 25, because the GSR always goes back to the range 34 to 38. For example, when the GSR went above 45 in 1984, gold prices were high relative to silver prices. A savvy investor should sell gold (since its price is high) and buy silver (since its price is low).

Ordinary investors don't have a hoard of gold that they can sell and they don't want to stockpile silver in the basement, but they can buy and sell futures contracts, which are wagers on the future prices of gold and silver. Selling gold futures is a bet that the price of gold will go down; buying silver futures is a bet the price of silver will go up. Selling gold futures and buying silver futures simultaneously is a bet that the GSR will fall.

On July 3, 1984, the GSR was 45.04 with gold at $369.75 and silver at $8.21. Suppose that you had bought 1 silver futures contract and sold 1 gold futures contract, counting on the GSR to return to the range 34 to 38.

Suppose, further, that you were right. Gold goes to $380 (a 2.8 percent increase) while silver goes to $10 (a 22 percent increase), bringing the GSR down to 38. A gold futures contract is for 100 ounces of gold; a silver futures contract is for 5,000 ounces of silver. So, your profit is $7,925:

Profit on silver	5,000($10.00 - $8.21)	=	$8,950
Loss on gold	100($369.75 - $380.00)	=	− $1,025
NET PROFIT			$7,925

In futures markets, there is a daily settlement in which investors who had losses that day transfer funds to investors who had profits. Brokers require their customers to have enough funds (called *margin*) in their accounts at the beginning of each day to cover the potential daily settlement. If you run out of money, the broker will liquidate your futures contracts.

Let's suppose that this margin is $2,500. If so, a profit of $7,925 on an investment of $2,500 is a mouthwatering 317 percent rate of return.

That's right, a modest drop in the GSR gives you a 317 percent return on your investment. This is because you have tremendous leverage, in that you put up $2,500 but are reaping the rewards on futures contracts worth about $40,000. Leverage is not money for nothing. Leverage is a proverbial double-edged sword that multiplies losses as well as gains. As it turned out, the GSR did not quickly fall back below 38 in 1984. Instead, the losses came quickly. On July 6, 1984, 3 days after initiating the trade, gold was $366, silver was $7.60, and the GSR was up to 48.16. Your position had a loss of $2,675, more than 100 percent of your initial investment. You either have to put up more margin or close your position. That's the power of leverage. You can lose your entire investment in 3 days.

If you had put up more margin, hoping for the GSR to fall, your losses would have kept mounting, month after month, year after year. Figure 17.2 shows that the GSR kept rising, peaking at 75 in 1986 before falling back to 50 in 1987. Then the GSR started rising again, topping 100 in 1991. The GSR briefly fell below 45 in 1998, and then rose again. It wasn't until 2011, 37 years after the gold-silver position was taken, that the GSR fell below 38. The average value of the GSR was 36 for the years 1970 through 1985, but 66 for the years 1986 through 2012.

Figure 17.2: The GSR 1970–2012

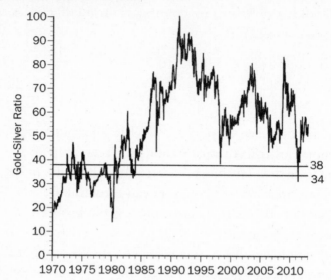

Very few investors could hold their position for 37 years, paying commissions every time futures contracts are renewed and putting up more margin after every losing day. When the GSR hit 75 in 1986, there was a $17,000 loss on your $2,500 investment. When the GSR hit 100 in 1991, the loss was $22,500. If you had invested more heavily—say $25,000—in this disastrous trade, your losses would have been ten times larger.

■ QUANTS

Quantitative financial analysts ("quants") use math and data to analyze stocks and other investments. They aren't interested in subjective evaluations of a CEO's personality or a product's potential. Don't try to talk to them about Steve Jobs or Warren Buffett or smartphones or Coca-Cola. Their battle cry is, "Just show me the numbers!"

Some of the pioneers of this approach were Harry Markowitz, Robert Merton, Fischer Black, and Myron Scholes. Markowitz, Merton, and Scholes were all awarded Nobel Prizes (Black was deceased) for their pathbreaking theories, but the misuse of their models has cost many investors dearly.

In the 1950s Markowitz developed mean-variance analysis to quantify risk. This is widely used by institutional investors and financial advisors. A major weakness is the reliance on historical data. Investors are tempted to assume that a stock that has been relatively safe in the past will be relatively safe in the future. A dangerous assumption!

In the 1970s Merton, Black, and Scholes determined the theoretically "correct" value of a call option, which gives the owner the right to buy a stock at a specified price and date. This is now called the Black-Scholes Model. A major weakness is that many of the underlying assumptions are false—for example, that changes in stock prices are like coin flips and that investors can trade stocks and options at no cost and with no sudden, large price movements.

Their pioneering work nicely illustrates the two main pitfalls of quantitative financial analysis: a naive confidence that historical patterns are a reliable guide to the future, and a dependence on theoretical assumptions that are mathematically convenient but dangerously unrealistic.

Statistical arbitrage is a more recent, and extreme, manifestation of quantitative finance. It, too, is mathematically and statistically sophisticated, but perilous because of its fragile empirical and theoretical assumptions.

■ CONVERGENCE TRADES

The GSR is an early example of statistical arbitrage in which so-called quants found a statistical pattern and assumed that deviations from this pattern are temporary aberrations that can be exploited. If the ratio of gold to silver prices has historically been between 34 and 38, they assume that whenever the GSR goes outside this range, it must soon return. This is called a *convergence trade*.

The investor is not betting on prices going up or down, but on prices converging to the historical relationship. Although the deviation from the historical relationship may be small, a leveraged bet can multiply a small convergence into huge profits.

Early convergence trades were based on simple patterns, like the ratio of gold prices to silver prices. Modern computers can ransack large databases looking for much more subtle and complex patterns. But the fundamental problem is the same. Data without theory is treacherous. If there is no underlying reason for the discovered pattern, there is no reason for deviations from the pattern to self-correct.

There is no logical reason why an ounce of gold should cost the same as 34-to-38 ounces of silver. Gold and silver are not like eggs sold by the dozen or half dozen where, if the prices diverge, consumers will buy the cheaper eggs. Nor are gold and silver like corn and soybeans, where if the price of corn rises relative to the price of soybeans, farmers will plant more corn.

Figure 17.3 shows that the prices of corn and soybean have generally moved up and down together since 1960.

Figure 17.4 shows that the ratio of the per-bushel prices of soybeans and corn averaged 2.5 over the years 1960 through 2012, because it cost about 2.5 times as much to produce a bushel of soybeans as to produce a bushel of corn. Year-to-year, the ratio rose and fell because of fluctuations in demand and supply. However, short-term fluctuations in the ratio around 2.5 were quickly corrected as farmers chose to plant more of whichever crop was more lucrative.

There is nothing similar about gold and silver. There is no reason why the GSR has to be between 34 and 38.

■ JUST SHOW ME THE DATA

Quants too often do not think about whether the patterns they discover make sense. "Just show me the data." Indeed, many quants have PhDs in physics or mathematics and only the most rudimentary knowledge of economics and finance. That does not deter them. If anything, their ignorance encourages them to search for patterns in the most unlikely places.

There is a joke about two finance professors who see a $100 bill on the sidewalk. As one professor reaches for it, the other one says, "Don't bother—if it were real, someone would have picked it up by now." Finance professors are fond of saying that financial markets don't leave $100 bills lying on the sidewalk, meaning that if there was an easy way to make money, someone would have figured it out by now.

Figure 17.3: Soybean and Corn Prices

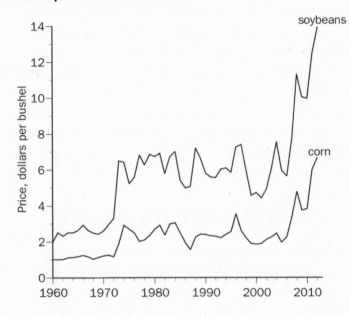

Figure 17.4: The Soybean-Corn Ratio

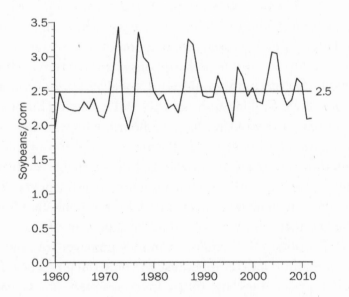

This is not completely true. Stocks and bonds *are* sometimes mispriced. During speculative booms and financial crises, financial markets leave suitcases full of $100 bills on the sidewalk. Still, when you think you have found a mispricing, you should ask if there is a logical explanation. If the price of gold is rising relative to the price of silver, is the market stupidly leaving $100 bills on the sidewalk? Or is there a logical explanation?

Finding a historical correlation between gold and silver prices is no more convincing than finding a historical correlation between marriage and beer consumption. All it demonstrates is that we looked long enough to find a correlation.

■ PICKING UP NICKELS IN FRONT OF A BULLDOZER

John Meriwether made his reputation and fortune at Salomon Brothers in the 1980s exploiting bond market imperfections—finding small aberrations in interest rates and betting that the aberrations would disappear. He bought bonds that had too-high interest rates and sold bonds with too-low interest rates, which is a bet that the interest rates will converge.

After Meriwether left Salomon, he founded Long-Term Capital Management in 1994. Long-Term's management team included several MIT PhDs who had been part of Salomon's arbitrage group; two mathematical finance professors (options wizards Myron Scholes and Robert C. Merton) who would win Nobel prizes in economics in 1997; and David Mullins, another MIT PhD, who left his position as vice-chairman of the Federal Reserve Board, where he was expected to succeed Alan Greenspan as Fed chair.

With these star-studded credentials, Long-Term had no trouble attracting investors even though the minimum investment was $10 million and the only thing investors were told about Long-Term's strategy was that the management fees would be 2 percent of assets plus 25 percent of profits. One prominent money manager told me that he did not invest in Long-Term because the only thing he knew for sure was that they were greedy. Other investors were not so cautious. Long-Term raised more than $1 billion.

One of their early strategies involved US Treasury bonds of slightly different maturities—for example, a thirty-year bond that had just been issued and a thirty-year bond that had been issued a few months earlier. The interest rates should be virtually identical, but newly issued bonds tend to be more actively traded and therefore more desirable for traders who jump in and out of the market. The bond market prices the earlier issue to have a slightly higher interest rate because it is harder to find buyers.

The convergence wager is that when a new thirty-year bond is issued, the earlier bonds will be virtually identical and their interest rates will converge. So, Long-Term bought the early bond, sold the current bond, and waited for their interest rates to converge. In contrast to picking up $100 bills on the sidewalk, Scholes characterized Long-Term as a giant vacuum cleaner sucking up nickels that everyone else overlooked.

With leverage of 25 to 1, Long-Term's vacuum cleaner earned (before management fees) 28 percent in 1994, 59 percent in 1995, 57 percent in 1996, and at least 22 percent in 1997. The problem with such massive leverage is that if the anticipated convergence turns, even temporarily, into a divergence, Long-Term could be mortally wounded.

Here's a simple, hypothetical example of their strategy and its risks. Suppose you buy a futures contract that commits you to paying $20 for a bottle of wine ten years from now. You also sell a futures contract that commits you selling a bottle of wine ten years from now for $21. If it is the same bottle of wine, there is a market inefficiency that guarantees you a $1 profit on the delivery date when you pay $20 for the wine and simultaneously sell it for $21.

The profit is not guaranteed if the wines are different. If the wine you buy is a cabernet sauvignon and the wine you sell is a Riesling, there is no guarantee that you can trade one for the other on the delivery date. Perhaps you have observed that these two wines generally sell for about the same price and you are hoping that this will be true on the delivery date. Your plan is to pay $20 for the cabernet on the delivery date and sell it for whatever the market price is that day, using the proceeds to buy the Riesling, which you sell for $21. Table 17.1 shows that, if all goes as planned, you will have your $1 profit, no matter whether the cabernet and Riesling prices are $10 or $30 on the delivery date. All that matters is that they are the same.

Table 17.1: A Profitable Wine Convergence

	Both Wine Prices are $10	Both Wine Prices are $30
Buy cabernet	- $20	- $20
Sell cabernet	$10	$30
Buy Riesling	- $10	- $30
Sell Riesling	$21	$21
Net profit	$1	$1

As long as the two prices converge on the delivery date, you will have your profit. However, as the old English proverb goes, "There's many a slip twixt the cup and the lip." The fact that these cabernet and Riesling prices have been close in the past is no guarantee that they will be close in the future.

In addition, even if the prices do converge on the delivery date, you are only assured a profit on that date. After all, if the wines have different prices today, there is no reason why the price difference couldn't be even larger tomorrow. Both of these risks, magnified by their enormous leverage, contributed to Long-Term's downfall.

Long-Term made complicated trades in bonds, stocks, and mortgages whose prices had been correlated historically. Other trades involved options and other securities whose prices depend on their perceived riskiness. When prices changed because other investors believed risk had increased, Long-Term wagered that perceived riskiness would soon return to its historical norm.

In every case, their strategy was to buy the relatively cheap asset, sell the relatively expensive asset, leverage the heck out of it, and count the profits. The inclusion of "long-term" in Long-Term's name is an apparent reference to the belief that in the long-term, prices will converge and profits will emerge. However, as the great British economist John Maynard Keynes observed during the Great Depression:

This long run is a misleading guide to current affairs. In the long
run we are all dead. Economists set themselves too easy, too useless
a task if in tempestuous seasons they can only tell us that when the
storm is long past the ocean is flat again.

Keynes was mocking the belief that in the long-run the economy
will be calm and everyone who wants a job will have a job. Keynes
believed that the storm of an economic recession is more important
than a hypothetical long run that no one will ever live to see.

In retrospect, Long-Term was blindly picking up nickels in front
of a bulldozer—grabbing small profits while ignoring the possibility
of a catastrophic storm. One of Long-Term's errors was a belief that
historical data were a reliable guide to the future. A Long-Term manager argued that, "What we did is rely on experience. And all science
is based on experience. And if you're not willing to draw any conclusions from experience, you might as well sit on your hands and do
nothing."

Well, doing nothing is better than doing something stupid. Not
trading gold and silver would have been better than assuming the GSR
will always return to the range 34 to 38. In Long-Term's case, doing
nothing would have been better than assuming the future will be just
like the past.

Some of their trades had a logical basis—for example, the interest
rates on newly issued and recently issued Treasury bonds *should be*
approximately the same. Other trades were based on historical patterns that were not much more reliable than the gold-silver ratio. For
example, Long-Term made large bets on the relationship between
United Kingdom, French, and German interest rates. World interest
rates often move in the same direction, but there is no logical reason
why they should move in lockstep.

World interest rates are related because investors can choose
which bonds to buy. If one nation's bonds paid lower interest rates
than the bonds issued by an identical country, then no one would buy
the first country's bonds. So the interest rates have to be the same.
Fair enough, *if* the countries are identical. But countries aren't identical, and their bonds aren't identical. Investors may fear that one

country is more likely to default on its bonds. Investors may fear that one country's currency will depreciate, reducing the realized return on its bonds. Investors may fear that one country may change its tax laws, or that one country's bond market may dry up, making it harder to find buyers.

Figure 17.5 shows the interest rates on ten-year bonds issued by the French and German governments during the thirty-five-year period 1960 through 1995. These two interest rates were closely related, except when they weren't. If you had seen the French and German interest rates separate in 1975 and made a convergence bet that these interest rates would soon get back together again, you would have had to wait fifteen long years for it to happen. That's very much like making a convergence bet on cabernet and Riesling wines and hoping for the best. It is not a riskless bet.

Long-Term also bet that there is a close relationship between US mortgage rates and Treasury bond rates though these, too, do not move in lockstep. The default risks are quite different and mortgages have the added complexity that homeowners pay off their mortgages early when they move or when they refinance at lower interest rates. These confounding factors change over time and are notoriously difficult to predict. A manager later lamented, "We had academics who came in with no trading experience and they started modeling away. Their trades might look good given the assumptions they made, but they often did not pass a simple smell test."

A second error was the assumption that diverse bets (for example, in Italian bonds, German stocks, and US mortgages) were largely uncorrelated because this had been true historically. It turned out Long-Term's bets had two things in common that they overlooked.

Long-Term's net worth at the beginning of 1998 was nearly $5 billion. In August, an unforeseen storm hit. Russia defaulted on its debt and perceived measures of risk rose throughout financial markets. Long-Term had placed bets in many different markets, but an awful lot of them were bets that risk premiums would decline. After the Russian default, historically uncorrelated investments were suddenly highly correlated. Risk premiums rose everywhere, and the bulldozer ran over the nickel picker.

Figure 17.5: Interest Rates on Ten-Year French and German Government Bonds

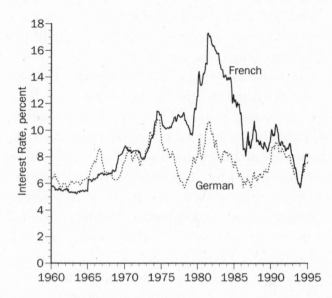

In addition, inspired by Long-Term's success, many copycat firms either figured out the bets Long-Term was making and made the same bets or used similar statistical models that led to the same bets. When these bets went sour, a lot of copycat firms closed their positions, which they did by selling what Long-Term had bought and buying what Long-Term had sold. Prices diverged instead of converging and Long-Term was in trouble, big trouble.

Long-Term argued that all it needed was time for financial markets to return to normal, but they didn't have time. Their tremendous leverage created enormous losses. Long-Term lost $550 million on August 21 and $2.1 billion for the entire month, nearly half its net worth. The firm tried to raise more money so that it could weather the storm, but frightened lenders didn't want to loan Long-Term more money. They wanted their money back.

Keynes was not only a master economist—he was also a legendary investor. One of his enduring observations was that, "Markets can remain irrational long than you can remain solvent." Perhaps markets overreacted to the Russian default. Perhaps Long-Term's losses would have eventually turned into profits. But it couldn't stay solvent long enough to find out.

On September 23, Warren Buffett faxed Long-Term a one-page letter offering to buy the firm for $250 million, roughly 5 percent of its value at the beginning of the year. The offer was take it or leave it, and would expire at 12:30 p.m., about an hour after the fax had been sent. The deadline passed and the funeral preparations began.

The Federal Reserve Bank of New York feared that the domino effects of a Long-Term default would trigger a global financial crises. The Federal Reserve and Long-Term's creditors took over Long-Term and put in enough money to buy time for an orderly liquidation of its assets. The creditors got their money back, Long-Term's founding partners lost $1.9 billion, and the other investors got an expensive lesson in the power of leverage and the fragility of statistical relationships.

After Long-Term collapsed, Meriwether and many of the other Long-Term partners started new funds based on largely the same strategies. Most folded during the 2007—2009 financial crisis, typically for the same reasons that Long-Term failed. No problem. Meriwether promptly launched yet another fund.

Fool me once, shame on you. Fool me twice, shame on me. Fool me three times . . . well, you know the rest.

■ THE FLASH CRASH

A 2011 article in the wonderful technology magazine *Wired* was filled with awe and admiration for computerized stock trading systems. These systems are called *algorithmic traders* because the computers decide to buy and sell using computer code ("algorithms") in place of human judgment. Humans write the algorithms that guide the computers but, after that, the computers are on their own.

Some of these systems track stock prices, others dissect news stories. They all look for patterns that would have been profitable signals in the past. Then, when this pattern reappears, they move fast, buying thousands of shares in a few seconds and then typically selling these shares seconds later. Done over and over, day after day, a profit of a few pennies (or even a fraction of a penny) in a few seconds on thousands of shares can add up to real money. *Wired* marveled that these automated systems are "more efficient, faster, and smarter than any human."

Well, these programs do process data faster than any human, but they are no smarter than the humans who write the code that guides the computers. If a human tells a computer to look for potentially profitable patterns—no matter whether the discovered pattern makes sense or not—and to buy or sell when the pattern reappears, the computer will do so whether it makes sense or not. Indeed, some of the human brains behind the computers boast that they don't really understand why their computers decide to trade. After all, their computers are smarter than them, right? Instead of bragging, they should have been praying.

It's similar to the data dredging using by Long-Term Capital Management, but even worse because *all* human judgment is removed. And it is even worse because the copycat problem is magnified a hundred fold. If humans give hundreds of computers very similar guidelines, then hundreds of computers may try to buy or sell the same thing at the same time, wildly destabilizing financial markets. To *Wired*'s credit, they recognized the danger of unsupervised computers moving in unison: "[A]t its worse, it is an inscrutable feedback loop . . . that can overwhelm the system it was built to navigate."

On May 6, 2010, the US stock market was hit by what has come to be known as the "flash crash." Investors that day were nervous about the Greek debt crisis and an anxious mutual fund manager tried to hedge its portfolio by selling $4.1 billion in futures contracts. The idea was that if the market dropped, the losses on the fund's stock portfolio would be offset by profits on its futures contracts. This seemingly prudent transaction somehow triggered the computers. The computers bought many of the futures contracts the fund was selling, then sold them seconds later because they don't like to hold positions for very long. Futures prices started falling and the computers decided to buy and sell more heavily. The computers were provoked into a trading frenzy as they bought and sold futures contracts among themselves, like a hot potato being tossed from hand to hand.

Nobody knows exactly what unleashed the computers. Remember, even the people behind the computers don't understand why their computers trade. In one 15-second interval, the computers traded 27,000 contracts among themselves, half the total trading volume, and ended up with a net purchase of only 200 contracts at the end of this 15-second madness. The trading frenzy spread to the regular stock market, and the flood of sell orders overwhelmed potential buyers. The Dow Jones industrial average fell nearly 600 points in 5 minutes. Market prices went haywire, yet the computers kept trading. Proctor & Gamble, a rock solid blue chip company, dropped 37 percent in less than 4 minutes. Some computers paid more than $100,000 a share for Apple, Hewlett-Packard, and Sotheby's. Others sold Accenture and other major stocks for less than a penny a share. The computers had no common sense. They blindly bought and sold because that's what their algorithms told them to do.

The madness ended when a built-in safeguard in the futures market suspended all trading for five seconds. Incredibly, this five-second stabilization of prices was enough to persuade the computers to stop their frenzied trading. Fifteen minutes later, markets were back to normal and the temporary six hundred-point drop in the Dow was just a nightmarish memory.

There have been other flash crashes since and there will most likely be more in the future. Oddly enough, Proctor & Gamble was hit again on August 30, 2013, on the New York Stock Exchange (NYSE) with a mini flash crash, so called because nothing special happened to other stocks on the NYSE and nothing special happened to Proctor & Gamble stock on other exchanges.

Inexplicably, nearly 200 trades on the NYSE, involving a total of about 250,000 shares of Procter & Gamble stock occurred within a 1-second interval, triggering a 5 percent drop in price, from $77.50 to $73.61, and then a recovery less than a minute later. One lucky person happened to be in the right place at the right time, and bought 65,000 shares for an immediate $155,000 profit. Why did it happen? No one knows. Remember, humans aren't as smart as computers.

Yeah, right.

■ **Don't be Fooled:** Don't bet the bank on historical patterns and relationships that have little or no logical basis. The price of gold may be 34-to-38 times the price of silver for years, but there is no reason it has to stay in that range. The US mortgage market may have been uncorrelated with the Russian bond market for years, but a panic could have similar effects on both markets. Don't just look at numbers. Think about reasons.

18

THEORY WITHOUT DATA

MANY OF THE EXAMPLES IN THIS BOOK INVOLVE THE DODGY practice of ransacking data without having any underlying theory or well-defined purpose—other than to uncover an interesting statistical relationship that might lead to fame and funding. This is data without theory.

The other end of the spectrum is theory without data—a semi-plausible theory that is presented as fact without ever confronting data. A theory is just a conjecture until it is tested with reliable data. For predictions decades or even centuries into the future, that is pretty much the norm.

■ ON A ROAD TO NOWHERE

When Albert Einstein was asked the most important concept he had ever learned, he immediately said "compounding." Not statistical mechanics. Not quantum theory. Not relativity. Compounding.

Suppose you invest $1,000 at a 10 percent annual interest rate. The first year, you earn $100 interest on your $1,000 investment. Every year after that, you earn 10 percent on $1,000 plus *interest on the interest you have already earned*, which is what makes compounding so powerful, bordering on the miraculous. After 50 years of compound interest, your $1,000 grows to $117,391. A seemingly modest rate of return, com-pounded many times, turns a small investment into a fortune. The miracle of compounding doesn't just apply to investments. It applies to anything growing at a compound rate, including population and resource usage.

The miracle of compounding figures prominently in a 1972 report, *The Limits to Growth*, sponsored by the mysterious-sounding Club of Rome. Is this a secret brotherhood, perhaps related to the Freemasons or the *Da Vinci Code*? The Club of Rome is more prosaic. In 1968 an Italian industrialist assembled an international group in Rome to support an interdisciplinary, long-term analysis of the world's prospects. An ambitious undertaking! He called this small group with the big agenda the Club of Rome.

The Limits to Growth was very popular. It was translated into thirty languages and sold more than twelve million copies. The lead author, Donella ("Dana") Meadows, had an undergraduate degree in chemistry and a PhD in biophysics and was a part of an MIT team assembled by Jay W. Forrester to create World3, a model of the world socioeconomic system.

Forrester began his career as an electrical engineer but moved from engineering to management, developing what came to be known as "system dynamics" for understanding complex phenomena. In order to understand the dynamic evolution of a system— for example, the creation, production, and marketing of a new product—it is crucial to understand the feedback, interactions, and delays among the various parts of the system. Because the models are so complex, computer simulations are used to analyze the system's evolution.

Forrester was invited to a Club of Rome meeting, where he was asked if system dynamics could be used to model the "predicament of mankind" caused by the demands of a growing population on a planet with finite resources. Of course he could. Even though he had no formal training in economics, Forrester sketched his model, called World1, on his plane ride back to the United States. He fiddled with the model—now called World2 and involving forty-three variables— and described several computer simulations of his model in a 1971 book called *World Dynamics*.

Forrester's conclusion was that the world standard of living in 1971 might be the maximum level the planet could sustain. He concluded that, "From the long view of a hundred years hence, the present efforts of underdeveloped countries to industrialize may be unwise." To maintain the 1971 standard of living, he recommended reducing the birth rate by 30 percent, food production by 20 percent, and natural resource usage by 75 percent.

The World3 model that was developed by Meadows's team has many more variables and equations than World2, but has the same core assumptions and pessimistic conclusions. It also has the same flaws. At the most fundamental level, the problem is that Forrester and Meadows are not economists and seem to have no more than a passing acquaintance with economic theory or data. *None* of the equations are based on economic growth models; *none* of the equations are estimated from historical data.

Extrapolating decades or centuries into the future is extraordinarily challenging. And in this case they tried to do it without using theories that had been tested by others or testing their own theories. Their models are an extreme example of garbage in, gospel out, in that the people who were persuaded by their models' predictions were persuaded because the predictions came from a computer, not because the model made any sense.

The disconnect between the model and reality is strikingly illustrated by the recommendation they made in a twenty-year update of *The Limits to Growth*:

> [The scenario] shows a simulated world . . . with a definition of "enough." This world has decided to aim for an average industrial output per capita of $350 per person per year—about the equivalent of that in South Korea, or twice the level of Brazil in 1990. . . . If this hypothetical society could also reduce military expenditures and corruption, a stabilized economy with an industrial output per capita of $350 would be equivalent in material comforts to the average level in Europe in 1990.

William Nordhaus, a distinguished Yale economist and persistent critic of these models, made the following sardonic observation about the model (which he called Limits II) in a paper titled "Lethal Model 2":

[T]he factual predicates of the recommendation are so faulty that one wonders whether Limits II is referring to another planet. A rough estimate of global per capita GNP in 1990 would be $4200, while that of OECD countries would be $20,170. South Korea's per capita GDP in purchasing-power-parity terms in 1990 was $7190, not $350. . . . The Limits II proposals would limit our material aspirations to attaining the living standards of Somalia or Chad. . . . The world could not afford to undertake the investments to slow global warming or the research and development to develop resource-saving technological change. The [Limits to Growth] prescription would save the planet at the expense of its inhabitants.

The models constructed by Forrester and Meadows involve the complex interactions of many variables and equations, but the key to their apocalyptic predictions is very simple: compound growth can deplete finite resources surprisingly soon.

Figure 18.1: Doomsday is Inevitable

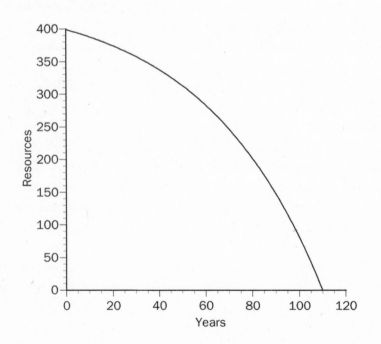

The World2 model assumes that the world's resources are 400 times the world's current annual consumption of resources. These resources would last 400 years if consumption were constant, but will be exhausted sooner if consumption increases each year as the population grows. Compound growth has the power to enrich or destroy. With a modest 2 percent growth rate, annual consumption will be 7 times the current level in 100 years and, as shown in Figure 18.1, the world's resources will be exhausted in 110 years.

This compound growth model is not sensitive to the assumed level of resources or the consumption growth rate in the sense that no matter how high the initial level of resources and no matter how fast the annual increase in consumption, finite resources will eventually be exhausted. What is newsworthy is that with compound growth, the world's resources will be depleted surprisingly soon. The World2 model published in 1971 predicted that the world standard of living would peak in 1990 and then decline inexorably.

The solution? Forrester's models assume that the birth rate is positively related to living standards in general and to food production in particular. Because he believes that an increase in food production will increase the birth rate, he recommends that *less* food be produced! Specifically, he argued that world governments should reduce the world supply of food by 20 percent, so that people will be persuaded to have fewer children, or starve. (You might think he was joking. He wasn't.)

Doomsday population predictions have been around at least since Malthus's 1798 *Essay on the Principle of Population*. At the time, many intellectuals believed that the human race had reached a point where society could improve without limit. In contrast to this unfettered optimism, Malthus argued that, throughout history, the population tended to increase faster than the supply of food. Indeed, improvements in agricultural productivity only lead to higher birth rates, until there are again too many people and not enough food. This crisis is resolved by famine, disease, and war—which mask the underlying problem: overpopulation. Then the cycle repeats. Economics is sometimes labeled "the dismal science" because of Malthus's bleak analysis.

Malthus argued that instead of using high death rates to resolve the problem of too many people and not enough food, it could be resolved by lower birth rates through celibacy, birth control, abortion, and prostitution. Yes, the good reverend saw virtue in abortion and prostitution.

So far, Malthus has been wrong. Incredible technological advances have allowed the world population to increase by a factor of seven. Nonetheless, Forrester and Meadows essentially repeat Malthus's 1798 assumptions and conclusions. Resource usage grows at a compound rate while the supply of resources does not. If new resources are discovered, the higher standard of living increases the birth rate so that the growing population soon overwhelms resources.

One obvious problem with Malthus, Forrester, and Meadows is that abundance does *not* increase the birth rate. Since Malthus's time, we have invented effective means of birth control and, whether we compare nations or look at a single nation, higher living standards clearly lead to *slower* population growth. Today, the rate of population growth is near zero or even negative in some developed countries.

In addition, there is no empirical basis for their assumption that resource consumption grows at a compound rate while the world's supply of resources is fixed. Technological progress that allows a more efficient utilization of resources may also grow at a compound rate. Malthus, Forrester, and Meadows completely ignore the role of prices in persuading people to adapt to changing conditions. If something becomes scarce, it will become more expensive and people will use less of it and discover less-expensive alternatives.

Forrester and Meadows lump all natural resources together into a single bundle called *resources*. In reality, there are many different kinds of natural resources, some more plentiful than others (think oxygen and gold), and humans are endlessly creative in thinking of ways to substitute more-plentiful resources for less-plentiful ones. We have figured out how to use nuclear fuels in place of fossil fuels; e-mail in place of snail-mail; plastic in place of wood, metal, and glass. No one knows what substitutions will take place over the next one hundred years, but we can be certain that there will be substitutions.

The underlying problem with Malthus, Forrester, and Meadows is that their reasoning has a plausible ring to it, but they do not make any attempt to see whether historical data support or refute their theories. We are asked to believe because they believe.

Just as we can be fooled by data without theory, so we can be fooled by theory without data.

■ **Don't be Fooled:** We need both theory and data. Don't be persuaded by one without the other.

If somebody ransacks data to find a pattern, we still need a theory that makes sense. On the other hand, a theory is just a theory until it is tested with persuasive data.

No matter who has done the study, it needs to pass the common sense test and it needs to be tested with data that are unbiased and have not been corrupted by data grubbing.

19

WHEN TO BE PERSUADED
AND WHEN TO BE SKEPTICAL

THESE DAYS WE ARE DELUGED BY DATA, AND AT THE SAME TIME WE are often duped by data.

Sometimes, data help us evaluate competing claims and make good choices. Governments choose policies that reduce unemployment and eradicate cholera, polio, and smallpox. Business create products that improve our lives and can be produced at reasonable cost. Investors buy low-cost mutual funds and choose diversified portfolios of attractively priced stocks. Patients are given medicines and treatments that can literally save their lives. Consumers choose products that work and are competitively priced. We stop smoking and start exercising.

Other times, we are deceived by data and make bad choices that have expensive, even disastrous, consequences. Governments impose rent controls and raise taxes in the midst of an economic recession. Businesses follow the latest management fad and rely on surveys that are hopelessly biased. Investors chase hot stocks and trust their money to con artists. Patients misinterpret test results and take medications and treatments that are worthless, or worse. Consumers follow the latest diet craze and buy homes because housing prices always go up. We think the successful are jinxed and that the unsuccessful are due for good luck.

When it comes to data, there are times to be persuaded and times to be skeptical.

■ SEDUCED BY PATTERNS

We are hardwired to make sense of the world around us—to notice patterns and invent theories to explain these patterns. We underestimate how easily patterns can be created by inexplicable random events—by good luck and bad luck.

We should aspire to recognize that we are susceptible to the lure of patterns. Instead of being seduced, we should be skeptical. Correlations, trends, and other patterns by themselves prove nothing. Every pattern is just a pattern, unless there is a sensible explanation. Every sensible theory should be tested with fresh data.

■ MISLEADING DATA

Experiments often involve changing one thing while holding confounding factors constant and seeing what happens. For example, plants can be given varying doses of fertilizer while holding water, sunlight, and other factors constant. In the behavioral sciences, however, experiments involving humans are limited. We can't make people lose their jobs, divorce their spouses, or have children and see how they react. Instead, we make do with observational data—observing people who lost their jobs, divorced, or have children. It's very natural to draw conclusions from what we observe. We all do it, but it's risky.

Self-selection bias occurs when we compare people who made different choices without thinking about *why* they made these choices. Students who choose colleges with low graduation rates may do so because they would be less likely to graduate from other colleges. Students who choose to go to college may be more talented and motivated than those who choose not to go.

Our conclusions would be more convincing if choice was removed—for example, if randomly selected students were compelled to attend different colleges or not to go to college at all. Fortunately, scientists are not allowed to ruin people's lives in order to collect data for their research papers. Unfortunately, we need to be wary of data that are susceptible to selection bias.

Another common problem with theorizing about what we observe is the survivor bias that can occur because we don't see things that no longer exist. A study of the elderly does not include people who did not live long enough to become elderly. An examination of planes that survived bombing runs does not include planes that were shot down. A survey of people staying in certain hotels, flying on certain airlines, or visiting certain countries does not include people who did it once and said, "Never again."

A compilation of the common characteristics of great companies does not include companies that had these characteristics but were less successful, even failed. Our conclusions would be more persuasive if, before looking at the data, we enumerated the factors we think make a difference and identified companies that have these characteristics and companies that do not. Then see how things turn out.

Don't overlook the possibility of errors in recording data or writing computer code. Reinhart and Rogoff bolstered the case for reducing government spending and raising taxes in the midst of a great recession by inadvertently omitting data that undercut their argument and by calculating averages in an unusual and unpersuasive way. Levitt and Donohue argued that legalized abortion in the United States reduced the crime rate, but their study had several glitches, including a programming error.

■ MANGLED GRAPHS

Visual displays—graphs—can help us interpret data and draw inferences. A useful graph displays data accurately and coherently and helps us see tendencies, patterns, trends, and relationships. A picture can be worth a thousand numbers.

However, graphs can also distort data. Watch out for graphs that exaggerate differences by omitting zero from a graph's axis. Remember the CEO who thought a modest decline in revenue was a crisis, until zero was put back on the axis.

Be doubly skeptical of graphs that have two vertical axes and omit zero from either or both axes. A clever artist can make it seem that income has gone up much faster than consumer prices, or vice versa, by fiddling with the range of numbers shown on the axes.

Watch out for graphs that omit data, use inconsistent spacing on the axes, reverse the axes, and clutter the graph with chartjunk.

■ CALCULATING WITHOUT THINKING

There is a natural tendency to focus on the accuracy of numerical calculations without thinking hard enough about whether they are the right calculations.

In the infamous Monty Hall problem, the existence of two possibilities—one good and one bad—doesn't mean that good and bad outcomes are equally likely. Even more strikingly, experts have repeatedly abandoned common sense by arguing that the gender of an unseen child depends on whether this child is older than a sibling, has an unusual name, or is born on a Tuesday. Before you double-check someone's arithmetic, double-check their reasoning.

A very common logical error is to confuse two conditional statements. The probability that a person who has a disease will have a positive test result is *not* the same as the probability that a person with a positive test result has the disease.

As the population grows over time, so do many human activities (including the number of people watching television, eating oranges, and dying) which are unrelated but nonetheless statistically correlated because they grow with the population. Watching television does not make us eat oranges and eating oranges does not kill us. Correlation is not the statistical term for causation. No matter how close the correlation, we still need a logical explanation.

Comparisons are often critical in empirical studies. However, we need to watch out for superficial comparisons: comparisons of the percentage changes in big numbers and small numbers, comparisons of things that have nothing in common except that they increase over time, and comparisons of irrelevant data.

■ LOOKING FOR CONFOUNDING FACTORS

When you hear a puzzling assertion (or even one that makes sense), think about whether confounding factors might by responsible.

Sweden has a higher female mortality rate than Costa Rica—because there are more elderly women in Sweden. Berkeley's graduate programs admitted fewer female applicants—because women applied to more selective programs. One type of surgery was more successful than another—because it was used in easier cases. Patients with pancreatic cancer drank more coffee than other patients—because many of the other patients had ulcers and stopped drinking coffee.

Confounding factors are often present in observational studies, where we can't control the choices people make, but they can also be present in experimental settings where the researcher forgot to control for a confounding influence.

■ HOT STREAKS

When a fair coin is flipped 10 times, a streak of 4 heads in a row seems too remarkable to be explained by chance, even though streaks this long, or longer, can be expected 47 percent of the time. We are tempted to think that something must be unusual about the coin or the person flipping the coin.

When a basketball player makes several shots in a row, we are tempted to conclude that the player is hot—and a hot player is very likely to make the next shot. We are too quick to discount the possibility that the player was lucky. The same is true in all sports, and outside sports.

There is credible evidence that athletes do sometimes get hot, but the fluctuations in their abilities are much smaller than players and fans imagine. The same is no doubt true outside of sports.

■ REGRESSION TO THE MEAN

A student (let's call her Rachel) who receives the highest score on a test probably benefited from good luck (in the questions that were asked and the answers that were guessed) and consequently did well not only compared to other students, but also relative to her own ability. Rachel's ability is most likely not as far from the average ability as her test score is from the average score. Rachel's score on a second test is consequently likely to be closer to the average—to regress to the mean. Similarly, the ability of the student with the lowest test score is probably not as miserable as the test score—this student will probably do somewhat better on a second test.

The same is true of the most and least successful companies, athletes, employees, employers, and potential soulmates. Don't be fooled by successes and failures. Those who appear to be the best are probably not as far above average as they seem. Nor are those who appear to be the worst as far below average as they seem. Expect those at the extremes to regress to the mean.

■ THE LAW OF AVERAGES

A very different—and very incorrect—argument is that successes must be balanced by failures (and failures by successes) so that things average out. Every coin flip that lands heads makes tails more likely. Every red at roulette makes black more likely. A baseball player who gets several base hits is due for an out. A house that has never had a fire is due to burn down. An airline passenger who has had many safe flights is due for a crash. These beliefs are all incorrect.

Good luck will certainly not continue indefinitely, but do not assume that good luck makes bad luck more likely, or vice versa.

■ THE TEXAS SHARPSHOOTER

Researchers seeking fame and funding often turn into Texas sharpshooters, firing at random and painting a bullseye around the area with the most hits. It is easy to find a theory that fits the data if the data are used to invent the theory. Finding something only proves someone looked for a data cluster or some other pattern. What is found is not persuasive unless it makes sense and is tested with un-contaminated data.

Other Texas sharpshooters fire at hundreds of targets and only report the hits. Test hundreds of theories and only report the theory that fits the data best. Look at hundreds of characteristics of cancer victims and only report the characteristic that is the most common.

Eventually stumbling on a theory that is supported by the data only proves that we tested lots of theories. The theory still needs to be sensible and confirmed with fresh data.

Sometimes researchers are coy about being Texas sharpshooters and it takes a bit of detective work to uncover their mischief. Look for unnatural groupings of data. Be suspicious when it seems that the researchers only reported some of their statistical tests. Don't be easily convinced by theories that are consistent with data but defy common sense. When a theory is generated by ransacking data, these plundered data don't provide a fair test of the theory.

■ WATCH OUT FOR PRUNED DATA

Watch out for studies where data were omitted, especially if you suspect that the omitted data were discarded because they do not support the reported results. Some clues are data that start or end on unusual dates ("baseball players born between 1875 and 1930") or are grouped in unusual ways ("women over the age of 75," "years when government debt exceeded 90 percent of GDP")

What these studies really demonstrate is that people chasing promotion, tenure, and grants can find support for preposterous theories by discarding data that don't support their preposterous theories.

■ DATA WITHOUT THEORY ARE JUST DATA

Ever hopeful, people scour data looking for ways to beat the stock market and win the lottery, and come up with ridiculous theories involving the Super Bowl or having a friend named Mary buy their lottery tickets. Don't fall for such nonsense.

We can always find patterns—even in randomly generated data—if we just look hard enough. No matter how striking the pattern, we still need a plausible theory to explain the pattern. Otherwise, we have nothing more than coincidence.

If a theory doesn't make sense, be skeptical. If a statistical conclusion seems unbelievable, don't believe it. If you check the data and the tests, there is usually a serious problem that wipes out the conclusion.

■ A THEORY WITHOUT DATA IS JUST A THEORY

People believe in comforting things—because they are comforting. Evidence to the contrary is discounted or discarded. It is easier to dismiss inconvenient facts than to admit that we are wrong. Determined to make sense of the world, even the most intelligent people can be stubborn and foolish.

Just as people can be fooled by data without theory, so they can be fooled by theory without data. We need both theory and data. Ransacking data for a pattern is not enough. The pattern has to be explained by a theory that makes sense and needs to be tested with new data. At the other extreme, a theory is just a conjecture until it tested with reliable data.

■ A LOVELY DAY TO BE BORN

The origin of Valentine's Day is as mysterious as love, the sometimes inexplicable passion it celebrates. Legend has it that a man named Valentine defied Roman Emperor Claudius II by marrying Christian couples and aiding Christians who were persecuted by the Romans. Claudius arrested Valentine and tried to persuade him to convert to Roman paganism. When Valentine refused and instead tried to convert Claudius to Christianity, he was beaten with clubs and stoned. Valentine survived the beating, so he was beheaded.

A Saint Valentine was buried on February 14 beside a road north of Rome, but we do not know if this Saint Valentine was the Valentine who had the legendary conversation with Claudius, or even if that conversation ever happened.

It is also not known how Valentine's Day came to be associated with romantic love. In 1392, the English poet Geoffrey Chaucer wrote a poem celebrating the anniversary of the May 2 engagement of King Richard II and Anne of Bohemia, who married when they were fifteen years old. Chaucer wrote that, "For this was Saint Valentine's Day, when every bird cometh there to choose his mate." However, Chaucer was probably referring to May 2 (the day for celebrating Saint Valentine of Genoa) and not February 14, which is the middle of winter in

England and not a likely time for lovebirds to mate. Nonetheless, February 14 has somehow evolved into an international sales event for flowers, candy, jewelry, and dust catchers.

Love, marriage, and a baby carriage. A pregnant woman's "due date" is approximately forty weeks after the first day of her last normal menstrual period. This is an average, around which there is considerable variability—much like a weather forecast made weeks in advance. Even using estimates based on a woman's age and ethnicity and whether this is her first child, there is only about a 5 percent chance that the birth will be on the due date. Twenty percent of all births are more than 2 weeks away, either before or after the due date.

A 2011 study using US data for 1996 through 2006 concluded that mothers can choose to give birth on Valentine's Day. This is an interesting and provocative finding because spontaneous births are generally considered, well, spontaneous in that women cannot control the timing.

This study found that, not only can women choose Valentine's Day, the day of love, they can avoid having their child born on Halloween, the day of death.

Not so fast. Many people with Halloween birthdays were indignant when they heard of this study, proclaiming Halloween to be their favorite holiday. One person wrote that, "I loved trick or treating on my birthday," and another wrote that, "I loved having Birthday/Halloween parties with everyone wearing costumes."

Survey says: Christmas is the favorite holiday in the United States, followed by Thanksgiving and Halloween. Valentine's Day is tied with Hanukkah for tenth. With its lethal combination of guilt and disappointment, the only poll Valentine's Day wins is for least favorite holiday.

And yet, and yet. There is that study, by two Yale professors no less.

What do you think?

SOURCES

Chapter 1: Patterns, Patterns, Patterns

CBS News, "World Cup Final a Battle of Octopus vs. Parakeet," July 14, 2010.

Daily Mail (2010). "World Cup 2010: Paul the Psychic Octopus Has Competition as Mani the Parakeet Pecks Holland as his Winners," Mail Online, July 9, 2010.

Daily Mail Foreign Services (2010). "He's No Sucker: Paul the Oracle Octopus is Right For the Seventh Time After Picking Germany to Beat Uruguay to Third Place," Mail Online, July 10, 2010.

Ria Novsti (2010). "German Octopus Predicts Spanish Victory in World Cup," July 9, 2010.

Sy Montgomery (2010). "Deep Intellect: Inside the Mind of an Octopus," Orion.

Jennifer A. Mather, Roland C. Anderson, and James B. Wood, Octopus: The Ocean's Intelligent Invertebrate, Timber Press, 2010.

Bernard Kettlewell, The Evolution of Melanism: The Study of a Recurring Necessity, with Special Reference to Industrial Melanism in the Lepidoptera, Oxford: Oxford University Press, 1973.

M. E. N. Majerus, Melanism: Evolution in Action, Oxford: Oxford University Press, 1998.

A. P. Møller (1992). "Female Preference for Symmetrical Male Sexual Ornaments," Nature 357: 238–40.

A. P. Møller Sexual Selection and the Barn Swallow. Oxford: Oxford University Press 1994.

A. C. Little, B. C. Jones, C. Waitt, B. P. Tiddeman, D. R. Feinberg, D. I. Perrett, C. A. Apicella, and F. W. Marlowe. "Symmetry is Related to Sexual

Dimorphism in Faces: Data Across Culture and Species," *PLOS one* 3(5): e2106. doi:10.1371/journal.pone.0002106.

G. Rhodes (2006). "The Evolutionary Psychology of Facial Beauty," *Annual Review of Psychology* 57: 199–226.

John Maynard Smith, David Harper, *Animal Signals,* Oxford: Oxford University Press, 2003.

Ewen Callaway (2010). "Report Finds Massive Fraud at Dutch Universities," *Nature* 479: 15.

Michael Shermer (2008). "Patternicity: Finding Meaningful Patterns in Meaningless Noise," *Scientific American* 299 (6).

Michael Shermer, *The Believing Brain: From Ghosts and Gods to Politics and Conspiracies—How We Construct Beliefs and Reinforce Them as Truths*, New York: Henry Holt, 2011.

Kevin R. Foster and Hanna Kokko (2009). "The Evolution of Superstitious and Superstition-Like Behavior," 276 PROC. R. SOC. B. 31, 31.

A. J. Wakefield, S. H. Murch, A. Anthony, J. Linnell, D. M. Casson, M. Malik, M. Berelowitz, A. P. Dhillon, M. A. Thomson, P. Harvey, A. Valentine, S. E. Davies, and J. A. Walker-Smith (1998). "Ileal-Lymphoid-Nodular Hyperplasia, Non-Specific Colitis, and Pervasive Developmental Disorder in Children," *The Lancet* 351 (9103): 637–41.

Brian Deer, "Revealed: MMR Research Scandal," *The Sunday Times* (London), February 22, 2004.

Brian Deer (2011). "Secrets of the MMR Scare: How the Case Against the MMR Vaccine Was Fixed," *BMJ*: 342.

Fiona Godlee (2011). "Wakefield's Article Linking MMR Vaccine And Autism Was Fraudulent," *BMJ*: 342.

Phil Plaitt (2013). "Andrew Wakefield Tries to Shift Blame for UK Measles Epidemic," *Slate*.

J. P. A. Ioannidis (2005). "Why Most Published Research Findings Are False," *PLoS Medicine* 2 (8): e124.

Steven Goodman and Sander Greenland (2007), "Assessing the Unreliability of the Medical Literature: A Response to 'Why Most Published Research Findings Are False,'" Johns Hopkins University, Department of Biostatistics.

Steven Goodman and Sander Greenland (2007). "Why Most Published Research Findings Are False: Problems in the Analysis," *PLoS Medicine* 4 (4): e168.

J. P. A. Ioannidis (2007). "Why Most Published Research Findings Are False: Author's Reply to Goodman and Greenland," *PLoS Medicine* 4 (6): e215.

J. P. A. Ioannidis (2005). "Contradicted and Initially Stronger Effects in Highly Cited Clinical Research," *JAMA: the Journal of the American Medical Association* 294 (2): 218–28.

Chapter 2: Garbage In, Gospel Out

Associated Press, "Anger Doubles Risk of Attack of Heart Attack Victims," *The New York Times*, March 19, 1994.

Charles Babbage, *Passages from the Life of a Philosopher*, London: Longman, Green, Longman, Roberts, & Green; 1864, reprinted, New Brunswick: Rutgers University Press, 1994.

Jonathan Shaw, "Why 'Big Data' Is a Big Deal," *Harvard Magazine*, March-April 2014, p. 30.

Jason Stanley and Vesla Waever, "Is the United States a 'Racial Democracy'?," *The New York Times*, Online January 12, 2014.

E. Scott Geller, Nason W. Russ, Mark G. Altomari (1986). "Naturalistic Observations of Beer Drinking Among College Students," *Journal of Applied Behavior Analysis* 19: 391–96.

Steven Reinberg, "Too Much TV May Take Years Off Your Life," HealthDay.

French survey: Cynthia Crossen, "Margin of Error: Studies Galore Support Products and Positions, but Are They Reliable?," *The Wall Street Journal*, November 14, 1991.

J. Lennert Veerman, Genevieve N. Healy, Linda J. Cobiac, Theo Vos, Elisabeth A. H. Winkler, Neville Owen, and David W Dunstan (2011). "Television Viewing Time and Reduced Life Expectancy: a Life Table Analysis," *British Journal of Sports Medicine* Online: doi:10.1136/bjsm.2011.085662.

William G. Bowen, Matthew M. Chingos, and Michael S. McPherson, *Crossing the Finish Line: Completing College at America's Public Universities*, Princeton: Princeton University Press, 2009.

David Leonhardt. "Colleges are Failing in Graduation Rates," *The New York Times*, September 9, 2009.

Sharon Jayson, "College Drinking is Liberating, and a Good Excuse," *USA Today*, August 22, 2011.

Edward R. Murrow, speech to the Radio and Television News Directors Association (RTNDA) Convention, Chicago, October 15, 1958.

Boykin v. Georgia Pacific 706 *F.2d* 1384, 32 *FEP Cases* 25 (5th Cir. 1983).

The Steering Committee of the Physicians' Health Study Research Group (1988). "Preliminary Report: Findings From the Aspirin Component of the Ongoing Physicians' Health Study," *New England Journal of Medicine*, January 28, 1988, 262–64.

Daniel Nasaw, "Who, What, Why: How do Cats Survive Falls From Great Heights?," *BBC News Magazine*, March 24, 2012.

Wayne Whitney and Cheryl Mehlhaff collected the data reported in Jared Diamond, "How Cats Survive Falls from New York Skyscapers," *Natural History*, 98: 20–26 (August 1989).

Jim Collins, *Good to Great,* New York: HarperCollins, 2001.

Tom Peters and Robert H. Waterman, Jr., *In Search of Excellence*, New York: Harper & Row, 1982.

Bruce G. Resnick and Timothy L. Smunt (2008). "From Good to Great to . . ." *Academy of Management Perspectives* 22(4): 6–12.

Phil Rosenzweig, *The Halo Effect*, New York: The Free Press, 2007.

Gabrielle Baum and Gary Smith (2013). "Great Companies: The Secrets of Success are Still a Secret," unpublished.

Chapter 3: Apples and Prunes

L. L. Miao, "Gastric Freezing: An Example of the Evaluation of Medical Therapy by Randomized Clinical Trials," in J. P. Bunker, B. A. Barnes, and F. Mosteller, editors, *Costs, Risks and Benefits of Surgery*, New York: Oxford University Press, 1977.

J. Bruce Moseley, Kimberly O'Malley, Nancy J. Petersen, Terri J. Menke, Baruch A. Brody, David H. Kuykendall, John C. Hollingsworth, Carol M. Ashton, and Nelda P. Wray (2002). "A Controlled Trial of Arthroscopic Surgery for Osteoarthritis of the Knee," *New England Journal of Medicine* 347: 81–88.

Alexandra Kirkley, Trevor B. Birmingham, Robert B. Litchfield, J. Robert Giffin, Kevin R. Willits, Cindy J. Wong, Brian G. Feagan, Allan Donner, Sharon H. Griffin, Linda M. D'Ascanio, Janet E. Pope, and Peter J. Fowler (2008). "A Randomized Trial of Arthroscopic Surgery for Osteoarthritis of the Knee," *New England Journal of Medicine* 359: 1097–1107.

Susan Milton, "Wellfleet the Victim in Statistical Murder Mystery," *Cape Cod Times*, December 12, 1994.

Wheeler's Market Intelligence (2011). "Analysis of Potential Impacts of Liberty Quarry on the Tourism Industry and Property Values in Temecula, California."

John E. Husing (2007). "Liberty Quarry: Economic Impact on Riverside County & Its Southwestern Area."

Diane Hite (2006). "Summary Analysis: Impact of Operational Gravel Pit on House Values, Delaware County, Ohio," Auburn University.

Peter Berck, "A Note on the Environmental Costs of Aggregate," Liberty Quarry Environmental Impact Report, FEIR Sections, Appendix U.

Peter Berck, letter submitted by Gary Johnson to the Riverside County Board of Supervisors, January 28, 2012.

Manfred Keil and Gary Smith (2011). "The Estimated Costs and Benefits of the Proposed Liberty Quarry," Rose Institute of State and Local Government.

T. Odean (1998). "Volume, Volatility, Price and Profit When All Traders Are Above Average." *J. Finance* 53(6): 1887–1934.

P. Slovic, B. Fischhoff, S. Lichtenstein (1976). "The Certainty Illusion," *ORI Res. Bull* 16(4): 1–38.

E. J. Langer, J. Roth (1975). "Heads I Win, Tails It's Chance: The Illusion of Control as a Function of the Sequence of Outcomes in a Purely Chance Task." *J. Personality Soc. Psych.* 32(6): 951–55.

D. T. Miller, M. Ross (1975). "Self-serving Bias in Attribution of Causality: Fact or Fiction?" *Psych. Bull.* 82(2): 213–25.

Chapter 4: Oops!

John J. Donohue and Steven D. Levitt (2001). "The Impact of Legalized Abortion on Crime," *Quarterly Journal of Economics*, 116: (2), 379–420.

Christopher L. Foote and Christopher F. Goetz (2008). "The Impact of Legalized Abortion on Crime: Comment," *Quarterly Journal of Economics* 123 (1): 407–23.

Steven D. Levitt (2002). "Using Electoral Cycles in Police Hiring to Estimate the Effects of Police on Crime: Reply," *American Economic Review* 92 (4): 1244–50.

Steven D. Levitt (1997). "Using Electoral Cycles in Police Hiring to Estimate the Effect of Police on Crime," *American Economic Review* 87(3): 270–90.

John R. Lott Jr. and John Whitley (2007). "Abortion and Crime: Unwanted Children and Out-of-Wedlock Births," *Economic Inquiry* 45 (2): 304-324.

Justin McCrary (2002). "Do Electoral Cycles in Police Hiring Really Help Us Estimate the Effect of Police on Crime?, Comment," *American Economic Review* 92 (4): 1236–43.

Rick Nevin (2000). "How Lead Exposure Relates to Temporal Changes in IQ, Violent Crime, and Unwed Pregnancy," *Environmental Research* 83 (1): 1–22.

Rick Nevin (2007). "Understanding International Crime Trends: The Legacy of Preschool Lead Exposure," *Environmental Research* 104 (3): 315–336.

C. M. Reinhart and K.S. Rogoff (2010a). "Growth in a Time of Debt," *American Economic Review: Papers & Proceedings* 100 (3): 573–78.

C. M. Reinhart and K.S. Rogoff (2010b). "Growth in a Time of Debt," Working Paper 15639, National Bureau of Economic Research, http://www.nber.org/papers/w15639.

Carmen M. Reinhart, Vincent R. Reinhart, and Kenneth S. Rogoff (2012). "Public Debt Overhangs: Advanced-Economy Episodes Since 1800," *Journal of Economic Perspectives* 26(3): 69–86.

Paul Ryan (2013). *The Path to Prosperity: A Blueprint for American Renewal,* Fiscal Year 2013 Budget Resolution, House Budget Committee, http://budget.house.gov/uploadedfiles/pathtoprosperity2013.pdf.

Thomas Herndon, Michael Ash, and Robert Pollin (2013). "Does High Public Debt Consistently Stifle Economic Growth? A Critique of Reinhart and Rogoff," Political Economy Research Institute, University of Massachusetts Amherst.

James Kwak, "The Importance of Excel," http://baselinescenario.com/2013/02/09/the-importance-of-excel.

Washington Post editorial, "Debt Reduction Hawks and Doves," January 26, 2013.

Arindrajit Dube (2013). "Reinhart/Rogoff and Growth in a Time Before Debt," unpublished.

Chapter 5: Graphical Gaffes

Thomas L. Friedman, "That Numberless Presidential Chart," *The New York Times*, August 2, 1981.

The medical cost figure is an update of a graph printed in *The Washington Post* in 1976, using data for 1939–1976 and using pictures of doctors instead of hearts.

The Yankee ticket price example is based on a figure created by the Associated Press that, by reversing the axes, seemed to show that state and local government expenditures had slowed down when they had actually accelerated: Associated Press, 1974, from David S. Moore, *Statistics: Concepts and Controversies*, New York: W. H. Freeman, 1979.

David Frum, "Welcome, Nouveaux Riches," *The New York Times*, August 14, 1995; reprinted in *Reader's Digest*, December 1995, p. 123.

William Playfair, *The Commercial and Political Atlas*, 1786.

National Science Foundation, *Science Indicators, 1974*, Washington: General Accounting Office, 1976.

Ithaca Times cover, December 7, 2000.

Arthur Schlesinger, Jr. "Inflation Symbolism vs. Reality," *The Wall Street Journal*, April 9, 1980.

Dan Dorfman, "Fed Boss Banking on Housing Slump to Nail Down Inflation," *Chicago Tribune*, April 20, 1980.

The tedious parade of numbers quotation is from *Time*, February 11, 1980, p. 3.

The shrinking dollar is an update of a graph that appeared on the front page of *The Washington Post* on October 25, 1978, comparing the purchasing power of one dollar from Dwight Eisenhower to Jimmy Carter. Their figure was further embellished by replacing the picture of George Washington on the one dollar bill with pictures of the respective presidents.

I did the casino study. The unhelpful graph was created solely for this book and combines many enhancements that people do to enliven graphs.

"Abreast of the Market," *The Wall Street Journal*, October 19, 1987.

Felix Rohatyn, a general partner in Lazard Freres & Co., quoted in James B. Stewart and Daniel Hertzberg, "How the Stock Market Almost Disintegrated," *The Wall Street Journal*, October 30, 1980.

The Colorado teachers example is from William A. Spurr and Charles P. Bonini, *Statistical Analysis for Business Decisions*, revised edition, Homewood, Illinois: Irwin, 1973.

Joint Economic Committee of the United States Congress, "The Concentration of Wealth in the United States," July 1986, pp. 7–43.

Chapter 6: Common Nonsense

Steve Selvin (1975). "A Problem in Probability (letter to the editor)," *American Statistician* 29 (1): 67.

Steve Selvin (1975). "On the Monty Hall Problem (letter to the editor)," *American Statistician* 29 (3): 134.

Marilyn vos Savant, "Ask Marilyn," *Parade*, September 9, 1990.

Marilyn vos Savant, "Ask Marilyn," *Parade*, December 2, 1990.

Marilyn vos Savant, "Ask Marilyn," *Parade*, February 17, 1991.

John Tierney, "Behind Monty Hall's Doors: Puzzle, Debate and Answer?," *The New York Times*, July 21, 1991.

Martin Gardner. *The Scientific American Book of Mathematical Puzzles and Diversions*, New York: Simon and Schuster, 1954.

Martin Gardner, *The Second Scientific American Book of Mathematical Puzzles and Diversions*, New York: Simon & Schuster, 1959.

L. Mlodinow, *The Drunkard's Walk: How Randomness Rules Our Lives*, New York: Pantheon Books, 2008.

John Allen Paulos, *Innumeracy: Mathematical Illiteracy and its Consequences*, New York: Hill and Wang, 1988.

Maya Bar-Hillel and Ruma Falk (1982). "Some Teasers Concerning Conditional Probabilities," *Cognition*, 11: 109–122.

John E. Freund (1965). "Puzzle or Paradox?," *The American Statistician*, 19 (4): 29, 44.

Stephen Marks and Gary Smith (2011). "The Two-Child Paradox Reborn?," *Chance*, 24 (1): 54–59.

P. Meier and S. Zabell (1980). "Benjamin Peirce and the Howland Will." *Journal of the American Statistical Association.* 75: 497–506.

Supreme Court of California, *People v. Collins*; see also William B. Fairly and Frederick Mosteller, "A Conversation About Collins," in Fairly and Mosteller, *Statistics and Public Policy*, Reading, MA: Addison-Wesley, 1977, pp. 355–79.

Arnold Barnett, "How Numbers Can Trick You," *Technology Review*, October 1994, p. 42.

David Eddy, "Probabilistic Reasoning in Clinical Medicine: Problems and Opportunities," in Daniel Kahneman, Paul Slovak, and Amos Tversky, *Judgment Under Uncertainty: Heuristics and Biases*, Cambridge, UK: Cambridge University Press, 1982, pp. 249–67.

Alexis Madrigal (2009). "Scanning Dead Salmon in MRI Machine Highlights Risk of Red Herrings," *Wired*, http://www.wired.com/wiredscience/2009/09/fmrisalmon.

Craig M. Bennett, Abigail A. Baird, Michael B. Miller, and George L. Wolford, "Neural Correlates of Interspecies Perspective Taking in the Post-Mortem Atlantic Salmon: An Argument For Proper Multiple Comparisons Correction," *Journal of Serendipitous and Unexpected Results* 1 (1): 1–5.

Chapter 7: Confound It!

Steven Johnson, *The Ghost Map: the Story of London's Most Terrifying Epidemic, and How it Changed Science, Cities and the Modern World*, New York: Penguin, 2006.

John Snow, *On the Mode of Communication of Cholera*, London: J. Churchill, 1849. A second edition including the results of his study of the 1854 epidemic was published in 1855.

A. H. Hassall, *A Microscopical Examination of the Water Supplied to the Inhabitants of London and the Suburban Districts*, London: S. Highley, 1850.

H. Markel (2013). "Happy Birthday, Dr. Snow," *Journal of the American Medical Association* 309 (10): 995–96.

K.B. Thomas and John Snow in: *Dictionary of Scientific Biography*. Vol. 12. New York: Charles Scribner's Sons; 1973: 502–503.

P. J. Bickel, E. A. Hammel, and J. W. O'Connell, "Sex Bias in Graduate Admissions: Data from Berkeley," *Science*, February 7, 1975.

Joel E. Cohen, "An Uncertainty Principle in Demography and the Unisex Issue," *The American Statistician*, February 1986, pp. 32–39.

Cari Tuna, "When Combined Data Reveal the Flaw of Averages," *The Wall Street Journal*, December 2, 2009.

C. R. Charig, D. R. Webb, S. R. Payne, and O. E. Wickham (1986). "Comparison of Treatment of Renal Calculi by Open Surgery, Percutaneous

Nephrolithotomy, and Extracorporeal Shockwave Lithotripsy," *British Medical Journal (Clinical Research)* 292 (6524): 879–82.

Steven A. Julious and Mark A. Mullee (1994). "Confounding and Simpson's Paradox," *British Medical Journal* 309 (6967):1480-1481.

S.M. Stigler (1980). "Stigler's Law of Eponymy," *Transactions of the New York Academy of Sciences* 39: 147–58 (Merton Frestschrift Volume, F. Gieryn (ed.))

P. Cole (1971). "Coffee-Drinking and Cancer of the Lower Uninary Tract," *The Lancet*, 297: 1335–1337.

Catherine M. Viscoli, Mark S. Lachs, and Ralph I. Horowitz, "Bladder Cancer and Coffee Drinking: A Summary of Case-Control Research," *The Lancet*, June 5, 1993, 1432–37.

G. López-Abente and A. Escolar (2001). "Tobacco Consumption and Bladder Cancer in Non-Coffee Drinkers," *Journal of Epidemiology and Community Health*, 55: 68–70.

B. MacMahon, S. Yen, D. Trichopoulos, et al. (1981). "Coffee and Cancer of the Pancreas," *New England Journal of Medicine*, 304: 630-33.

A. R. Feinstein, R. I. Horwitz, W. O. Spitzer, and R. N. Battista (1981). "Coffee and Pancreatic Cancer: The Problems of Etiologic Science and Epidemiologic Case-Control Research," *Journal of the American Medical Association*, 246: 957–961.

"Coffee Nerves," *Time*, March 23, 1981, Vol. 117 Issue 12, p. 77.

C. C. Hsieh, B. MacMahon, S. Yen, D. Trichopoulos, K. Warren K, and G. Nardi (1986). "Coffee and Pancreatic Cancer (Chapter 2)". *New England Journal of Medicine* 314: 587–89.

American Cancer Society. *1996 Guidelines on Diet, Nutrition and Cancer Prevention*, Atlanta: The American Cancer Society 1996 Dietary Guidelines Advisory Committee, 1996.

Neal D. Freedman, Yikyung Park, Christian C. Abnet, Albert R. Hollenbeck, and Rashmi Sinha (2012). "Association of Coffee Drinking with Total and Cause-Specific Mortality," *New England Journal of Medicine* 366: 1891–1904.

Chapter 8: When You're Hot, You're Not

Neil Paine "Ray Allen's Hot Streak," http://www.basketball-reference.com /blog/?p=6353.

Baxter Holmes, "Celtics' Ray Allen Sets Record for Three-Pointers," *Los Angeles Times*, June 07, 2010.

J. A. Adande, "Unusual Night all Around in Los Angeles," ESPN.com, June 7, 2010, http://sports.espn.go.com/nba/playoffs/2010/columns/story ?columnist=adande_ja&page=Bryant-100607.

Associated Press, "Rondo Takes Over for Sharp-Shooting Allen as Celtics take Game 2," ESPN.com, June 7, 2010, <http://espn.go.com/nba /recap ?gameId=300606013>

A. Tversky and D. Kahneman (1971). "Belief in the law of small numbers," *Psychological Bulletin* 76: 105–110.

A. Tversky and D. Kahneman (1974). "Judgment Under Uncertainty: Heuristics and biases." *Science* 185: 1124–31.

A. Tversky and T. Gilovich (1989). "The Cold Facts About the 'Hot Hand' in Basketball." *Chance* 2: 16–21.

A. Tversky and T. Gilovich (1989). The "Hot Hand": Statistical Reality or Cognitive Illusion?" *Chance*, 2: 31–34.

R. L. Wardrop (1999). "Statistical Tests for the Hot-Hand in Basketball in a Controlled Setting," working paper.

T. Gilovich, R. Vallone, and A. Tversky (1985). "The Hot Hand in Basketball: On the Misperception of Random Sequences." *Cognitive Psychology*, 17 (3): 295–314.

D. L. Gilden and S. G. Wilson (1995). "Streaks in Skilled Performance." *Psychonomic Bulletin & Review*, 2: 260–65.

L. D. Goodfellow (1938). "A Psychological Interpretation of the Results of the Zenith Radio Experiments in Telepathy," *Journal of Experimental Psychology*, 23(6): 601–32.

Gary Smith (2003). "Horseshoe Pitchers' Hot Hands," *Psychonomic Bulletin & Review*, 10: 753–758.

Reid Dorsey-Palmateer and Gary Smith (2004). "Bowlers' Hot Hands," with, *The American Statistician*, 58: 38–45.

A. Bandura (1977). "Self-Efficacy: Toward a Unifying Theory of Behavioral Change." *Psychological Review*, 84: 191–215.

D. E. M. Taylor (1979). "Human Endurance: Mind or Muscle?," *British Journal of Sports Medicine* 12: 179–184.

L. R. Nelson and M. L. Furst (1972). "An Objective Study of the Effects of Expectation on Competitive Performance." *Journal of Psychology*, 81: 69–72.

Chapter 9: Regression

John Maynard Keynes, *The General Theory of Employment, Interest and Money*, London: Macmillan, 1936.

Union Carbide was acquired by Dow Chemical in 2001; Sears was acquired by Kmart in 2005. The Addition and Deletion portfolio calculations reported in the text assume that the proceeds from these acquisitions are invested equally in the stocks remaining in the portfolio.

Horace Secrist, *The Triumph of Mediocrity in Business*, Evanston, Ill: Northwestern University, 1933.

R. F. Elder (1934). "Review of The Triumph of Mediocrity in Business by Horace Secrist," *American Economic Review* 24 (1): 121–122.

"Current Notes," *Journal of the Royal Statistical Society*, 96 (4): 721–722

W. I. King (1934). "Review of The Triumph of Mediocrity in Business by Horace Secrist," *Journal of Political Economy* 42 (3): 398–400.

R. Riegel (1933). "Review of The Triumph of Mediocrity in Business by Horace Secrist," *Annals of the American Academy of Political and Social Science* 170: 178–79.

Harold Hotelling, review of Horace Secrist, "The Triumph of Mediocrity in Business," *Journal of the American Statistical Association* 28, 1933, pp. 463–65. Secrist and Hotelling debated this further in the 1934 volume of this journal, pp. 196–99. Open Letters Author(s): Horace Secrist, Harold Hotelling, M. C. Rorty, Corrado Gini, and Willford I. King. Source: *Journal of the American Statistical Association* Vol. 29, 186 (1934), pp. 196–205.

Albert O. Hirschman, *Exit, Voice, and Loyalty*, Cambridge, Massachusets: Harvard University Press, 1970.

W. J. Baumol, S. A. B. Blackman, and E. N. Wolff, *Productivity and American Leadership: The Long View*, Cambridge and London: MIT Press, 1989.

E. F. Fama and K. R. French (2000). "Forecasting Profitability and Earnings," *Journal of Business* 73: 161–175.

M. Friedman (1992). "Do Old Fallacies Ever Die?" *Journal of Economic Literature* 30 (4): 2129–32.

William F. Sharpe, *Investments*, third edition, Englewood Cliffs, New Jersey: Prentice-Hall, 1985.

J. G. Williamson (1991). "Productivity and American Leadership: A Review Article," *Journal of Economic Literature* 29 (1): 51–68.

A. Tversky and D. Kahneman (1973). "On the Psychology of Prediction," *Psychological Review* 80: 237–51.

Francis Galton (1886). "Regression Towards Medicrity in Hereditary Stature," *Journal of the Anthropological Institute* 15: 246–63.

Anita Aurora, Lauren Capp, and Gary Smith (2008). "The Real Dogs of the Dow," *The Journal of Wealth Management* 10 (4): 64–72.

Alexander Wolff (2002). "The Cover No One Would Pose for: Is the SI Jinx for Real?" *Sports Illustrated.*

Teddy Schall and Gary Smith (2000). "Baseball Players Regress toward the Mean," *The American Statistician*, 54: 231–35 (also *1999 Proceedings of the Section on Statistics in Sports*, American Statistical Association, 2000, 8–13).

Chapter 10: Even Steven

Marilyn vos Savant, "Ask Marilyn," *Parade,* July 12, 1992.

Marilyn vos Savant, "Ask Marilyn," *Parade,* July 1, 1990.

Charlotte Gazette (WV), July 29, 1987.

Chapter 11: The Texas Sharpshooter

Nancy Wertheimer and Ed Leeper, "Electrical Wiring Configurations and Childhood Cancer," *American Journal of Epidemiology* 109 (3): 273–84.

Atul Gawande, "The Cancer-Cluster Myth," *The New Yorker*, February 8, 1999, 34-37. http://www.pbs.org/wgbh/pages/frontline/programs/transcripts/1319.html.

Jon Palfreman (2006). "The Rise and Fall of Power Line EMFs: The Anatomy of a Magnetic Controversy," *Review of Policy Research* 23 (2): 453–472.

Kenneth J. Rothman, "A Sobering Start for the Cluster Busters' Conference," *American Journal of Epidemiology* 132 (1): Supplement S6-S13.

David A. Savitz, Neil E. Pearce, and Charles Poole (1989). "Methodological Issues in the Epidemiology of Electromagnetic Fields and Cancer," *Epidemiological Reviews* 11: 59–78.

UK Childhood Cancer Study Investigators, "Exposure to Power-Frequency Magnetic Fields and the Risk of Childhood Cancer," *The Lancet* Dec. 4, 1999; 354(9194): 1925–31.

Maria Feychting and Anders Ahlbom (1994). "Magnetic fields, leukemia, and central nervous system tumors in Swedish adults residing near high-voltage power lines," *Epidemiology* 5: 501–509. If ailments are completely unaffected by power lines, we expect 5 percent (40 out of 800 risk ratios) to show a statistically significant pattern—half with higher risk ratios and half with lower risk ratios.

Paul Brodeur, *The Great Power-Line Cover-Up: How the Utilities and the Government Are Trying to Hide the Cancer Hazard Posed by Electromagnetic Fields*, Boston: Little, Brown, 1993.

Paul Brodeur, "Annals of radiation: Calamity on Meadow Street," *The New Yorker* 66; July 9, 1990; 38-72.

Paul Brodeur, "Department of amplification," *The New Yorker,* November 19, 1990; 134-150.

Paul Brodeur, "Annals of radiation: The Cancer at Slater School," *The New Yorker* 68; December 7, 1992; 68 86-119.

William Feller, *An Introduction to Probability Theory and Its Applications*, New York: Wiley, 1968.

R. D. Clarke (1946). "An Application of the Poisson Distribution," *Journal of the Institute of Actuaries (1886–1994)* 72(3): 481.

A. Tversky and D. Kahneman (1972). "Subjective Probability: A Judgment of Representativeness," *Cognitive Psychology* 3: 430–54.

David Johnson, *V-1 V-2: Hitler's Vengeance on London*, New York: Stein and Day, 1981.

Chapter 12: The Ultimate Procrastination

D. P. Phillips, "Deathday and Birthday: an Unexpected Connection," in J.M. Tanur ed. *Statistics: a Guide to the Unknown*. San Francisco: Holden-Day, 1972.

D. P. Phillips and E. W. King (1988). "Death Takes a Holiday: Mortality Surrounding Major Social Occasions," *The Lancet* 2: 728–32.

D. P. Phillips and D. G. Smith (1990). "Postponement of Death Until Symbolically Meaningful Occasions," *JAMA* 263: 1947–51.

D. P. Phillips and K. Feldman (1973). "A Dip in Deaths Before Ceremonial Occasions: Some New Relationships Between Social Integration and Mortality," *American Sociological Review* 38: 678–96.

D. P. Phillips, C. A. Van Voorhees, T. E. Ruth (1992). "The Birthday: Lifeline or Deadline?" *Psychosomatic Medicine* 54: 532–42.

H. Royer and G. Smith (1998). "Can the Famous Really Postpone Death?" with Heather Royer, *Social Biology* 45: 302–305.

P. Lee and G. Smith (2000). "Are Jewish Deathdates Affected by the Timing of Holidays?" with Peter Lee, *Social Biology* 47: 127–34.

Gary Smith (2004). "Asian-American Deaths Near the Harvest Moon Festival," *Psychosomatic Medicine* 66: 378–81.

J. A. Skala and K. E. Freedland (2004). "Death Takes a Raincheck," *Psychosom Med* 66: 383–86.

Chapter 13: Serious Omissions

Robert J. Shiller, "Investor Behavior in the October 1987 Stock Market Crash: Survey Evidence," Yale University, November 1987.

"Black Monday: What Really Ignited The Market's Collapse After Its Long Climb," *The Wall Street Journal*, December 16, 1987.

Nicholas Brady (1989). "Report of the Presidential Task Force on Market Mechanism," Washington DC: Government Printing Office.

Lester C. Thurow, "Brady Group's Answers Miss the Key Questions," *Los Angeles Times*, January 24, 1988.

Felix Rohatyn, a general partner in Lazard Freres & Co., quoted in James B. Stewart and Daniel Hertzberg, "How the Stock Market Almost Disintegrated A Day After the Crash," *The Wall Street Journal*, October 30, 1980.

James Gleick, "Hole in Ozone Over South Pole Worries Scientists," *The New York Times*, July 29, 1986.

Report of the Presidential Commission on the Space Shuttle Challenger Accident, 1986, Volume 1, p. 145.

L. Tappin (1994). "Analyzing Data Relating to the *Challenger* Disaster," *Mathematics Teacher*, 87(6): 423–26.

Siddhartha R. Dalal, Edward B. Fowlkes. and Bruce Hoadley (1989). "Risk Analysis of the Space Shuttle: Pre-Challenger Prediction of Failure," *Journal of the American Statistical Association* 84(408): 945–57.

D. P. Phillips, G. C. Liu, K. Kwok, J. R. Jarvinen, W. Zhang, and I. S. Abramson (2001). "The Hound of the Baskervilles Effect: Natural Experiment on the Influence of Psychological Stress on Timing of Death," *British Medical Journal* 323: 1443–46.

D. P. Phillips, T. E. Ruth, and L. M. Wagner (1993). "Psychology and Survival," *The Lancet* 342: 1142–45.

Gary Smith (2002). "Scared to Death?" *British Medical Journal* 325: 1442–43.

Gary Smith (2006). "The Five Elements and Chinese-American Mortality," *Health Psychology* 25 (1): 124–29.

Chapter 14: Flimsy Theories and Rotten Data

Michael Lewis, *Moneyball: The Art of Winning an Unfair Game*, New York: W.W. Norton, 2003.

Bill James, *Baseball Abstract*, annual editions, self-published 1977–1980, New York: Ballentine Books, 1981–88.

Sean Lahman's Baseball Archive, http://seanlahman.com.

P. Erwin and A. Calev (1984). "The Influence of Christian Name Stereotypes on the Marking of Children's Essays," *British Journal of Educational Psychology* 54: 223–27.

H. Harari and J. McDavid (1973). "Name Stereotypes and Teachers' Expectations," *Journal of Educational Psychology* 65: 222–25.

M. Levine and F. Willis (1994). "Public Reactions to Unusual Names," *The Journal of Social Psychology* 134: 561–68.

J. McDavid and H. Harari (1966). "Stereotyping of Names and Popularity in Grade-School Children," *Child Development* 37: 453–59.

N. Christenfeld, D. Phillips and L. Glynn (1999). "What's in a Name: Mortality and the Power of Symbols," *Journal of Psychosomatic Research* 47: 241–54.

Coke-Pepsi Slugfest; July 26, 1976, *Time*, 64–65.

S. Morrison and G. Smith (2005). "Monogrammic Determinism?" *Psychosomatic Medicine* 67: 820–24.

Gary Smith (2011). "Another Look at Baseball Player Initials and Longevity," *Perceptual and Motor Skills* 112 (1): 211–16.

L. Pinzur and G. Smith (2009). "First Names and longevity," *Perceptual and Motor Skills* 108: 149–60.

E. L. Abel and M. L. Kruger (2009). "Athletes, Doctors, and Lawyers With First Names Beginning With 'D' Die Sooner." *Death Studies*, 34, 71-81.

Gary Smith (2012). "Do People Whose Names Begin With 'D' Really Die Young?" *Death Studies*: 36: 182–89.

E. L. Abel and M. L. Kruger (2005). "Birth Month and Suicide Among Major League Baseball Players," *Perceptual and Motor Skills* 101: 21–24.

E. L. Abel and M. L. Kruger (2005). "The longevity of Baseball Hall of Famers Compared to Other Players," *Death Studies* 29: 959–63.

Gary Smith (2011). "Birth Month is Not Related to Suicide among Major League Baseball Players," *Perceptual and Motor Skills* 112 (1): 55–60.

Gary Smith (2011). "The Baseball Hall of Fame is Not the Kiss of Death," *Death Studies* 35: 949–55.

Chapter 15: Don't Confuse Me With Facts

Irving Langmuir, "Pathological Science," transcribed and edited by Robert N. Hall, *Physics Today*, October 1989, pp. 36–48.

J. B. Rhine and Louisa E. Rhine (1927). "One Evening's Observation on the Margery Mediumship," *The Journal of Abnormal and Social Psychology* 21(4): 401–21.

J. B. Rhine, *Parapsychology, Frontier Science of the Mind*, Springfield, IL: Charles C. Thomas, 1957.

J. B. Rhine, *Extra-Sensory Perception*, Boston, MA: Bruce Humphries, 1934.

Arthur Conan Doyle, *The Coming of the Fairies*, New York, Toronto and London: Hodder & Stoughton, 1922.

Martin Gardner, *Fads and Fallacies in the Name of Science*, second edition, New York: Dover, 1957.

Martin Gardner (1966). "Funny Coincidence," *The New York Review of Books* 6: 9.

Martin Gardner (1980). "An Expense of Spirit," *The New York Review of Books* 27: 8.

Martin Gardner (1977). "ESP at Random," *The New York Review of Books* 24: 12.

W. Kaempffert, "The Duke Experiments in Extra-Sensory Perception," *The New York Times* October 10, 1937.

C. E. M. Hansel, *ESP: A Scientific Evaluation*, New York: Charles Scribner's Sons, 1966.

L. D. Goodfellow (1938). "A Psychological Interpretation of the Results of the Zenith Radio Experiments in Telepathy," *Journal of Experimental Psychology* 23:6 601–32.

Erich Von Däniken, *Chariot of the Gods?*, New York: Putnam, 1968.

Ronald Story, *The Space Gods Revealed*.

Clifford Wilson, *Crash Go The Chariots*, New York: Lancer, 1972.

Nova, "The Case of the Ancient Astronauts," Season 5, Episode 9, 1978.

James Randi, "Geller a Fake, Says Ex-Manager," *New Scientist*, April 6, 1978.

Po Bronson, "A Prayer Before Dying: The Astonishing Story of a Doctor Who Subjected Faith to the Rigors of Science—and then Became a Test Subject Herself," *Wired*, December 2002.

Allen Spraggett with William V. Rauscher *Arthur Ford: The Man Who Talked with the Dead* New American Library, Inc., 1973.

Francis Galton (1872). "Statistical Inquiries into the Efficacy of Prayer," *Fortnightly Review* 12: 125–35.

F. Sicher, E. Targ, D. Moore, and H. Smith (1998). "A Randomized Double-Blind Study of the Effect of Distant Healing in a Population with Advanced AIDS. Report of a Small Scale Study," *The Western Journal of Medicine* 169 (6): 356–63.

J. Astin, J. Stone, D. Abrams, D. Moore, P. Couey, R. Buscemi, and E. Targ (2006). "The Efficacy of Distant Healing for Human Immunodeficiency Virus—Results of a Randomized Trial." *Alternative Therapies in Health and Medicine* 12 (6): 36–41.

Susy Smith, *The Book of James (William James, That Is)*, New York: Putnam, 1974.

H. Benson, J. Dusek, et al (2006). "Study of the Therapeutic Effects of Intercessory Prayer (STEP) in Cardiac Bypass Patients: a Multicenter Randomized Trial of Uncertainty and Certainty of Receiving Intercessory Prayer," *American Heart Journal* 151 (4): 934–42.

Arthur Moses, "Houdini Speaks Out: I Am Houdini! and You Are a Fraud!," Xlibris Corporation, 2007.

James Randi, *Flim-Flam! Psychics, ESP, Unicorns, and Other Delusions*, New York: Prometheus Books, 1988.

William Kalush and Larry Sloman, *The Secret Life of Houdini: The Making of America's First Superhero*, New York: Atria Books, 2006.

Chapter 16: Data Without Theory

Abraham Lincoln, *Second Annual Message*, December 1, 1862.

Mark Twain, *Life on the Mississippi*, 1883.

Sue Avery, "Market Investors Will be High on Redskins Today," and "Morning Briefing: Wall Street 'Skinnish' on Big Game," *Los Angeles Times*, January 22, 1983.

James Bates, "Reality Wears Loser's Jersey in Super Bowl Stock Theory," *Los Angles Times*, January 22, 1989.

Floyd Norris, "Predicting Victor in Super Bowl," *The New York Times*, January 17, 1989.

D. Gardner and T. Gardner *The Motley Fool Investment Guide: How the Fools Beat Wall Street's Wise Men and How You Can Too*, New York: Simon and Schuster 1996.

D. Gardner, and T. Gardner (2000). "Farewell, Foolish Four," retrieved August 28, 2013, from http://www.fool.com/ddow/2000/ddow001211.htm.

G. McQueen, and S. Thorley (1999). "Mining Fool's Gold," *Financial Analysts Journal* 55 (2): 61-72.

R. Sheard, (1997). "The Daily Dow," Retrieved August 28, 2013, from http://www.fool.com/DDow/1997/DDow971230.htm.

This example is based on price charts I created and sent to a technical analyst in the 1970s.

Sporting Age, 1988.

Gail Howard, *State Lotteries: How to Get in It . . . and How to Win It!*, 5th edition, Ben Buxton, 1986.

Alex Michelini, "$40m Jackpot Bring Out the Big Numbers," *New York Daily News*, November 8, 1996.

Irene Gardner Keeney, "Court Puts Mail Order Scams Out of Business, Refunds Due," *Albany Times Union* May 16, 1991.

Shelby Gilje, "FTC Again Takes Action Against Manufacturer of Aids 'Cure,'" *The Seattle Times*, February 12, 1991.

Figures 1 and 2 use a logarithmic scale to show the fluctuations better.

Jack W. Wilson and Charles P. Jones. "Common Stock Prices and Inflation: 1857–1985," *Financial Analysts Journal*, July/August 1987, 67–71.

Because they only had S&P 500 data back to 1926 and CPI data back to 1913, Wilson and Jones spliced these to other stock price and consumer price indexes going back to 1857. Oddly enough, the conclusion they drew from their comparison of actual and real stock prices was that either the CPI would have to fall (correct) or the S&P 500 would have to *increase* (incorrect):

In order for real stock prices to once again *equal nominal prices, one of
two extreme alternatives (or some combination between these extremes)
would have to occur over the next "generation" of 25 years (by 2011).
If the CPI remained at its 1985 level, the S&P index would have to increase 557.6 percent (7.58 percent per annum) to a level of 1247.65.
Alternatively, if the S&P remained at the 1985 level of 186.84, the CPI
would have to drop 85.3 percent—to the 1941–43 base level of 1.0—
or fall by 7.04 percent per annum.

Chapter 17: Betting the Bank

Roger Lowenstein, *When Genius Failed: The Rise and Fall of Long-Term
Capital Management*, New York: Random House, 2000.

Harry Markowitz, *Portfolio Selection: Efficient Diversification of Investments*, New York: John Wiley & Sons, 1959.

Fischer Black and Myron Scholes (1973). "The Pricing of Options and Corporate Liabilities," *Journal of Political Economy* 81 (3): 637–54.

Robert C. Merton (1973). "Theory of Rational Option Pricing," *Bell Journal
of Economics and Management Science* 4 (1): 141–83.

Espen Gaarder Haug *Derivatives: Models on Models*, New York: Wiley &
Sons, 2007

Hume & Associates, *The Superinvestor Files: The GSR Trade*, Atlanta, GA:
Hume Publishing, 1986.

John Maynard Keynes, *A Tract on Monetary Reform*, London: Macmillan,
1923.

Pablo Triana. *Lecturing Birds on Flying: Can Mathematical Theories Destroy
the Financial Markets?* New York: Wiley & Sons, 2009.

Ludwig Chincarini, *The Crisis of Crowding: Quant Copycats, Ugly Models,
and the New Crash Normal*, Bloomberg Press, 2012.

Felix Salmon and Jon Stokes, "Bull vs. Bear vs. Bot," *Wired*, January 2011,
90-93.

Chapter 18: Theory Without Data

William D. Nordhaus (1973). "World Dynamics: Measurement Without
Data," *The Economic Journal* 83(332) 1156–83.

William D. Nordhaus, Robert N. Stavins, and Martin L. Weitzman (1992). "Lethal Model 2: The Limits to Growth Revisited," *Brookings Papers on Economic Activity* 1992(2): 159.

Jay W. Forrester, *World Dynamics,* Cambridge, Mass., Wright-Allen Press, Inc., 1971.

Donella H. Meadows et al., *The Limits to Growth*, New York, Universe Books, 1972.

Donella H. Meadows, Dennis L. Meadows, and Jorgen Randers, *Beyond the Limits,* Post Mills, VT: Chelsea Green Publishing Company, 1992.

Malthus's 1798 *Essay on the Principle of Population*, London: J. Johnson, 1798.

INDEX

A League of Ordinary Gentlemen
(film), 131
Abel, Ernest, 205–211
addition portfolio, 152–153
austerity, 57–59
aggregated data, 113–117
Ahlbom, Anders, 170
AIDS, 229–231
alcohol abuse, 31–32
algorithmic traders, 276
Allen, Ray, 123, 125
American Cancer Society, 121
American Economics Association, 65
American Heart Association (AHA), 19
American Psychological Association,
31–32
American Statistical Association, 175
Ash, Michael, 59
aspirin study, 18–19, 28

Babbage, Charles, 25–27; and Differ-
ence Engine, 26; and Analytical
Engine, 26
Bacon, Francis, 234
Baird, Abigail, 102
Baskervilles Study, 191–195; and Chi-
nese birth year study, 192–195
Beanie Babies, 254–255
Bennett, Craig, 101
Black Monday (1987), 185
Black, Fischer, 266–267; and Black-
Scholes Model, 267
Boggs, Wade, 203
bombings, 163–167
Boston Celtics, 123
Boston Herald, 218
Boston Red Sox, 203–204

Bowen, William, 27–28
Brady Commission, 186–187
British Medical Journal, 16
British Royal Air Force, 37
British Royal Family, 225
Brodeur, Paul, 167, 172; and *The Great
Power-Line Cover-Up: How the
Utilities and Government Are Try-
ing to Hide the Cancer Hazard
Posed by Electromagnetic Fields*
(Brodeur), 168
Buxton, Ben, 250

Cal Poly, 131
calculators, 25–27
Cameron, David, 59
Carter, Jimmy, 85, 86, 87
Challenger (space shuttle), 188–190
Chandler v. Miller, 98
chartjunk, 88–90, 292
Chicago Cubs, 204–205
cholera, 105–111, 233, 289
Churchill, Winston, 234
Clarke, R. D., 166
Club of Rome, 282
Coase, Ronald, 5
coffee, 117; and bladder cancer, 119;
and pancreatic cancer, 120–121,
293; and health benefits, 121
Collins, Jim, 38–41
compounding, 281, 285-286
computational errors, 55–57; and
NASA, 55; and the "London
Whale" debacle, 56–57; and the
Reinhart-Rogan Study, 57–64; and
the Donohue/Levitt study, 65–69,
291

conditional probabilities, 97, 103, 292
confirmation bias, 51
confounding effects, 8, 111, 118
confounding factor, 9, 105, 111, 113, 115–117, 128, 274, 290, 292, 293
Consumer Price Index (CPI), 256, 259–260
convergence trade, 267–268, 271–272
Cornell University, 83, 127
Crandon, Mina (Margery), 217
Crossing the Finish Line (Bowen, McPherson), 27

Dallas Morning News, The, 10
Dallas Zoo, 10
Dartmouth Salmon Study, 100–102
data clusters, 166–167, 173, 294; and cancer 167–169; and Legionnaires' disease 169–170; and leukemia 170–172
data-mining, 242–243
Debreu, Gerard, 64
Deer, Brian, 15–16; and the British Press Award, 16
deletion portfolio, 152–153
Detroit Tigers, 204
DiMaggio, Joe, 83
direct positive correlation, 50; and Temecula Valley 47–50; and marriage and drinking, 50–51
discrimination, 34–35; and Georgia Pacific Sawmill, 34; and *Hazelwood School District v. United States,* 35
Donohue, John, 65–69
dot-coms, 250–259; and Old Economy, 251; and New Economy, 251
Doyle, Sir Arthur Conan, 216–218, 232; and *The Coming of the Fairies* (Doyle), 217
drinking, *see* alcohol abuse
Dube, Arindra-jit, 64
Dubner, Stephen, 65
Duke University, 218
Durant, Kevin, 97

Eastern Michigan, 28–29
economic value, 253–254
Einstein, Albert, 19, 281; and Theory of Relativity, 19

electromagnetic fields (EMFs), 167, 170–172
English Royal College of Surgeons, 26
Essay on the Principle of Population (Malthus), 285-286
European Football Championships (2008), 8
evolution, 12; and natural selection, 12–13
extrasensory perception (ESP), 17, 18, 126, 215–231

False-Positive Problem, 97–103
Fannie Mae, 40
Federal Reserve, 186–187, 253, 270, 276
Fenway Park, 203
Feychting, Maria, 170
Feynman, Richard, 171, 190; and Feynman Trap, 171
flash crash, 277–278
Flick, Elmer, 211
Ford, Gerald 86, 87
Forrester, Jay W., 282–286; and World3, 282–283; and World2, 285; and system dynamics, 282; and *World Dynamics,* 282; and birth rate, 285–286
Foshee, Gary, 96
Fourth Amendment, 98
Freakonomics: A Rogue Economist Explores the Hidden Side of Everything (Dubner, Levitt), 64, 70
Friedman, Milton, 149
Frum, David, 75
futures (stock), 264–266, 271, 277

Galbraith, John Kenneth, 56
Galton, Sir Francis, 144, 229; and prayer 225–226
Gardner brothers, 241–243; and Foolish Four Strategy, 242–243; and UV4, 243; and *The Motley Fool Investment Guide: How the Fools Beat Wall Street's Wise Men and How You Can too* (Gardner brothers), 241
Gardner, Martin, 94, 96
Gathering for Gardner, 96

GDP and inflation adjusted growth, 57–64
Gehrig, Lou, 83
Geis, Gilbert, 176
Geller, E. Scott, 31
Geller, Uri, 228
George Mason University, 92
Gergen, David, 74
Gilovich, Thomas, 127–129
gold-silver ratio (GSR), 263; 267–268, 273; and statistical arbitrage, 267
Good to Great (Collins), 38–40
Gordon, David M., 56
Gottfried Wilhelm Leibniz, 25
Great Depression, 56, 86, 137, 138, 272
Greater Fool Theory, 254–256
Greenspan, Alan, 253, 270
Guinness Book of World Records, The, 92

Hamilton, Josh, 154
Harvard, 27, 57, 65, 102, 119, 175, 217, 227, 231
Harvest Moon Festival, 181-182
Hassall, Arthur, 107; and A Microscopical Examination of the Water Supplied to the Inhabitants of London and the Suburban Districts (Hassall), 107
Herndon, Thomas, 59
Hogg, Ima, 195–196
Holmes, Sherlock, 11, 216
Home Depot, 150–152
hot hands phenomenon, 127–129, 131–135
Hotelling, Harold, 140, 148
Houdini, Harry, 217, 222–224, 227, 231
House Ways and Means Committee, 73
Howard, Gail, 248
Hume & Associates, 263; and The Superinvestor Files, 263

In Search of Excellence (Peters, Waterman), 41
incautious extrapolation, 234–238
Institute for Parapsychology, 17
International Business Machines (IBM), 235–238, 258

International Monetary Fund, 59
Ioannidis, John, 20; and "Why Most Published Research Findings Are False", 21
Ithaca Times, 83

Jaggers, William,161
James, Bill, 201
James, Henry, 93
James, LeBron, 97
James, William, 227
John Bates Clark Medal, 65
Johnson, Magic, 97
Joint Economic Committee of Congress, 56
Jordan, Michael, 97
Journal of the American Medical Association, 45, 182

Kahneman, Daniel, 125, 143–144
Keynes, John Maynard, 137–138, 244, 272; and The General Theory of Employment, Interest and Money (Keynes), 138
King Gustav III, 118–119
Kmart, 151–152
Kruger, Michael, 205–211

Lahman, Sean, 201, 210
Lambeth Company, 107–108
Landgrebe, Earl, 214
Langmuir, Irving 219–221
LaPlace, Pierre-Simon, 91
Larson, Gary, 32
law of averages, 127, 160–162
Lee, Peter, 179–180
Leeper, Ed, 167, 170
Leonhardt, David 27–30
Let's Make a Deal, 91, 93
Levitt, Steven, 65–69
Levy, Walter J., 17–18
Lincoln, Abraham, 234
location values, 88
London Science Museum, 26
Long-Term Capital Management, 270–276; and world interest rates, 273–276
Los Alamos National Laboratory, 93
Los Angeles Lakers, 123

Los Angeles Times, 240, 241
lottery, 247–250, 295

MacMahon, Brian, 119–121
Madden NFL, 4, 153, 155
Major League Baseball (MLB), 154,
　201–211; and superstitions 203–
　205; and World Series, 204–205;
　and players' names, 205–207; and
　suicide, 207–209; and Hall of
　Fame kiss of death, 210–211
Major League, 203
Mantle, Mickey 83
manufactured data, 14, 16–17
margin, 265
Maris, Roger, 153
Markowitz, Harry, 266–267; and
　mean-variance analysis, 267
Mars Climate Orbiter, 55
McDougall, William, 217
Meadows, Donella, 282, 286; and *The
　Limits to Growth* (Meadows), 282
medical studies, 20–21
Medicare, 79
Mendel, Gregor, 22; and Pea plant
　study, 22; and Mendel's Laws of
　Inheritance, 22
Meriwether, John, 270, 276
Merton, Robert 266–267, 270; and
　Black-Scholes Model, 267
miasma theory, 105–111
Michelson, Albert, 19
Minnesota Zoo, 10
MIT, 65, 270, 282
Mlodinow, Leonard, 94–96;
　and *The Drunkard's Walk*
　(Mlodinow), 94
Moneyball (Lewis), 202
Monty Hall Problem, 91–93, 103, 292
Moore's Law, 252–253
Morley, Edward, 19
Mullins, David, 270
Murrow, Edward R., 32

National Academy of Sciences, 172
National Basketball Association (NBA),
　97, 123, 125, 128, 129
National Football League (NFL), 10,
　240

National Health Service (NHS), 15
National Institute of Health (NIH), 230
National Oceanic and Atmospheric
　Administration's Aeronomy
　Laboratory, 187
National Science Foundation (NSF), 74,
　75
New England Aquarium, 9
New England Journal of Medicine, 45,
　120–121
New School for Social Research, 56
New York Mets, 203
New York Times, 27, 29, 30, 65, 75,
　93, 214, 218, 241
New York Yankees, 83, 159, 204
New Yorker, 167, 172
Newton, Sir Isaac, 256
Nightingale, Florence, 106
Nixon, Richard, 213–215
Nobel Prize, 64, 65, 74, 75, 125, 143,
　148, 149, 190, 219, 266, 270
Nordhaus, William, 283–284; and
　"Lethal Model 2", 283–284
Northwestern University, 137

Oakland Athletics, 202
Obey, David, 56–57
Ohio State University, 97; and Compre-
　hensive Cancer Center, 182
outliers, 186–188, 199

Pascal, Blaise, 25; and Aritmatique,
　25–26
Paul the Octopus, 7–11, 13, 19
Paulos, John, 94; and *Innumeracy*
　(Paulos), 94
peppered moth, 12
pet predictions, 10–11; and Kanda the
　Great, 10; and Mindy, 10; and
　Mani the Parakeet, 11, 13
Peters, Tom, 41
pharmaceutical testing, 20–21
Philadelphia 76ers, 128
Phillips, David P., 175–182
Playfair, William, 79–80; and *The
　Commercial and Political Atlas*
　(Playfair), 79
Pollin, Robert, 59
positive initials, 4, 196–199

post hoc ergo propter hoc, 106
Princeton University, 175
Professional Bowlers Association (PBA),
130, 133–134
Pulitzer Prize, 27, 41

quantitative financial analysis, 266–267

Randi, James, 222, 228, 231
random-event generator, 18
Rare Disease Problem, 99–100
Reagan, Ronald, 64, 73, 86, 87
Red Lion Hotel, 36
regression to the mean, 141–148, 150,
153–157, 294; and standardized
tests, 142; and medical tests 142;
and investment success 142; and
height 144
Reinhart, Carmen, 57–64, 70, 291
Rhine, J.B., 18, 216–222, 232; and
Extra-Sensory Perception (Rhine),
218
Ripken, Jr., Cal, 211
Roe v. Wade, 66–68
Rogoff, Ken, 57–64, 70, 291
Royer, Heather, 179
Ruth, Babe, 83, 84, 153, 204; and
Curse of the Bambino, 204

sabermetrics, 201; and batting average,
201–202, 203; and on-base plus
slugging (OPS), 201
Schickard, Wilhelm, 25
Scholes, Myron, 266–267, 270, 271;
and Black-Scholes Model, 267
Scientific American, 94
Scorsese, Martin, 153; and *Taxi Driver,*
153; and *New York,
New York,* 153
Sears, 150–152
Seattle Aquarium, 9
Secrist, Horace, 137–141, 145,
148–149, 156; and *The
Triumph of Mediocrity in
Business* (Secrist), 139
Seinfeld, 159
selective reporting, 10, 220–222;
and publication effect, 221; and
decline effect, 221

self-selection bias, 28–30, 31, 32, 34,
42, 70, 112, 290
Short, Purvis, 123
Sianis, Billy, 204–205
Sicher, Fred, 230
Simpson, Edward, 113; and Simpson's
Paradox, 113–117
small numbers, law of, 125–126; and
gambler's fallacy, 125–126
Smith, Susy, 227, 231; and *The Book
of James (William James, That Is)*
(Smith), 227; and *Life is Forever:
Evidence for Survival after Death*
(Smith), 227; and *Prominent Amer-
ican Ghosts* (Smith), 227; and
Today's Witches (Smith), 227
Snow, John, 106–111; and *On the
Mode of Communication of
Cholera* (Snow), 106
Society of Experimental Social Psychol-
ogy, 16
Solomon, Susan, 187
South Sea Company, 255–256
Southwark and Vauxhall Water
Company, 107–108
Sports Illustrated, 3, 153, 155;
and SI Swimsuit Indicator, 241
St. Louis Cardinals, 83
Standard & Poors 500 Index, 152
Stanford University, 20, 127, 228, 229
Stapel, Diederik, 16
statistical proof, 8
statistical puzzles, 91
statistically significant, 8, 18–19, 133,
182, 202, 207, 209, 211, 221, 229
Stigler's Law, 113
Stock market, 4, 10, 24, 214, 235–247,
277, 295; and Dow Jones, 4, 150–
153, 185–186; and
Dow Jones Industrial Average, 46,
150, 186, 241, 252, 278;
and New York Stock Exchange,
39, 185–186, 278
streak probability, 123–135, 293
Student Life, 82
Sudoku, 21
Super Bowl, 4, 24, 252, 295; and
"Super Bowl Stock Market
Predictor", 240–241, 243

survivor bias, 35–38, 41, 42, 291
symmetry, 12–13

Targ, Elisabeth, 229–232; and
    distance healing, 229–231
Targ, Russell, 228; and remote
    viewing, 228
Targ, William, 226–227
technical analysis, 243–247
Terrible Tuesday, 186
Texas sharpshooter fallacy, 170–171,
    173, 182, 294
textjunk, 89
The Lancet, 14, 16, 107
Tilburg School of Social and
    Behavioral Sciences, 16, 17
Time, 85
Tufts University School of Medicine, 20
"The Cancer Cluster Myth"
    (New Yorker), 172
Tversky, Amos, 125, 127–129
Twain, Mark 235

U.S. News, 82, 83
UK Childhood Cancer Study, 172
UK General Medical Council, 16
under-matching, 28
University of California at Berkeley,
    113, 293
University of California at Irvine, 176
University of California at San Diego,
    175, 196–199
University of Chicago, 65, 216
University of Colorado, 39
University of Ioannina, 20
University of Massachusetts Amherst,
    59, 64
University of Michigan, 28–29

vaccines, 14–16; and MMR, 14–16;
    and autism, 14–16
Vallone, Robert, 127–129
Virginia Tech, 31
Volcker, Paul, 85
Von Däniken, Erich, 226; and Chariots
    of the Gods (Däniken), 226
vos Savant, Marilyn, 92–93, 160
voting, 30

Wakefield, Andrew, 14–16
Wald, Abraham, 37–38
Wall Street Journal, 10–11, 185
Warren Buffett, 242–243,
    256–259, 266, 276; and
    Berkshire Hathaway, 243,
    256–259
Washington Post, 58, 78
Watergate, 213–215
Waterloo, Battle of, 33
Waterman, Robert 41
Wayne State University, 205
Wendell, Turk, 203
Wertheimer, Nancy, 167, 170
Who Was Who in America, 176
Williams, Jr., Walter Ray, 130,
    276–277
World Cup (soccer), 7–11
World Series, 83
Wrigley, Phil, 204

Yankee Stadium, 83, 84
Young, Cy, 210–211
Young, Donn, 182–183

Zener, Karl, 17; and Zener Cards,
    17, 218–220
Zenith Radio Corporation, 126